W9-BBE-437

Mind, Modality, Meaning, and Method

SUNY SERIES IN PHILOSOPHY

Robert C. Neville, Editor

OTHER BOOKS BY THE SAME AUTHOR:

Truth and Denotation
The Notion of Analytic Truth
Toward a Systematic Pragmatics
Intension and Decision
Belief, Existence, and Meaning
Logic, Language, and Metaphysics
Whitehead's Categoreal Scheme and Other Papers
Events, Reference, and Logical Form
Semiotics and Linguistic Structure
Peirce's Logic of Relations and Other Studies
Pragmatics, Truth, and Language
Primordiality, Science, and Value
Logico-Linguistic Papers

MIND,

MODALITY,

MEANING,

AND

METHOD

R. M.

MARTIN

State University of New York Press

ALBANY

Published by
State University of New York Press, Albany
© 1983 State University of New York
For information, address State University of New York
Press, State University Plaza, Albany, N.Y., 12246

Library of Congress Cataloging in Publication Data
Martin, R.M. (Richard Milton), 1916–
    Mind, modality, meaning, and method.

    (SUNY series in philosophy)
    Includes bibliographical references and index.
    1. Philosophy—Addresses, essays, lectures.
2. Logic—Addresses, essays, lectures.   I. Title.
II. Series.
B29.M36777   1983   100   82-19440
ISBN 0-87395-721-0
ISBN 0-87395-722-9 (pbk.)

To the memory of

Erich Frank, Aron Gurwitsch, and Richard Kroner,

with gratitude for the privilege

of their friendship.

"Nay, I do not oscillate in Emerson's rainbow, but prefer rather to hang myself in my own halter than swing in another man's swing. . . . I would rather be a fool than a wiseman. I love all men who *dive*. Any fish can swim near the surface, but it takes a great whale to go downstairs five miles or more; & if he don't attain the bottom, why all the lead in Galena can't fashion the plummet that will. I'm not talking about Mr. Emerson now — but of that whole corps of thought-divers, that have been diving & coming up again with blood-shot eyes since the world began."

H. Melville

Contents

Preface

It is a commonplace to note that philosophy continually feeds upon, builds upon, or utilizes in one way or another the philosophy of the past, including the immediate past. No philosopher is an island, replete of himself. He is continually testing his ideas against those of others; he is reacting to them, either favorably or otherwise. His reactions help him to sharpen his own ideas as well as to lead him into pastures in which he might not otherwise graze. Also he may see important interconnections between or among his own ideas and those of others, interconnections that might at first sight seem rather remote or difficult to ascertain. Many of the papers of this volume are in effect reactions to the work of others, attempts to strengthen the underlying philosophical view by seeing how it may incorporate other seemingly disparate approaches. Dr. Johnson remarked to Boswell on one occasion: "A system, built upon the discoveries of a great many minds, is always of more strength than what is produced by the workings of any one mind. There is not so poor a book in the world that would not be a prodigious effort were it wrought out entirely by a single mind, without the aid of prior investigators. . . ." (*Life of Johnson,* report of 26 July 1763).

In all philosophical writing there is the ubiquitous undercurrent of *logic* continually asserting its presence and authority, whether we are aware of it or not. Much of the history of philosophy may be read as the history of trying to get our ideas straightened out in a logically satisfactory way, no matter what those ideas may be or may be concerned with. Logic underlies the most delicate and refined discussions of high moral, aesthetic, and metaphysical matters, quite as much as it does those in and concerning mathematics and the exact and experimental sciences. The fact that this is the case, however, is rarely recognized by either philosophers or the general reader, and is given little lip-service even by professional logicians. The result is of course that the state of logical culture among professional philosophers is at as low an ebb as ever, and this in spite of the great advances that have been made in the subject in recent years. Moreover, most philosophical arguments or presentations of a view or position lack the kind of rigor or scaffolding that is needed if they are to withstand even the minimum of logical criticism. And, worse, most philosophers do not even think that such a scaffolding is needed or even desirable. Most purported philosophical statements and arguments, even at the professional level, are such that, in the phrase of Peirce, a horse and four could pass through commodiously at almost any point. Whatever has happened to the logistic method in philosophy? it might thus profitably be asked. The fact is that it is very much alive and with us, as the various papers of this volume will help, it is hoped, to show.

In the world of affairs a professor is often said to be one who always thinks otherwise. In academe it is the philosopher of whom this seems to be said most frequently. Among philosophers, it is the logician who tends to think still otherwise, and among logicians it is the *fastidious* one — the one who retains his "robust sense of reality" and refuses to be lost in a "rich mud of conceptions" — who perhaps thinks the most otherwise of all. There has to be, of course, a limit to this, but there would seem to be no reason to stop at any point until a bedrock of "maximum logical candor" is reached. The phrase is Gilbert Ryle's, but the enterprise of trying to reach it far transcends anything he envisaged. To the fastidious logician a bedrock of maximum logical candor provides a basis with which to survey the strife of philosophical and scientific systems and argumentation with a certain detachment and equanimity. All philosophic and scientific activity is then grist to his mill and material to be assessed, pressed for its value, and properly reconstructed.

The titles of most of the papers of this book, it will be observed, are of the form 'On so and so'. The use of 'on' in this way is thought to call attention to a desirable tentativeness in the ensuing discussions. No paper is intended as final but rather as exploratory and adventuresome. Also the use of 'on' calls attention to the vastness of the subjects treated, and that the best one can do in a separate essay is to concern oneself with certain significant features of the subject under discussion, those that appear the most significant in the relevant context and at the present stage of research.

Although the papers here are concerned with a variety of seemingly disparate philosophical topics, all of them seek to get at fundamental foundational matters by means of a common methodology. The methodology may be referred to in different ways, in one paper as protometaphysics, in another as event logic, in another as general pragmatics or semiotics, and so on. The rose by any other name still holds its nectar, however, the unity of method being the important item and not the diversity of descriptions of it. Some descriptions seem appropriate for some papers, others for others. No matter how described, the hard work of fundamental logical analysis cannot be avoided anywhere in philosophy, it would seem, if we seek to probe deeply enough. The results of such probing need not be symbolized in the ways to be described here, of course. There are always alternatives to be explored and critically examined.

Some readers may object to the use of logical notation at some points in the various papers here. They will find the notation appropriate in logic and mathematics but not elsewhere. Elsewhere, they may contend, we all know perfectly well what is being said — if done so clearly in a natural language — and no logical notation is needed. This is rarely the case, however, as the use of logical symbolism in science, in analytic philosophy, and in the scientific study of language generally, has more and more brought to light in recent decades. Bertrand Russell once commented that a "good notation has a subtlety and suggestiveness about it which at times makes it seem almost like a live teacher . . . and a perfect notation would be a substitute for thought." The use of 'substitute' here is perhaps too strong — 'indispensable aid' would be better. A *perfect* notation, however, is not easy to come by and usually we must be satisfied with something far less. But the use of any good logical notation is better than none at all and serves also as an instrument of discovery, helping to bring to light new problems that had previously been passed over in dogmatic slumber. In a way, every advance in notation, like new discoveries in astronomy, say, leads to an increase of ignorance. The "Boole-Frege searchlight," as it has been called, is as great an aid to thought as the most powerful telescopes on Mount Palomar are to advances in astronomy and allied sciences. To object to the use of logical symbolism in philosophy seems not only philistine but *retardataire* in these closing decades of the twentieth century. As C. I. Lewis noted years back, "logistic is an instrument of such power as to make its eventual use almost certain."

For fruitful applications to philosophy, logistic should be expanded in the directions already hinted at. Notions providing for protometaphysics, event logic, or general pragmatics are needed. Several items here seem to be of especial importance, items that have come to light since the monumental work of Whitehead and Russell's *Principia Mathematica* of 1910–1913. The first is the semantical theory of *truth* and the exact *syntax* it presupposes. The second is the incorporation of some specifically *pragmatical relations* between the users of language and the items of language used. There is also the slow emergence of a suitable theory of *intensionality,* followed by a logical theory of *gerundives* for the handling of acts, events, states, and so on. Finally, there is the beginning of the process of sorting out the various *grammatical or quasi-grammatical relations* needed for the delineation of the inner intricacies of linguistic structure. Here we encounter such relations as being the agent of, being the patient or recipient of, being the object of, and so on, including all manner of relations for handling prepositions. The work along these lines has scarcely begun, but gives every indication of being fruitful in the emerging field of *logico-linguistics,* the new science in which an extended logistic is put to work in structural linguistics. All of these items have been called attention to in the author's previous writings, and will be commented on again here or there in the papers that follow. All such developments, as in the history of logic generally, take place slowly and with the inevitable trial and error. Only think how long — over two millenia — it has taken to disengage the quantifiers from the clinging mud of the wider linguistic contexts in which they are embedded. Such slowness and painful trial and error seem to be the hallmark of any true progress in logical matters.

Semantics is generally understood to be the study of the ways in which the expressions of a language are interrelated with the entities of which the language speaks. For the purposes of philosophical understanding the need for being clear concerning these interrelations cannot be overestimated. This is not to suggest that philosophy is exclusively this kind of study, for the objects spoken of have their own status irrespective of their role in semantics. The new way of words is merely a useful adjunct to the old way of things. This is a very obvious point, but one frequently misunderstood.

In the new way of words nothing is more important than the delineation of the relational structures involved. Modern logic, in its early stages, took on a new life with the explicit recognition of relations on a par with classes — not only dyadic ones, but relations of higher degree as well. Philosophers have been slow to embrace the riches of relational logic as relevant to and helpful for their work. In most metaphysical writing, for example, relations are continually spoken of but only rarely with much definiteness. The moment we stipulate a specific relation, as relating such and such a kind of entity with such and such another or others, we take an enormous step forward in clarity of statement. In the papers of this volume attention is continually called to specific relations thought to be of especial relevance for the topic or topics being discussed. The whole subject then becomes the theory of these relations and of how they interrelate or "interanimate" each other. The result is an exhibition of relational structure, however tentative and exploratory, which, it is hoped, helps to clarify and further the topics under discussion.

The various papers here thus cover a variety of philosophical subjects, united, however, in their concern with relational structure, with the theory of *mind* and of mental actions and states, with notions of both subjective and objective *modality,* with the analysis of *meaning* in terms of explicit logical forms, and with philosophic *method* generally. More specifically the papers are as follows. The first, I, consists of some introductory remarks concerning the status and role of criticism regarded as a central part of philosophic activity. II is a "reading" of one of *Whitehead's* most revealing early papers, his Presidential Address to Section A of the British Association in 1916, a paper almost wholly neglected by commentators. In II there is a critical but sympathetic discussion of *protometaphysics*, of the study of *being quā being,* and of notions of *subjective modality,* conceptions akin to those of *Panayot Butchvarov.* In IV a theory of *objective modality* is put forward, centering to some extent around a valuable suggestion due to *Ruth Marcus.* V consists of a discussion of the so-called *metaphysical presuppositions of logic* as well as of the *logical presuppositions of metaphysics.*

VI, VII, and VIII are concerned respectively with some work of *Sommers, Strawson,* and *Quine.* In VI a *semantics* is provided for Sommers' theory that singular terms should be handled predicatively. In VII there are some sympathetically critical remarks on Strawson's views concerning *subjects* and *predicates.* And in VIII the foundations of Quine's so-called *predicate-functor logic* are subjected to a careful scrutiny. In IX, which is a natural outgrowth of VIII, a *relational algebra* is put forward that is thought to avoid the undesirable features of Quine's work criticized in VIII. It amounts in essentials to a reformulation of the classical first-order logic in which there are *no variables* and hence of course *no quantifiers.* And with only minor adjustments of detail it may be reformulated so as to contain *no sentential connectives.* The result is a kind of natural equational algebra with an especially simple structure.

X is concerned with the study of *mental actions* and their role in *Roy Schafer's* reconstruction of the *language of psychoanalysis.* XI consists of a prolegomenon to the Prolegomena of *Husserl's Logische Untersuchungen,* and is probably the first attempt to show how intimately Husserl's concerns there are connected with developments in modern logic, semantics, event theory, and the like. In XII the relational algebra of IX is compared with *Whitehead's* conception of a *universal algebra* as discussed in his very first published book. With only slight adjustments of detail, relational algebra can be made to provide suitable logical foundations for the *later cosmology.* In the light of this a deeper kind of unity in Whitehead's thought can be seen than hitherto seems to have been noticed.

XIII is concerned with the problem of so-called *alternative logics,* the one standard *logic₁* versus the many *logics₂.* An argument is put forward to the effect that all logics₂ may be interpreted — and indeed *should* be interpreted — as special applications of logic₁. The paper opens with some incidental criticisms of *Quine's* views concerning *bivalence.* In XIV, a deep look is taken at *Goodman's* so-called *symbol systems,* by way of a reply to his objections made against a previous critique of his views. Quine and Goodman are perhaps the two most famous and influential American philosophers of their generation, and it is unfortunate that their views have not been subjected to the careful kind of logical scrutiny and critique they call for.

In XV a "rational reconstruction" of *Sir John Eccles' theory of the independent existence of the self-conscious mind* is put forward. The question of the appropriateness of this hypothesis as a "scientific" one is discussed, as well as its interest and relevance for a metaphysics based on objective idealism. In XVI there is a critique of the discussion of *intuitionistic logic* by Dag Prawitz presented at the meeting of the Institut Internationale de Philosophie in 1978 at Düsseldorf. In XVII, some of the material of XI is carried forward in the analysis of the notions of *purpose* and *obligation,* providing a new approach to the foundations of *deontic* logic. Finally, in XVIII, a critique is presented of five recent reviews, containing mainly misstatements based on misunderstanding, of some previous work of the author.

Only two of the papers presented here, XII and XVII, have been previously published. Thanks are due the editors and publisher of *The Monist* for permission to include XII and those of the *Analecta Husserliana* for XVII. II and XIII were presented at the Logic and Metaphysics Seminar of the International Society for Metaphysics, in 1980 and 1981 respectively. III is an expanded version of a review that appeared in *The Southwestern Journal of Philosophy* in 1981. VI is a reaction to a paper by Sommers presented at the Logic Forum, Boston, in October, 1980. VIII, the critique of Quine, was presented at the Boston Colloquium for the Philosophy and History of Science in December, 1980. X was prepared for presentation before the VIth International Congress for Psychoanalysis in New York in 1980. And XVII was presented at the XIth International Phenomenological Congress in September, 1981.

Inevitably there is some little overlap in the material of the various papers here. Some contain loose and exploratory formulations (such as III, IV, XI, and XVII); some are more formal and systematic (such as VI and IX). Some employ one kind of a semantics, others another. Some are in the main critical discussions (such as V, VIII, X, XIV, XV, and XVI), others primarily constructive. The papers may be read independently of each other and are more or less self-contained. Some of them consist of further development of notions put forward in previous publications. Readers familiar with these — at least to some extent — will thus inevitably have an advantage over those who are not.

Thanks are herewith expressed to Northwestern University and to the Boston University Center for the Philosophy and History of Science for support during the writing of the papers of this volume.

CHAPTER I

Some Remarks on Philosophic Criticism

"But you who seek to give and merit fame,
And justly bear a critic's noble name,
Be sure yourself and your own reach to know,
How far your genius, taste, and learning go;
Launch not beyond your depth, but be discreet,
And mark that point where sense and dulness meet."

Pope

Philosophical criticism is not an isolated enterprise but rather an integral part of philosophic activity. Of course there is always *self*-criticism in any philosophic writing, but it is mainly the professional criticism of *others,* both contemporary and past, that is to be considered here. Philosophy lives on in the criticism of others in ways that seem quite unique. Criticism of poetry is not ordinarily itself poetry, and a critical review or discussion of a scientific paper need not be a contribution to the science in question. Art criticism is an activity very different from the practice of art, and the criticism of musical performances can have nothing whatsoever to do with actual performance — the classical example being of a review in an Amsterdam newspaper of a purported piano-recital (by Irene Schreier Scott) that never took place! A critical paper in philosophy, however, may be as much or as little a contribution to philosophy as that of which it is a criticism. Philosophy seems to absorb its criticism in ways that are highly special. What is the function of philosophical criticism? What role does it play within philosophical activity generally? And, more specifically, what is it anyhow? And upon what is it based if not just on some alternative way of viewing the matters at hand? What varieties of philosophic criticism are there, and in what ways can they be helpful in philosophic progress, if there is any? Let us reflect a little upon these questions, if only indirectly and by way of some examples, especially in the light of the recent developments in modern logic and its application to the study of language.

A masterful statement of the aim and nature of philosophic criticism is to be found in the famous Epistle to the Reader with which John Locke prefaced his celebrated *An Essay concerning Human Understanding* in

1689. "The commonwealth of learning," Locke wrote, it will be recalled, "is not at this time without master-builders, whose mighty designs, in advancing the sciences, will leave lasting monuments to the admiration of posterity; but everyone must not hope to be a Boyle or a Sydenham; and in an age that produces such masters as the great Huyghenius and the incomparable Mr. Newton, with some others of that strain, it is ambition enough to be employed as an under-labourer in clearing the ground a little, and removing some of the rubbish that lies in the way to knowledge; — which certainly had been very much more advanced in the world, if the endeavours of ingenious and industrious men had not been much encumbered with the learned but frivolous use of uncouth, affected, or unintelligible terms, introduced into the sciences, . . . Vague and insignificant forms of speech, and abuse of language, have so long passed for mysteries of science; and hard and misapplied words, with little or no meaning, have, by prescription, such a right to be mistaken for deep learning and height of speculation, that it will not be easy to persuade either those who speak or those who hear them, that they are but the covers of ignorance, and hindrance of true knowledge. To break in upon the sanctuary of vanity and ignorance will be, I suppose, some service to human understanding."

Locke's comments here are both vivid and extremely relevant to the contemporary situation in philosophy. The more philosophy has changed during the past three centuries the more it seems to have remained precisely as Locke described it.

It is interesting to note that the "master-builders" here are natural or medical scientists, and not primarily philosophers in our present-day sense. Also, clearly Locke thinks of himself as an "under-labourer." Most of us now would regard him as one of the great philosophic master-builders of his time. More interesting still is the indication that, for Locke, under-laboring has to do primarily with the critique of language, to help remove "unintelligible" terms, "vague and insignificant forms of speech, and abuse of language," and "hard or misapplied words, with little or no meaning." The critique of language is becoming a very serious business in these closing decades of the twentieth century, thanks mainly to developments in the new logico-linguistics. But the neglect of these developments is still widespread, and most philosophers write as though they had never taken place. Even to mention them is to "break in upon the sanctuary [or sanctuaries] of vanity and ignorance," and few indeed are the nonlogically minded philosophers who "think they deceive or are deceived in the use [or misuse] of words" or that the particular school to which they belong "has any faults in it which ought to be examined or corrected." Indeed, the situation is so grim that it would not be conducive to their professional advancement for philosophers to think otherwise. *Quicquid multis peccatur, inultum est.*

Morton White observed keenly, back in 1956, that "unfortunately this hygienic job [of Locke's under-laboring] is never done, and the philosopher must take up his broom periodically, to clear the way not only for scientists, but also for himself, for *he too should advance and he too can build* [italics added]."[1] White's positive suggestions for these latter are illuminating and should be carried further. The main one is in calling attention to what is essentially the Fregean *Art des Gegebenseins*[2], although White's discussion centers rather around Moore and Austin. We must seize again "the clue which Moore gives us," White continues, "when he says that a natural attribute is the sort of attribute we ascribe to a thing in the course of *describing* it. Here we come to the element of profound truth in Moore's moral philosophy — the fact that describing is a kind of linguistic activity which is different from the activity we engage in when we sometimes use the word 'good'."

Of course we must not foist too much on Frege, or on Moore or Austin, but there can be no doubt that calling attention to certain types of linguistic activity is a first step toward developing a *theory* of it. Describing, or talking, under a given linguistic description (predicate or Russellian description), is one such type.[3] Other significant ones are, as White notes, commanding, prescribing, performing (in essentially Austin's sense), evaluating, to say nothing of apprehending, uttering, accepting, asserting, questioning, and so on.[4] The answer to White's question 'How Do We Go from Where?' is thus clear: we should embrace the contributions that logico-linguistics can make toward the clarification of these and allied notions as prolegomena to our philosophical discussion of their various uses or "meanings." It is often remarkable what such clarification reveals. White points out that one such result is that "mysterious intensionalism and indefensible universalism give way to a description [characterization] of the many different uses of specific bits of language with an eye to the removal of philosophical perplexity." The "indefensible universalism" spoken of here is, according to White, Moore's view that no natural attribute is identical with any ethical one.

White's main argument is, then, that a "reunion of philosophy . . . will be achieved only by recognizing that describing, doing, and evaluating are all of them important and connected parts of the [philosophic] enterprise." He points out correctly that it is the positivists and pragmatists who have, as a matter of historical fact, welcomed the need for logico-linguistic prolegomena more than philosophers of other "sects." But all philosophers whatsoever are in need of them, especially perhaps those who think that their work in this regard has no "faults in it which ought to be examined or corrected." As Locke pointed out, "the taking away of false [linguistic] foundations is not to the prejudice, but advantage, of truth, which is never injured or endangered so much as when mixed with or built on . . ." such foundations. Those who think that their work contains no false foundations are usually those whose work stands most in need of examination and correction.

The point of seeking appropriate logico-linguistic foundations for one's work is to help in the enterprise, to help do it better, to free it from obvious inadequacies of statement, inconsistencies, indecisiveness, and the like. Such seeking should thus not be regarded as an impediment, a straight-jacket, or a block in the road to inquiry, as is so often done. The situation is just the contrary. There is everything to gain in such seeking and nothing to lose except what should be lost anyhow.

In his *Philosophy and the Mirror of Nature*[5], Richard Rorty has distinguished between "pure" and "impure" kinds of philosophy of language. The pure kind, according to him, centers around "problems about how to systematize our notions of meaning and reference in such a way as to take advantage of quantificational logic, preserve our intuitions about modality, and generally produce a clear and intuitively satisfying picture of the way in which notions like 'truth', 'meaning', 'necessity', and 'name' fit together." The impure kind explicitly concerns itself with matters epistemological. In pure philosophy of language no epistemological *parti pris* is taken, and indeed, we are told, it has no "relevance to most of the traditional concerns of modern philosophy." This latter contention seems rather wide of the mark, however, and stems from a misunderstanding of the nature and function of semantics and of logico-linguistic theory.

Consider for the moment Rorty's pooh-poohing of Davidson's suggestion that, in Rorty's words (p. 261), "we probably just have to go ahead and quantify over persons, rather than 'reducing' them to things, in order to have a truth-theory for action-sentences. The philosophical interest . . . [of doing this] is, indeed, largely negative. . . . The actual results of the hard work on adverbial modification and the like which would result from concerted efforts to carry out Davidson's suggestions would do little to help or hinder any solution of any of the text-book problems of philosophy."

But surely if persons are in some sense "reducible" to things so that quantifiers over the latter are indeed quantifiers over them, the import for philosophy is enormous. Of course we can quantify over whatever we want. The point is that what we quantify over we regard as constituting the ontology of our theory, and in so far forth as constituting the beings or entities our theory takes as "real" in the most fundamental sense.[6] If

4

Davidson wants to quantify over persons in action theory, he is then taking an explicit stand as to what he regards as real. The import of doing this for his philosophy is thus very different from that of one who admits only quantifiers over just things that are non-persons. The two methods result from taking very different approaches to the text-book problem of the ontological status of persons *vis-a-vis* "things."

The real point here Rorty does not mention in this context. It is, namely, whether such "reduction" is possible without loss. Davidson plays it safe, so to speak, in allowing quantifiers over persons. Has anyone ever succeeded in adequately defining quantifiers over persons wholly in terms of quantifiers over only things as occurring in all possible contexts of use? The success or failure of such a reduction carries a theory of quantification along with it. Rorty seems to think that such a reduction takes place in some other way, and, more generally, that the substantive problems of philosophy get "solved" somehow quite independently of the logical techniques needed. But this is not the case, it would seem, every sentence of our philosophic talk being shot through and through with notions of logic fundamentally.[7] And similarly of course with the study of adverbials. The approaches to these of Reichenbach or Montague, for example, contrast with that of Davidson in basic respects, with very different ontologies involved, and hence with very different approaches to text-book philosophical problems.

Note that we do not speak here of helping or hindering the "solution" of any problem of text-book philosophy, as Rorty does. Whether there ever are solutions to philosophical problems, in any definitive sense anyhow, is dubious. Problems may be laid aside, no longer attract interest, give way to more refined problems, and the like. The point is that there is progress in clarification concerning some of them and that such progress is intimately linked with advances in the study of logic and language. The situation in philosophy is not very different in this respect from that in the sciences. Strictly there are no "solutions" to scientific problems either, that is, at least to theoretical ones. There are theories formulated to characterize the material in question, these theories in time often giving way to theories that are "better" in some respects, or more acceptable, or more fruitful. There is surely progress in the sciences, and "success" is measured in part by predictions that are realized in observables. But when such success obtains, we are not therewith assured that some still better theory would not entail the same predictions, or entail them in some better way — with fewer assumptions, say, or on the basis of more secure or acceptable ones. Much the same may be said of mathematics also, incidentally, where "solutions" to problems are always relative to a given vocabulary available and suitable assumptions concerning it —

even problems concerning solvability and unsolvability themselves!

Rorty seems to misunderstand the central role a *logica utens* must play in philosophy. He berates (p. 264) "Dummett's notion of a philosophy of language as 'first philosophy' as mistaken not because some other area is 'first' but because the notion of philosophy as having foundations is as mistaken as that of knowledge having foundations." Let us not quibble here about the word 'foundations'. The central point that Rorty misses is that wherever language is used, the study of its structure rears its noble head to try to help us understand the nature of the laws governing it. Rorty cannot consistently berate the "nostalgia for philosophy as an ar-chitectonic and encompassing discipline" or technique and think of it, as he does, as merely one more "voice in the conversation of mankind" (in Michael Oakeshott's phrase), which "centers on one topic rather than another at some given time not by dialectical necessity but as a result of various things happening elsewhere in the conversation. . . . " The "con-versation" takes place in languages, all of which have certain built-in structural features. A conversation in a language lacking such features, the theory of which constitutes its foundations, is a contradiction in terms. Rorty seems to have no nostalgia for the great architectonic views that have always haunted the greatest of philosophers. He remains an outsider to the whole philosophic enterprise, listening to the babel of the "conversation" from afar. He seeks to be neither a master-builder nor an under-laborer, but seems content with the role of being merely a be-wildered *voyeur.*

Let us turn now to some of the questions raised in the first paragraph above and suggest in a very rough way some answers to them. The main function of one kind of criticism in philosophy is no doubt to help the philosopher do better what he is trying to do. No one ever does what he is doing well enough to be exempt from all possibility of improvement.

> "Whoever thinks a faultless piece to see,
> Thinks what ne'er was, nor is, nor e'er shall be."

Also there is always the problem of determining the comparative value of what is being done, relative to both past and contemporary work of relevance. It is easy enough to dismiss types of philosophic work other than those in which one is immediately interested, but much more diffi-cult to give them their proper due. And just as the past continually asserts itself in the work of the present, so the latter continually changes our atti-tudes to and understanding of that of the past. A detached, objectively correct statement of the work of the past is next to impossible of achieve-ment. It is as difficult as, if not more so than, a logico-mathematically correct rendition of some contemporary view. The work of the past is thus no more exempt from critical surveillance and reconstruction than that of the present. Also there are divergent standards of formulation to which the critic should continually call attention. There are divergent standards as to the choice of an underlying logic, with respect to the delineation of conceptual structure, with respect to the relevance of what is known in the appropriate sciences, and with respect to the relevance of past work already done. Not all logics are on a par, a fact not sufficiently recognized even now. (See XIII below.) Some concepts are and remain "fuzzy" in undesirable ways. Some types of philosophical works owe their survival to neglect and ignorance of relevant scientific and other material. Moreover, ignorance of history often leads merely to the repetition of its errors.

There is of course also the hermeneutical function of the critic, which may be external or internal to a text or both. There is continually the problem of internal meaning analysis and the need to achieve consistency. An adequate meaning analysis is rare to come by and even a modicum of assurance of consistency is very difficult to achieve. Here we must distinguish between mere journalism and genuine philosophy, a distinction that seems to have been lost sight of almost completely in recent years. Also we must distinguish, as Hume urged us to do, between the "accurate and abstruse" kind of philosophy, as contrasted with the "easy and obvious" that is always given preference by the majority of even professional philosophers. Externally there are always all manner of interesting interconnections with other work to point out. There is always the haunting question of what one has failed to take into account, of failure of comprehensiveness, of failure to acknowledge significant influences, and so on.

It is the critic's business to be continually sensitive to the use of words, to the "abuse of language," to "hard and misapplied words," and so on. It is also his business to be tolerant of uses of language other than his own. Words are deceptive and need to be seen through to be understood properly. Especially in matters of technical terminology great care must be exercised. Every philosopher must be allowed his own terms in his own way.

There is also the matter of philosophic silence. A philosopher is often best known by what he fails to tell us, the main portion of his thought remaining dormant beneath the verbal surface. That this is the case usually reveals itself in the first few paragraphs, and becomes pellucid thereafter. In particular, it usually takes a considerable effort before the critic can eke out with any precision what the root or basic notions are, and just what is being assumed concerning them and why. That this is the case results often from a certain lack of probity of presentational style.

7

Such probity is best achieved, it would seem, by a more self-conscious attention to the methods and techniques of logical formalization than is usually given them.

Let us return for a moment to the respective tasks of under-laboring and master-building. It would be an error merely to identify philosophic criticism with the former. A foundation on which criticism must rest is needed and this can only be firm and secure if masterfully built. There are many examples of master-builders in the history of philosophy — to say nothing of any contemporaries — who were master-builders as well as master-critics: Aristotle surely, Chrysippus presumably, Plotinus, St. Thomas, Descartes, Leibniz, Spinoza, Kant, Peirce, and Whitehead, to name only a few. Without some imposition of prior standards, no criticism can take place in any but a quixotic sense. Perhaps we should distinguish here the kind of under-laboring that precedes the finished edifice, the groping after clarity, the tentative formulation, the trial and error, and the inevitable failure, from that which can take place only after the edifice has been completed or envisaged, at least to a certain degree. All criticism, including self-criticism, it would seem, is of one kind or another or a suitable mixture of the two.

There is also the problem as to how the philosopher is to react to the criticism of his or her work. The most appropriate answer is, no doubt, that one should reflect upon the criticism carefully and dispassionately and take into account all of the items raised, however adverse. One should then accept those that, after due deliberation, are seen to be justified but reject those that are not. To those that are justified one should make due amends. If, however, some of the unjustified criticisms seem too far-fetched or *outré* to pass the test of professional competence, one should then make known the grounds for this. Not to do so is to serve the cause of injustice and of erroneous evaluation just as the original criticism did. This appropriate type of response to criticism, however, is not common. More frequently to be found is either convenient disregard, if the criticism is really probing, or the shyster-like reaction of paying no heed to the crucial critical points and puffing up falsity on falsity by way of self-seeking defense. This last type of response to criticism, however, is of interest only from the point of view of publicity and reputation-building.

On the other hand, adequate, helpful, professionally competent philosophic criticism is rare to come by. One usually seeks it in vain. One usually finds in its stead vague, journalistic comments from another point of view — that perhaps of a salesman of some second-hand philosophy — or a superficial defense of some purported *status quō* from which, in our organization-man oriented society, no deviation is tolerated, or a list of typographical or other errata puffed up into fundamental "errors" or "mistakes," or an amateur, armchair dismissal of technical work that is too challenging for comfort, or a defense of the views of some influential writer of the past or present from which any deviation is intolerable, and so on and on.

It is very important for the critic to stick to the actual text he is considering, to be sure he has understood it, and not wander off into vague generalities and accusations. A view or an opinion should never, strictly, be ascribed to another except by precise textual reference. A critic should never say that so and so says such and such without justifying it — at least elsewhere if not in the immediate context. Criticism should thus be directed to the text, and not to some vague statement the author is supposed to have made. And in all of this the critic should exercise a certain generosity and should always be willing, as Frege urged his readers to do, to meet the author at least half-way. He should always try to see what the author is *trying* to say, even if inaccurately or badly.

Genuine criticism is not an easy way of winning friends or even of influencing people. It must always be dead honest and involves the risk of being unwelcome to those to whom it is addressed. It must always be Cordelia-like, and truth alone should be its dower. Some types of criticism only intercede "between the dragon and its wrath," but others may have a very positive function of calling attention to new areas of interest, to new problems, to how to do it better, and so on. Genuine criticism is thus an integral part of both under-laboring and master-building, and is as noble as it is rare.

CHAPTER II

On the Organization
of Thought: Whitehead

"Those rules of old, discover'd, not devis'd,
Are nature still, but nature methodiz'd:
Nature, like liberty, is but restrain'd
By the same laws which first herself ordained."
Pope

Metaphysics, like science itself, is essentially logical, we may note, paraphrasing and extending Whitehead somewhat in one of his most trenchant and revealing early papers.[1] "The nexus between its concepts is [in part] a logical nexus, and the grounds for its detailed assertions are [in part] logical grounds." To King James' "No bishops, no king," we may add "No logic, no metaphysics; no metaphysics, no logic."[2] "The reason for the instinctive dislike which most men of science [and metaphysics] feel towards the recognition of this truth is, I think," Whitehead continues, "the barren failure of logical theory during the past three or four centuries. We may trace this failure back to the worship of authority. . . . A science which hesitates to forget its founders is lost. To this hesitation I ascribe the barrenness of logic."

In the last 100 years or so a tremendous growth has taken place in logic, however, one phase of which culminated with the publication of the great *Principia Mathematica* of Whitehead and Russell in 1910–1913. The barrenness of logic even then was already a thing of the past. Significant developments have taken place more recently also, of which account should be taken if the relevance of logic for metaphysics is properly to be assessed.[3]

Whitehead, in the essay under discussion, went on to distinguish four branches of logical theory, in accord essentially with the *PM* view. These are what we nowadays refer to as the theory of the *truth-functional* connectives 'and', 'or', 'not', 'if . . . then', and 'if and only if', (2) the theory of *sentential functions* incorporating the *quantifiers* 'for all x' and 'there exists at least one x such that', (3) the theory of *classes, relations,* and *functions* of all (finite) logical types, and (4) the theory of *special mathematical notions,* such as that of a one-to-one correlation, serial relations, and so on, needed for the foundations of cardinal and ordinal arithmetic and geometry. The inclusion here of (3) and (4) is essential in order to maintain the so-called *logistic thesis* that all mathematical notions are definable in terms of the logical ones and that all mathematical theorems — to within undecidable ones, if there are any — are provable from the axioms of logic. It is essentially this view of logic that Whitehead had in mind as the background for his later philosophical writings.

There have been many advances in logic since the years during which Whitehead was actively concerned with it. Among these three items stand out as of preeminent interest for constructive metaphysical purposes. The first is the systematic development of *metalogic,* including logical *syntax,* extensional or denotational *semantics,* and systematic *pragmatics.*[4] But the semantical theory of *intensions* also has clamored for clear formulation, and the most suitable method of achieving this is thought to be in terms, not of Fregean *Sinne* or Carnapian *intensions,* but in terms of the Fregean *Art Des Gegebenseins,* or mode of linguistic description.[5] The third item, thought also to be of great philosophic relevance, is the development of the logical theory of *gerundives,* which provides a basis for handling events, states, acts, processes, becomings, changes, and the like.[6] Above all, it is this last that is needed if good logical sense is to be made of Whitehead's own later speculative writings.[7]

The view has also become widespread, since the publication of *PM,* that items (3) and (4) in Whitehead's list belong more properly to mathematics than to logic. Of course, one can construe 'logic' as widely or as narrowly as one might wish. But there is a traditional, customary, normal division of labor at work if (1) and (2) are regarded as the proper concerns of logic and (3) and (4) of mathematics. And alternative forms of (3) and (4) are provided by the various systems of axiomatic set theory that have been on the market these many years clamoring for buyers.

Another development in logic that has been taking place in recent years in a rather different direction is the exact analysis of language. Gone now is the day of the old-fashioned, Wittgensteinian, linguistic philosophy, with the emergence of the new *logico-linguistics* taking its place. Just as modern logic itself has come to maturity as a result of work by both mathematicians and philosophers, so logico-linguistics is developing as a result of fruitful cooperation on the part of linguistics and logicians alike. The results of this cooperation are of the highest relevance, it would seem, for the analysis of metaphysical language. There are, then, these two different layers of logical research to reflect upon in their connection with metaphysics. There is logic cum metalogic cum intension and gerundive theory, and there is the wider terrain of logico-linguistics, which may be construed as a further development of the former.

11

Whitehead urged, in the essay under review, "that the basis of science does not depend on the assumption of any of the conclusions of metaphysics, but that both science and metaphysics start from the same given groundwork of immediate experience, and in the main proceed in opposite directions in their diverse tasks. For example, metaphysics inquires how our perceptions of . . . [say, this] chair relate us to some true reality. Science gathers up these perceptions into a determinate class, adds to them ideal perceptions of analogous sort, which under assignable circumstances would be obtained, and this single concept of that set of perceptions is all that science needs." Metaphysics clearly requires a good deal more, in particular some account of what "true reality" is taken to be and of how the "determinate" classes and relations studied in the sciences are related to it — to say nothing of such matters as goodness, beauty, God, freedom, immortality, and the like. Thus, although science and metaphysics do "in the main proceed in opposite directions" in their appointed tasks, the study of the interrelation between their results brings the two closely together again.

To see in precise detail how the two are brought together, no better means would seem to be at hand than those of logico-linguistics. These latter are concerned with natural languages only and the logical forms needed for the exact "representation" of natural sentences. Although the sentences of any science are in actual practice natural sentences, it is now more or less commonly agreed upon that all such sentences may be given an exact logical form. The best way to study the logical structure of a science is, it would seem, to work upon the basis of such an assumption. But the logical forms required for a science are specifically geared to its needs, more particularly, to its specific vocabulary. Thus in the logic of science we go no deeper than the vocabulary of science warrants.

A metaphysics, when suitably articulated, consists usually of a multiplicity of natural sentences, subject to the overall grammatical rules of the language as a whole. It too will have its special technical vocabulary, which transcends that of the natural language in various ways. The best way to study the logical structure of a metaphysical system is thus also no doubt to assign suitable logical "representatives" to its special vocabulary and logical forms to its special sentences. Thus science and metaphysics each proceed in their own way. It would be more accurate to say here that they proceed in supplementary directions, however, rather than "opposite" ones. There should be no essential opposition between the two enterprises when properly viewed. The problem remains, however, as to how the vocabulary and special sentences of an articulated metaphysics relate to the logical representatives of the vocabularies and sentences of the special sciences.

Is it correct to maintain, as Whitehead does, "that the basis of science does not depend on the assumptions of any of the conclusions of metaphysics?" This is of course a much-debated point to which there is no simplistic answer. In general, it does seem that the deeper the sciences probe, the closer they tend to become concerned with the "true reality" of the metaphysician. "To see with God's eyes" has been said by one of its greatest practitioners, Einstein himself, to be the goal of science, or at least one of its goals, along with the need to articulate what it is that is thus seen.

A logical analysis of the language of metaphysics is of course a mere means and is not to be taken as a final goal. It was remarked above that in the logic of science we go no deeper than the vocabulary of science warrants. Similarly for logico-linguistics itself. We need go no deeper in the study of natural language than its vocabulary and the structure of its sentences warrant. The sentences of the metaphysical language, however, although framed within the logical forms required for the natural language, will go deeper in certain fundamental respects. An example will help to clarify this point as well as to help bring out the way in which natural sentences are to be interpreted scientifically, on the one hand, and metaphysically, on the other.

Let us consider Peirce's example of A's giving a gift B to C. Here A and C are presumed to be persons and B some concrete object.[8] A suitable logical form for sentences of the kind 'A gives B to C' (construed timelessly) is thought to be

(5)   '$(Ee)(\langle \text{Give} \rangle \ e \cdot \text{A Agent} \ e \cdot \text{B Object} \ e \cdot \text{C Patient} \ e)$',

expressing that A is the *agent* of some act of *giving* e — '$\langle \text{Give} \rangle$' here is the event-descriptive predicate representing the gerundive for acts of giving — of which B is the *object* and C the *patient*. For the purposes of the characterization of natural-language structure, this or some analogous form would seem to suffice. *Metaphysically* regarded, however, this form leaves much to be desired. In particular, an account of the ontologies involved, of acts, persons, and objects and how they are interrelated, is needed. Is any one "reducible" in some suitable way to another or to the others jointly? Are any of these types of entities components of the "truly real"? If so, how? And so on. Also, acts of giving are a certain type of complex occurrence, primarily within the human sphere, and remain to be interrelated with the "truly real." Of course, many of these questions are answered to some extent in the detailed working out of the grammar of the natural language. The specifically metaphysical questions concerning the truly real, however, are not therewith considered. As with science generally, so in particular with the science of linguistics:

the deeper one probes the more essential it may become at some point to attempt to view the subject, along with all of its ramifications, "with God's eyes."

How, now, is (5) to be interpreted *scientifically,* so to speak, more particularly, within some language for some domain of physics, say? For this, certain *bridge rules,* let us call them, are needed to "reduce" (or construct) persons, concrete objects, and human acts to (or in terms of) suitable congeries of whatever entities are admitted in that domain of physics. Such bridge rules are very different from so-called "coordinating definitions," which interrelate theoretical constructs with observables. The entities of the given domain of physics may or may not be theoretical constructs, and persons, objects, and so on, may or may not be observables. Perhaps coordinating definitions are a special case of bridge rules, but at any event the latter are clearly the more important. Bridge rules are often of a semantical nature and may be given within an explicative semantics.[9]

(5) of course is a logical form for a sentence of ordinary language given its interpretation or construal within a scientific or metaphysical language in the ways just described. Let us consider now two additional examples, one a specific statement of a science awaiting its construal metaphysically, and a specifically metaphysical statement awaiting the characterization of its mode of relationship, so to speak, with science. For the first, consider the (or at least *a*) law of gravitation as formulated within RG, the relativistic theory of gravitation, within which it plays the role of an accepted law. Within any adequate metaphysics, this "law" must at least be stateable. For this, every expression of the language of RG must occur as an expression of the metaphysical language. Such specifically physical expressions may play a mere ancillary role within metaphysics, but at least they should be present if only for the purposes of stating certain bridge laws. Two sorts of bridge laws here are to be distinguished, those connecting the physical entities with their "truly real" metaphysical counterparts, and those showing how the given law of gravitation, for example, occurs or is handled within the metaphysical language. Bridge laws of both kinds are regarded as essential, without which metaphysics would be forever closed to a purview of the sciences. All scientific notions and statements may be presumed mirrored in metaphysics in some such fashion so that it may have the necessary comprehensiveness and inclusiveness of scope. Without this there is danger lest the metaphysician tend to harbor an antiscientific attitude or at least one of indifference. The attitude expressed by "Scientia sunt, non leguntur" is surely as reprehensible on the part of the metaphysician as that of "Metaphysica sunt, non leguntur" is on the part of the scientist.

One way of mirroring scientific statements within the metaphysical language might be to adopt the *PM* device with respect to the *Axiom of Infinity* and the so-called *Multiplicative Axiom*. Whitehead and Russell, it will be recalled, were unwilling to assume these two axioms outright as logical principles. On the other hand, they are needed fundamentally in the derivation of some crucial mathematical theorems. A way of getting around this situation is to take these axioms as hypotheses where needed. Where 'InfAx' and 'MultAx' abbreviate the appropriate axioms, we now write

$$\text{'InfAx} \supset \text{-----' or 'MultAx} \supset \text{-----'}$$

rather than '-----' outright, where '-----' is provable only on the assumption of the one or the other respectively. Principles of mathematics depending on one or the other or both of these axioms are now always written with the axiom (or axioms) needed taken as hypothesis.

The principles of a science may now be taken to be included in metaphysics in this same, rather Pickwickian, way. They need not be assumed outright, but rather appear throughout merely as hypotheses. The law of gravitation in RG need not be assumed by the metaphysician, but rather taken as hypothesis to physical statements depending on it. In this way the metaphysical counterparts to scientific statements become merely hypothetical. For this of course, a mirroring of the *notions* of the given science within the metaphysical language, by bridge rules within an explicative semantics, is presupposed.

Consider, finally, some specifically metaphysical statement, to the effect, say, that "the world is rational and the rational is the truly real." Of course we must suppose that this very statement itself has a sharp meaning within the given metaphysical language, that this language is well articulated in modern terms within an exact syntax and semantics, and that it is suitably "understood" by its users — quite an assumption no doubt! What bridge rules could conceivable interrelate the vocabulary of this statement with that of science, or of some science? And what bridge rule or rules could interrelate the "truth" of this statement with presumed truths in the science?

To answer such questions in any detail would take us afield from the present discussion and would require a considerable formalization of the metaphysics involved. Some suggestions toward such a formulation however, have been provided elsewhere, in terms, for example, of suitable relations of "manifestation."[10] The truly real is assumed to "manifest" itself in the entities studied in the sciences. The bridge rules would thus, for such a metaphysics, be stated wholly in terms of manifestation. But general metaphysical principles do not "manifest" themselves in scientific laws. These general principles are rather to be regarded as *sui generis,* some of them being suitable to be taken as meaning postulates or axioms. The view here is thus that metaphysical principles always transcend those of the special sciences, but that the latter are always suitably to be provided for, perhaps merely as hypotheses, within the overall metaphysical language.

Metaphysics also has an important critical role to play in science, and also an integrative one. 'Science' has been used above in essentially the old positivist sense of the "unity of science." It is more correct, however, to speak of the sciences in the plural, the problem of their integration remaining an essentially metaphysical one. Even if we speak only of the science of physics, what is it we find upon close examination? A variety of special theories, some depending upon others, some contradicting others, some supplementary to others, but nowhere do we find an integrated theory embracing the whole of physical knowledge.[11] Even in mathematics there is no integrated theory, if one refuses to accept the notion of set and some accompanying axioms concerning it. The situation is even more acute in the other empirical sciences. Further, there is no science embracing all the sciences; at best these latter may perhaps be given a unified setting within an overarching metaphysical scheme. But even this seems never to have been done with anything like sufficient precision and attention to detail.

What critical role can be assigned to metaphysics, given the relatively backward state of its development as regards precision of formulation in comparison with the advances in this regard made in the sciences? Well, a metaphysics given a proper formulation in modern logico-linguistic terms may indeed be used fruitfully as a critical foundation for areas in science lacking such a formulation.

Among scientific laws those of logic itself, even as construed in the extended sense of the present discussion, might be included. These laws, however, have a generality of application beyond that of the special sciences. Further, they are subject-matter neutral, as has frequently been emphasized. The laws of logic transcend those of the special sciences, but in a way different from that in which metaphysical laws may be said to do so. Laws of logic become statements of a given science, for example, by suitably instantiating their bound variables; no bridge rules are required. What status then do such laws have relative to those of metaphysics? This is an important question, especially emphasized recently by Ivor Leclerc. Although there are technical differences in the ways in which the two sorts of laws function within the overall theory, and in the roles they play, these do not seem sufficient to justify a division of kind. No. We should perhaps regard the laws of logic as a sub-class of those of metaphysics, but a rather special sub-class all the same. They are needed in the formulation of the metaphysical system in essentially the same way they are needed in the formulation of a system for mathematics or physics. That this is the case has been forcefully argued by Heinrich Scholz.[12]

Whitehead makes much, in the passage cited, of the *experiential* basis of both science and metaphysics, in accord with the prevailing empiricism of the time at which he was writing. In the intervening years the presuppositions of this view have lost some of their sway among both philosophers and men of science — and indeed Whitehead himself seemed in effect to reject them in his later cosmological writings. What is needed, for a deeper appraisal of this matter, is some exact account of observation and of its role in framing scientific and other hypotheses, in "verifying" them, and so on. Most of the writing on this subject unfortunately has remained at a rather superficial, and even metaphorical, stage.

The assumption made above is of course that every metaphysics can be given an exact logical formulation. Those who question this assumption usually do so on the basis of some older conception of what logic is and fail to take into account the developments of recent years. Metaphysicians unfamiliar with these developments fail to recognize that they are implicitly using logical devices all the time, if only in their skillful handling of the complexities of natural language. Whitehead commented that "you cannot know too much of the methods which you always employ," a contention that takes on another meaning now in view of the way in which logical notions surround and infiltrate our natural sentences at every turn. No linguist would seriously contend now that the logical analysis of language distorts or disorients our natural language. No, such analysis merely helps to make explicit the structural features it has whether we realize it or no. In similar vein, the logical handling of a metaphysical view need not distort it one whit. On the contrary, it brings it into sharper focus, helps to bring to light hidden ideas and assumptions, helps us to be more aware as to what follows from what, as to how various parts of the subject are interrelated conceptually, and so on.

It is often objected also that the logical formulation acts as a "straight-jacket" to metaphysical thought, that it strangles it, cannot account for subtle shades of meaning, and so on. The fact of the matter, however, is precisely the opposite. As Whitehead noted at the end of his essay, "Logic, properly used, does not shackle thought. It gives freedom, and above all, boldness. Illogical thought hesitates to draw conclusions, because it never knows either what it means, or what it assumes, or how far it trusts its own assumptions, or what will be the effect of any modification of assumptions. Also the mind untrained in that part of constructive logic which is relevant to the subject in hand will be ignorant of the sort of conclusions which follow from various sorts of assumptions, and will be correspondingly dull in deriving the . . . [logical] laws. . . ." This lack of proper training is no longer due to the barrenness of logic, but to the very backward state of the teaching of it, which in recent years has been left almost wholly in the hands of mathematicians, or mathematicians *manqutés,* almost wholly lacking in philosophical interests. But this is another story altogether, in need of a detailed telling.

CHAPTER III

On Being Quā Being, Protometaphysics, and Epistemic Modality

> "Expression is the dress of thought, and still
> Appears more decent as more suitable."
> *Pope*

The topic of being *quā* being, in one fashion or another, has been at the very center of metaphysical discussion since antiquity. To say precisely what it is in modern terms, however, that is, to give some reasonable account of it, and of how to carry on discourse about it, in the light of modern semiotics, say, or in terms of some suitable alternative, has turned out to be very difficult. Let us follow Panayot Butchvarov for the moment in regarding inquiry into the topic as absolutely fundamental.[1] Let us follow him also in using the term 'protometaphysics' for this inquiry. Further, it is a "transcendental" enterprise, in the sense that the very notions constituting it, so to speak, are presupposed in more special inquiries and in fact are common to all of them. Transcendental protometaphysics in this sense is the very first chapter, indeed, the very first paragraph, of any metaphysical view, if it is to be regarded as acceptably formulated in modern terms.[2]

Butchvarov himself uses 'transcendental' in what appears to be a less felicitous sense. For him transcendental terms are those by means of which (p. 5) "we *must understand* what it is for *something* to be *in* the world, what it is for something to *have* a property or to be *related* to another thing, and what it is for something to *be* a property or a relation [italics added]." Further, such terms "apply to any possible world; indeed nothing would be a world were it not for their applicability to it." The italicized words are of special import, involving necessity (in some sense), understanding, the very notion of thinghood, and the notion of being "in" the (or a) world, to say nothing of properties and relations and possible worlds.

Butchvarov is concerned with four, more or less traditional "puzzles," about existence (and non-existence), identity, and accidental and necessary predication. These puzzles correlate with four senses of the verb 'to be', or rather with their metaphysical counterparts. Further, the four notions are regarded as intimately interrelated, but that of identity is the basic one and "the other three are to be understood in terms of it."

Fundamental to Butchvarov's discussion is a distinction between "objects" and "entities." He refers to "the domain of the logically first application of our conceptual apparatus, that is, the application of the concepts of identity and existence, as the domain of *objects,* and to the domain that emerges from it by virtue of these applications as the domain of *entities.*" The distinction, however, is said not to be a real distinction but rather "a distinction of reason, a distinction due wholly to the application of concepts." A distinction also is drawn between *material* and *formal* identity statements, the former being of the form '*x* is the same as *y*' where *x* and *y* are entities, and the latter '*x* is the same as *x*' where *x* is an object. The distinction between objects and entities thus depends wholly upon our "conceptual apparatus" — whatever that is supposed to be. Clearly the apparatus must play a fundamental role in the theory, and expressions for it must explicitly be brought in in some fashion.

Let us reflect upon saying that

(1)   *x* and *y* are two objects

but that

(2)   *x* and *y* are only one entity.

"The criterion for determining (1) is simply the fact that *x* and *y* appear to be distinct things, that they are *singled out differently* [italics added]" rather than *identified.* Thus it appears that relations of singling out and of identifying are needed at the very beginning. Presumably you and I single out and identify very differently in our conceptual and linguistic activity, and each of us even very differently at different times and on different occasions. How can these relations be adequately symbolized? One suggestion would be in terms of the Fregean *Art des Gegebenseins.*[3] Let

(3)   '*p* SO$_e$ *x,a*'

express that person *p* singles out, in some conceptual or linguistic act *e*, a thing (object) *x* as being such that the one-place predicate *a* denotes or applies to it.

For example, suppose *a* is the predicate '$\{y \ni y = y\}$', for the universal virtual class. To say then that *p* SO$_e$ *x,a* is to say that in the act *e* person *p* singles *x* out as being self-identical (or in the universal class). Let 'α' and 'β' be distinct proper names or Russellian descriptions. To say then that *p* SO$_e$ α, *a*, where *a* is the form '$\{y \ni y = \beta\}$', is to say that *p* singles α out in e as being identical with β. In fact we could let

$$`p \ \text{Id}_e \ \alpha, \beta`$$

abbreviate the expression for this, thus gaining a form for identifying. Similarly we could let

(4)   '$p \ \text{Dist}_e \ \alpha, \beta$' abbreviate '$p \ \text{SO}_e \ \alpha, `\{y \ni \ \sim y = \beta\}`$'',

gaining an expression for *distinguishing*.

Butchvarov notes that in the course of his book he has been compelled to "introduce notions and propose theses of unusual difficulty" and that they are such "is an unavoidable consequence of the nature of the problems they are designed to solve." The notion of singling out, and presumably also that of identifying, he believes, "can be made clear only by the uses to which they are put throughout . . . , not by initial explanation." However, there is nothing in the nature of the problems dealt with that prevents formulation in terms such as those of (3) or cognate forms. Nor is there anything in the nature of (3) that prevents *some* explicit initial explanation. The situation here is not unlike that of some formulation of a set theory in terms of a membership relation ϵ. Some initial explanation is at hand, but only in the course of the development of the theory do the various characteristics of ϵ emerge with the necessary clarity.

It might be objected that (3) and cognate forms are metalinguistic and thus bring in a linguistic factor unnecessarily. Such an objection would be ill-founded, however, it being now almost universally recognized that natural languages contain their own metalanguages. Hence any natural language for protometaphysics must contain its own metalanguages. One cannot be sure in advance whether a given natural sentence requires a metalinguistic representation or not.[4] And anyhow one can always eliminate the metalinguistic factor in suitable instances by appropriate use of disquotation.[5]

The question arises now as to whether the vocabulary of protometaphysics should be taken to include epistemic forms such as (3). Such forms belong properly to a pragmatics, in which the user of language is brought in fundamentally. Varying conceptions of protometaphysics will emerge, depending upon precisely what forms are allowed. Of course ultimately *all* suitable forms must be allowed to provide the full resources of a natural language. The question here is one of classification, of deciding which are to be regarded as protometaphysical and which not.

It might be proposed to equate protometaphysics with the logical theory of the truth-functional connectives and quantifiers. But this would clearly be too narrow. The next suggestion would be to add the formal theory of identity. This, too, would seem too narrow, protometaphysics being then identified with quantificational logic with identity. This proposal is essentially that of Heinrich Scholz, although he does not explicitly use the term 'protometaphysics'.[6]

Let us consider next some rendition of Leśniewski's mereology, or the theory of the part-whole relation. Quantification theory with mereology would seem a more likely candidate to be equated with protometaphysics. The part-whole relation between individuals seems to have a more metaphysical cast to it than the identity relation does. However, this is probably illusory, for identity (in one sense) can be regarded merely as mutual part-to-whole. The next candidates for inclusion are the various subdivisions of semiotics — syntax, semantics, and pragmatics. Syntax is concerned wholly with structural features of language, and its addition surely can do no harm. Semantics is concerned with structural features of language in connection with the various relations between linguistic items and whatever it is that the language talks about. Such features and relations have been of paramount interest throughout the long history of metaphysics, but have been brought into sharp focus only very recently. The inclusion of semantics in its modern form in protometaphysics would thus seem a most natural next step. The use of semantical notions and principles is now so closely related to the use of logical principles themselves, that semantics has become merely modern logic in full dress.

Thus far, it is to be noted, there has been no suggestion to admit pragmatic forms. Pragmatics is a field of study that now includes the theory of knowledge. This latter, in its pragmatic format, we may call 'epistemics'. A useful classificatory distinction seems to be achieved if epistemics is *excluded* from protometaphysics. One reason is that the distinction accords well with tradition; another is the very character of the problems involved. Pragmatical problems go well beyond mere matters of structure; they are usually of much greater complexity, involving reference to the individual knower (or "subject") or user of language, his activities in such use, the occasions of use, changes in usage over time, and so on. Further, we can make little progress in pragmatics, and hence in epistemics, without a prior delineation of semantical structure. To draw the line between protometaphysics and whatever comes after at just this point is useful, but nothing very fundamental need depend upon it. One will merely take what comes after as conveniently belonging to metaphysics proper, or theory of knowledge, or whatever, rather than to the protometaphysical *Grundlagenforschung*.

Let us be sure now that, in characterizing protometaphysics in this way, we have not lost sight of the study of being *quā* being. The point may well be controversial if looked at historically and without regard to the very basically *ontological* character of semantics. Let us take 'Den' for multiple denotation as the basic semantical relation, so that

(5)   '*a* Den *x*'

expresses that the one-place predicate *a* denotes or applies to the individual *x, x* being perhaps merely one out of many.[7] In the admission of this bland form (5) nothing is assumed concerning *x* other than that it be one of the items in the *Bereich,* or domain of discourse or of individuals, of our language. In (5) *x* is thus considered merely an item of being, concerning which discourse can be or is being carried out. *x* is considered merely as a being *quā* being and not as possessing this or that special property. To be sure, if '*a* Den *x*' holds for a given *a* and *x, a* truly applies to it. But even so, the *x* in (5), prior (so to speak) to the mention or use of (5), is to be regarded merely as a being *quā* being, rather than as a being denoted by *a*.

Similar remarks hold of the bland form

(6)   '*x* = *y*',

for identity. In any sentence of the form (6), or the special case of it '*x* = *x* ', the *x* and *y* are taken merely as beings *quā* being. Note that we speak here of sentences, not of statements or assertions, which involve the epistemic factor of being stated or asserted (by someone).

From speaking of *a* being *quā* being, in the singular, and of beings *quā* being, in the plural, how do we go on to the abstract general phrase 'being *quā* being'? The problem is akin to how 'a man', 'men', and 'man' are interrelated. No theory of language has yet been devised, it would seem, in which this problem can be handled to everyone's satisfaction. Three possibilities immediately suggest themselves within the present framework. The phrase 'being *quā* being' might be taken as an expression for the virtual class of individuals in the domain. Or it might be taken as the fusion of that class, that is, the mereological sum of its members. A third possibility is to define it in terms of an Harrisian appropriateness relation, or a typicality relation, or the like.[8]

Howsoever 'being *quā* being' is handled as a technical term within protometaphysics, one additional item should be noted. Beings undergo changes of state, of location, they move or are moved, they do such or suffer such and such to be done to them, and so on. Our protometaphysical talk of beings might seem rather restricted if explicit provision is not allowed for events, happenings, processes, acts, states, and the like.[9] Let us use 'event' here as the blanket rubric. Are events themselves beings, not the only ones perhaps but *ex pluribus*? In any case, technical provision must be made for them at some point. The subject is of course closely allied with the study of temporality, which might be thought to lie beyond protometaphysical purview. The study of events, and of what comes tumbling along with them, need not depend on anything but the most general features of temporality, however, features that must be provided for long before we get on to the study of time, space, space-time, and the like, as needed in physics or cosmology. These latter we should not wish to regard as protometaphysical, but some minimum core of the former might well be. Again, as in the case of pragmatics generally, the problem is one of delicacy of classification, and not too much need depend upon the decisions made.

The view of protometaphysics here contrasts sharply in several respects, as already in effect noted, with that of Butchvarov. For him, as for Scholz, identity is the fundamental notion, whereas here the part-whole relation of mereology is at least as fundamental if not more so. Butchvarov seems to have no concern with mereology, although some of its notions are probably needed by him (e.g., in his handling of "clusters" of qualities). Butchvarov, unlike Scholz, is not explicit as to the role of quantification in protometaphysics. Neither Butchvarov nor Scholz are concerned with the specific character of either the syntax or semantics presupposed. And neither worries very deeply as to the status of events, states, acts, and the like.

Scholz is explicit in not recognizing any pragmatic predicates, whereas Butchvarov needs them fundamentally, as already noted, in speaking of singling out, identifying, and the like. The form (3) above is already a pragmatical form, containing parameters 'p' for the human person, 'e' for an epistemic act, and 'a' for the *Art des Gegebenseins*. It will not be without interest to reflect upon (3) and cognate forms a little more fully than above and to toy with some notions definable in terms of them, in particular, with some epistemic modalities.

A word is needed concerning syntax, about which very little has been said. It is important to emphasize that, when we speak of the protometaphysical language, we do not speak of it merely as such but also in relation to what it talks about. But as a preliminary to this latter, some basic notational matters must be properly arranged. This may be done in terms of sign designs or shapes (types) or in terms of sign events or inscriptions (tokens). In either case, a relation or operation of *concatenation* is needed, to enable us to form compound expressions out of shorter ones, the very shortest being the primitives. Throughout this chapter the approach via shapes is used, being somewhat simpler in structure than the approach based on inscriptions.

The first item to consider now is that of the *Art des Gegebenseins* itself. How is this to be handled in general, (3) embodying merely a special case? Perhaps the best way is to introduce a triadic Under relation in contexts

$$\text{'}x \text{ Under } a,e\text{'}$$

expressing that the individual x is taken under the one-place predicate description a in the intentional act or state e. i.e., that in e x is taken under the *Art des Gegebenseins a.*[10]

A Limitation Principle for Under is then that

Under R1. $\vdash (x)(a)(e)(x \text{ Under } a,e \supset (\text{Ind } x \cdot \text{PredConOne } a \cdot \text{Int } e))$,

where 'Ind', 'PredConOne', and 'Int' are appropriately construed as predicates for being an individual, a one-place predicate constant, and for being an intentional act or state. Also we should have a *Consistency Principle*, that in the same e, nothing can be taken under contradictory predicate descriptions.

Under R2. $\vdash (x)(a)(e) (x \text{ Under } a,e \supset \sim x \text{ Under } \ulcorner -a \urcorner,e)$.

A word of explanation is perhaps needed concerning the notation. The values for the expressional variables 'a', 'b', and so on, are taken as shapes of object-language expressions. Suppose a is a PredConOne. Then $\ulcorner -a \urcorner$ is the shape of the negative of a, i.e., the result of writing '$-$' (for virtual-class negation) followed by or concatenated by the shape a. Similarly, where a and b are PredConOne's, $\ulcorner (a \cup b) \urcorner$ is the shape '(' concatenated with a concatenated with '$\cup$' (for the logical sum of virtual classes) concatenated with b concatenated finally with the shape ')'. Although the use of corners within a formula, as here, is somewhat unusual, it is clear how it may be explained away in terms wholly of concatenation and shape descriptions. Once familiarity with the use of corners in this way is gained, it is seen to facilitate the notation considerably.

Let 'a Prphrs b' express that the predicate constants a and b are paraphrases of each other, in the sense used by linguists. Then also we have an Equivalence Principle, that

Under R3. $\vdash(x)(a)(b)(e)(a \text{ Prphrs } b \supset (x \text{ Under } a,e \equiv x \text{ Under } b,e))$.

A Conjunctive Principle obtains, that

Under R4. $\vdash (x)(a)(b)(e)((\text{PredConOne } a \cdot \text{PredConOne } b) \supset ((x \text{ Under } a,e \cdot x \text{ Under } b,e) \equiv x \text{ Under } \ulcorner (a \cap b) \urcorner,e))$,

and also a Disjunctive Principle, that

Under R5. $\vdash (x)(a)(b)(e)((\text{PredConOne } a \cdot \text{PredConOne } b \cdot (x \text{ Under } a,e \vee x \text{ Under } b,e)) \supset x \text{ Under } \ulcorner(a \cup b)\urcorner,e)$,

but of course not conversely. Clearly also

Under R6. $\vdash (x)(a)(e)(x \text{ Under } a,e \supset x \text{ Under } '\{y \ni y = y\}',e,)$

and

Under R7. $\vdash \sim (Ex)(Ee)x \text{ Under } '\{y \ni \sim y = y\}',e.$

UnderR6 and *UnderR7* are respectively the Principles of the Universal and Null Predicate Descriptions. Also, more generally,

Under R8. $\vdash (x)(a)(e)(b) ((\text{PredConOne } a \cdot \text{LogThm } \ulcorner(y)ay\urcorner \cdot x \text{ Under } b,e) \supset x \text{ Under } \ulcorner y \ni ay\urcorner,e)$

and

Under R9. $\vdash \sim (Ex)(Ea)(Ee)(\text{PredConOne } a \cdot \text{LogThm } \ulcorner(y)ay\urcorner \cdot x \text{ Under } \ulcorner\{y \ni \sim ay\}\urcorner,e).$

Here of course 'LogThm c' expresses that c is a logical theorem.

These Under principles are merely preliminary — and somewhat tentative — and help lay the foundations for some epistemic modalities. It might be better to think of them as Principles of Rationality, as principles of rational mental behavior, or the like. Human beings are, to some extent anyhow, rational animals, and their mental and other behavior reflects this fact more or less. However, this need not be insisted upon here. The Under principles characterize certain features of rational mental states and acts, but may not always hold with full generality. Rational *patterns* of human behavior are in any case important, patterns of nonrational or even irrational behavior, less so. Similar remarks are to apply throughout when intentional relations are under consideration — and *a fortiori* when these other relations depend upon are or introduced in terms of 'Under'.

Of course epistemics is a vast subject, the exact study of which has scarcely gotten off the ground. It is a pity that such study has in general lagged far behind the developments in formal semiotics. The comments to follow are intended to provide a kind of first step to help remedy this situation, on what is thought to be a secure foundation in protometaphysics.

Let us consider here only six basic epistemic relations, for *appearing*, for *perception*, for *conception*, for acceptance or *belief*, for *knowing*, and for *asserting*. Let

(7)   'x Appear$_e$ a,p'

(8)   '$p\,\mathrm{Prcv}_e\,x,a$',

(9)   '$p\,\mathrm{Cncv}_e\,x,a$',

(10)   '$p\,\mathrm{Blv}_e\,x,a$',

(11)   '$p\,\mathrm{Kn}_e\,x,a$',

and

(12)   '$p\,\mathrm{Assrt}_e\,a,x,q$'

be the respective forms for these relations. The symbolization is merely a first step, and should not be mistaken — as is often done — for a full analysis. Strictly speaking, it is only *after* an acceptable symbolization is at hand that we can go on to give the analysis either by suitable definitions or by citing meaning postulates (in the manner of *UnderR1–UnderR9* with 'Under' taken as a primitive). For the present, it may be left open as to which of the relation expressions occurring in (7)–(12) are to be primitives and which defined (and precisely how). In general such decisions are very difficult, and indeed, impossible to make short of a full system characterizing these notions jointly. The concern with them here is less far-reaching than this, and is merely to show how each can be used as a basis for a distinct family of interrelated modal notions.

The order of the parameters occurring in (7)–(12) should be remarked. (8)–(11) may be read essentially as (3) above, *mutatis mutandis*. (7) of course is to the effect that *x* appears, in person *p*'s act *e,* to have *a* apply to it. And (12) expresses that *p* asserts *to* person *q* in act *e* that *a* applies to *x*.

In all of the forms (7)–(12), parameters occur for both the person and the act. Of the two, the ones for the act seem the more fundamental. We might wish to reflect upon the acts independently of the person. For the epistemic modalities, the acts or states are useful, but relativity to the person is not. Presumably there is no appearing except *to* a person (or sum of such), and no perceiving, believing, knowing, or asserting except *by* a person (or sum of such). Are there states or acts of *con*ceiving other than as person-relative? A metaphysical idealist would allow for such, and perhaps also for the other kinds, or at least some of them, as well. In any case the following notations are useful, enabling us to skirt such matters if they are not of immediate relevance. And because the *conceptual modalities* seem to be the most interesting from the point of view of modal theory in general, let us begin with them.

Let '⟨Cncv⟩' be an event-descriptive predicate for acts or states of conceiving in the epistemic (not reproductive!) sense, and let '⟨Cncv⟩ *e*' express that e is such an act or state. We can leave open the question as to whether or not every conceiving involves a conceiver. But we cannot leave open that conceptions are *of* objects. Let

$$\text{'}e\,\text{Of}_{\text{Object}}\,x\text{'}$$

express that e is of x as object. $\text{Of}_{\text{Object}}$ is merely one of the many relations for which 'of' in English is used as a blanket term.[11]

The notion of being a proper name will be used here in a somewhat extended sense. The appropriate definition in terms of 'Den' for the relation of denotation, where 'InCon b' expresses that b is an individual constant, is that

'a PrNm x' abbreviates '$(Eb)(\text{InCon } b \cdot \ulcorner\{y \ni y = b\}\urcorner \text{ Den } x) \lor (\text{Pred ConOne } b \cdot \ulcorner\{y \ni (by \cdot (z)(bz \equiv z = y)\}\urcorner \text{ Den } x))$'.

In view of this definition, proper names can be handled as one-place predicates so as to allow 'x Under a,e' to be significant even where a is a proper name. Relations of designation may also be introduced if desired. Thus

'a Des$_{\text{InCon}}$ x' may abbreviate '$(\text{InCon } a \cdot \ulcorner\{y \ni y = a\}\urcorner \text{ Den } x)$'

and

'$\ulcorner(\iota a)\urcorner$ Des$_{\text{Descr}}$ x' may abbreviate '$(\text{PredConOne } a \cdot \ulcorner\{y \ni (z)(az \equiv z = y)\}\urcorner \text{ Den } x)$'.

What now is a conceptual *necessity*? Let us let

'a Nec$_{\text{Cncpt}}$ x,b' abbreviate '$(\text{PredConOne } a \cdot b \text{ PrNm } x \cdot (e)((\langle \text{Cncv} \rangle) e \cdot e \text{ Of}_{\text{Object}} x \cdot x \text{ Under } b,e) \supset x \text{ Under } a,e))$.

The definiens here is to the effect that it is necessary conceptually that x *quā* b (where b is a proper name or description of x) is taken under a, i.e., that in every act or state e of conceiving x under b, x is taken under a in e — or that x *quā* b cannot be conceived without a's being taken to denote it. We can then let

'a Psbl$_{\text{Cncptl}}$ $x\,b$' abbreviate '$(\text{PredConOne } a \cdot \sim \ulcorner -a \urcorner \text{ Nec}_{\text{Cncptl}} x,b)$'

and

'a Cntgnt$_{\text{Cncptl}}$ x,b' abbreviate '$(a \text{ Psbl}_{\text{Cncptl}} x,b \cdot \sim a \text{ Nec}_{\text{Cncptl}} x,b)$'.

Thus a *possibly* applies (conceptually) to x *quā* b provided its negative does not do so necessarily, and *contingently* so if it does so possibly but not necessarily.

A kind of quasi-modal logic can be developed on the basis of these notions, a few principles of which are as follows.

Pr1. $\vdash (a)(b)(x)(a\ \text{Nec}_{\text{Cncptl}}\ x,b \supset a\ \text{Psbl}_{\text{Cncptl}}\ x,b)$.

The proof utilizes *UnderR2* and the existence law that

$$\vdash (x)(\text{E}e)(\text{E}b)(\langle\text{Cncv}\rangle\ e \cdot e\ \text{Of}_{\text{Object}}\ x \cdot x\ \text{Under}\ b,e).$$

Pr2. $\vdash (a)(b)(c)(x)((\text{PredConOne}\ a \cdot \text{PredConOne}\ b) \supset (\ulcorner(a \cap b)\urcorner$
$\text{Nec}_{\text{Cncptl}}\ x,c \equiv (a\ \text{Nec}_{\text{Cncptl}}\ x,c \cdot b\ \text{Nec}_{\text{Cncptl}}\ x,c)))$,

in view of *UnderR4*, and

Pr3. $\vdash (a)(b)(c)(x)((\text{PredConOne}\ a \cdot \text{PredConOne}\ b \cdot (a\ \text{Nec}_{\text{Cncptl}}\ x,c$
$\text{v}\ b\ \text{Nec}_{\text{Cncptl}}\ x,c)) \supset \ulcorner(a \cup b)\urcorner\ \text{Nec}_{\text{Cncptl}}\ x,c)$,

in view of *UnderR5*. Note that the corresponding principle with ' $\equiv$ '
does *not* obtain. And of course

Pr4. $\vdash (x)(a)(b)((\text{PredConOne}\ a \cdot \text{LogThm}\ \ulcorner(y)ay\urcorner \cdot b\ \text{PrNm}\ x) \supset$
$\ulcorner\{y \ni ay\}\urcorner\ \text{Nec}_{\text{Cncptl}}\ x,b)$,

in view of *UnderR8*.

Concerning conceptual possibility, we have that

Pr5. $\vdash (a)(b)(c)(x)((\text{PredConOne}\ a \cdot \text{PredConOne}\ b \cdot \ulcorner(a \cap b)\urcorner$
$\text{Psbl}_{\text{Cncptl}}\ x,c) \supset (a\ \text{Psbl}_{\text{Cncptl}}\ x,c \cdot b\ \text{Psbl}_{\text{Cncptl}}\ x,c))$,

in view of *Pr3, UnderR3*, and the lemma that

$\vdash (a)(b)(x)((\text{PredConOne}\ a \cdot \ulcorner-a\urcorner\ \text{Psbl}_{\text{Cncptl}}\ x,b) \supset\ \sim a\ \text{Nec}_{\text{Cncptl}}$
$x,b)$

and an adaptation of DeMorgan's law that

$\vdash (a)(b)\ ((\text{PredConOne}\ a\ \cdot\ \text{PredConOne}\ b) \supset\ \ulcorner(a \cap b)\urcorner\ \text{Prphrs}$
$\ulcorner-(-a \cup -b)\urcorner)$.

Also it obtains that

Pr6. $\vdash (a)(b)(c)(x)((\text{PredConOne}\ a \cdot \text{PredConOne}\ b) \supset (\ulcorner(a \cup b)\urcorner$
$\text{Psbl}_{\text{Cncptl}}\ x,c \equiv (a\ \text{Psbl}_{\text{Cncptl}}\ x,c\ \text{v}\ b\ \text{Psbl}_{\text{Cncptl}}\ x,c)))$,

the proof utilizing *Pr2*.

For a full development of the theory here suitable rules governing
'Cncv' must of course be adopted.

What now is an essence, more particularly, the *conceptual essence* of
an individual *x*? Clearly it should consist of just the one-place predicates
a such that *a* $\text{Nec}_{\text{Cncptl}}\ x,b$. Thus

'ess$_{Cncptl}$ '*x,b*' may abbreviate '$\{a \ni a \, \text{Nec}_{Cncptl} \, x,b\}$'.

This definition would seem to supply an especially clean-cut rendition for an otherwise rather murky notion.

To return a moment to one of Butchvarov's puzzles. *Accidental* predication may be handled merely as predication in the object language. *Essential* predication — essential *conceptual* predication — seems fully handled by means of 'Nec_{Cncptl}'. A one-place predicate *a* is essentially predicable of *x* just where it is a member of the conceptual essence of *x*. What, strictly, is an *object*? Merely a self-identical individual or a member of the universal class. And what is an *entity*? For the handling of this there must be some reference to some conceptual, or at least intentional, act of which it is an object in the sense of belonging to the counterdomain of Of$_{Object}$. Let 'Int *e*' express (as above) that *e* is an intentional act or state of the appropriate kind. Then we may let

$$\text{'}x \text{ Ent } e\text{'} \quad \text{abbreviate} \quad \text{'}(\text{Int } e \cdot e \text{ Of}_{Object} x)\text{'}.$$

Finally, how is *existence* to be treated? We may let N be the null individual, the one individual that, according to Leśniewski, does not exist.[12] To exist, then, is merely not to be identical with N.

How now is *relational* predication handled? Clearly accidental relational predication is object-linguistic, handled in terms of the application of a two-place (or three-or-more-place) predicate to two (or more) arguments taken in order. But how about *essential* relational predication? Let '*x* R *y*' express as usual that *x* bears the dyadic relation R to *y*, or that 'R' is accidentally predicated of *x* and *y* in this order. Two kinds of essential predication suggest themselves, one relative to *x* and one relative to *y*. Clearly if

$$\text{''}\{z \ni \alpha \text{ R } z\}\text{'} \text{ Nec}_{Cncptl} \, \beta, \text{ '}\beta\text{''}$$

holds (for constant 'α' and 'β' designating *x* and *y* respectively), then it is conceptually necessary for β that α bear R to it; whereas if

$$\text{''}\{z \ni z \text{ R } \beta\}\text{'} \text{ Nec}_{Cncptl} \, \alpha, \text{'}\alpha\text{''}$$

holds, it is conceptually necessary for α that it bear R to β. Of course both of these might obtain, but need not in general.[13] If they do, we have a third type of conceptual relational predication. We may speak of these types as being relative to the first argument, relative to the second, and relative to both. And similarly for triadic relations with seven types of conceptually necessary relational predication; and in general $2^n - 1$ types for *n*-adic relations.

We have spoken thus far only of conceptual necessity, possibility, contingency, and essences. But clearly the other relations, embodied in the forms (7), (8), (10), (11), and (12), likewise give rise to alternative kinds of modal theory. In this way we can distinguish *aspectual, perceptual, doxastic, sapiential* or *noetic,* and *assertoric* modalities, respectively, leaving open the further exploration of the specific features of these various types.

Are there, in addition to the foregoing — which might all be thought of as *subjective* modalities because they involve reference to the person or at least to acts or states — *objective* modalities? If so, a full characterization of them should be given within a suitable protometaphysical vocabulary. This appears not to have been done. Instead, objective modalities are usually handled in terms of *ad hoc* primitives 'Nec' or '□' or the like that are not defined away in terms of appropriate protolinguistic primitives, a good deal of mystery thereunto appertaining as a result. (See, however, IV below.)

If the various suggestions above concerning the epistemic modalities are sound, we would seem to have in protometaphysics as conceived here a suitable means for extricating ourselves from the kinds of epistemic and other puzzles Butchvarov considers. No doubt the suggestions here can be improved upon in various ways. But enough has been shown surely to see the great relevance of exact semiotics for epistemics. It is a pity the latter has been lagging so far behind the former, and that epistemologists have not availed themselves of the very techniques most appropriate for their very needs.

CHAPTER IV

On Actuality and
Objective Modality

> "Be not the first by whom the new are tried,
>   Nor yet the last to lay the old aside."
>
> *Pope*

What is the actual? The question is reminiscent of Richard Kroner's "What is the really real?"[1] Of course no one knows how to answer either of these questions. Whatever the really real is, it seems to be made "manifest" in various ways to constitute the various items of our cosmos and of our discourse concerning them. To get at either the actual or the really real is to make use of language, at the really real perhaps only in highly metaphysical terms, and at the actual in terms of our everyday experience, performative, perceptual, and conceptual. The actual is always relative to the time-span of specific acts or events as well as to particular ways of denoting or describing what it is that is actual. Discourse about actuality must thus, it would seem, make use of a *triadic* relation with one argument for a really real entity, with another for the way in which it is denoted or described, and a third for the act or occasion in or during which the really real entity is actually actual. The really real abides and undergoes change, coming into being, passing out of being, and so on, whereas the actual abides only during the occasions of being actual as described in such and such ways.

Let us reflect upon these difficult matters, tentatively and by way of exploration, by letting

(1) $\qquad\qquad\qquad$ 'x Actl$_e$ a'

express primitively that the really real entity or individual x is actual as described by the one-place predicate a during the time span of the occasion e. The person Socrates, for example, is actual at or during an e during his lifetime and as described by 'living Greek phiolsopher', 'living and snub-nosed', 'husband of Xantippe', and so on. But if e is some occasion occurring in the twelfth century, A.D., say, then Socrates is not actual at e as described by any of these predicates. For given instances of (1) to be true, with suitable constants replacing the variables, a suitable tensed sentence must be true, namely, that x at or during the time span of e be a member of the virtual class designated by a. Of course there may be many such states or occasions e, which we can group together into the virtual class $\{e \ni x \; \text{Actl}_e \; a\}$.

Another way of reading (1) is in terms of the notion *quā*. (1) could be read 'e is an occasion of x *quā a*'s being actual' or 'x *quā a* is actual at e'. For this purpose no technical term — for the moment anyhow — need be introduced to represent ' x *quā a* '. Rather '*quā*' takes on its character here wholly in terms of locutions of the form (1). Let us think of the really real as beings *quā* beings — as physico-chemical in some sense, as bits or manifestations of mind stuff, as congeries or pulsations of energy, or as combinations of such, *quodlibet*. In this way we need not run into difficulties concerning the conservation of energy, personal identity, and the like. Actual entities thus come into being and pass out of being with preservation of some fundamental *housia* that undergoes the change. The really real are thus the individuals that are assumed to exist independent of change. This, in any case, is the view under consideration.

Let us go on now to try to connect this notion of actuality with a notion of objective modality. In so doing, a few constructive steps, it is hoped, will be taken towards developing a systematic theory.

First we must ask what it can mean to say that the really real entity x permanently "ceases to be" such and such at e? In terms of 'Actl' we may let

'x Cease$_e$ a' abbreviate '$(Ee_1)(\text{Mom } e_1 \cdot e_1 \text{ Before}_{\text{Time}} e \cdot \sim (Ee_2)$ $(e_1 \text{ Before}_{\text{Time}} e_2 \cdot e_2 \text{ Before}_{\text{Time}} e) \cdot x \text{ Actl}_{e_1} a \cdot \sim x \text{ Actl}_e a \cdot (e_2)(e \text{ Before}_{\text{Time}} e_2 \supset \sim x \text{ Actl}_{e_2} a))$'.

Thus x ceases to have the one-place predicate constant a apply to it at e just when x is not actual *quā a* at e but was such at an immediately preceding momentary event e_1, and x continues to be non-actual *quā a* into the future. Here 'Before$_{\text{Time}}$' stands for the relation between events of occurring wholly before and 'Mom' for the notion of being a momentary event.

In a similar fashion we may introduce the notion that x *quā a* is *not yet* actual at e and never has been prior to e. Let

'x NotYet$_e$ a' abbreviate '$(Ee_1)(\text{Mom } e_1 \cdot e \text{ Before}_{\text{Time}} e_1 \cdot \sim (Ee_2)$ $(e \text{ Before}_{\text{Time}} e_2 \cdot e_2 \text{ Before}_{\text{Time}} e_1) \cdot \sim x \text{ Actl}_e a \cdot x \text{ Actl}_{e_1} a \cdot (e_2)$ $(e_2 \text{ Before}_{\text{Time}} e \supset \sim x \text{ Actl}_{e_2} a))$'.

What now might it mean to say the a one-place predicate constant a is *objectively necessary* for x as a b (or *quā b*) where b is a proper name? Let us let

'a Nec$_{\text{Obj}} x, b$' abbreviate '$(a \text{ Den } x \cdot b \text{ PrNm } x \cdot (Ee')(x \text{ Actl}_{e'} a \cdot x$

$Actl_{e'}$ b) · (e)(x $Cease_e$ a ⊃ (∼ x $Actl_e$ b · (e')(e $Before_{Time}$ e' ⊃ ∼ x $Actl_{e'}$ b))) · (e)(x $NotYet_e$ a ⊃ (∼ x $Actl_e$ b · (e')(e' $Before_{Time}$ e ⊃ ∼ x $Actl_{e'}$ b))))'.

The purported answer to this query is thus: just where a denotes x, b is a proper name of x^2, there is an occasion at which x is actual *quā a* and *quā b,* and x *quā b* fails to be actual at any occasion or any subsequent one at which a ceases to apply to x as well as at any occasion or prior one at which a does not yet apply to x. Thus, in effect, x fails to exist *quā b,* or to be the thing it is as designated by b, whenever a ceases to, or does not yet, apply to it.

Ruth Marcus has hinted at two ways of exploring objective modalities, one in terms of "ceasing to exist" and one in terms of "ceasing to be the thing it is."[3] More specifically, for her a property might be said to be necessary for x just where if x ceases to have it, x ceases to exist, or else x ceases to be the thing x is. Both of these phrases are troublesome and in need of a good deal of logical reconstruction, as Marcus would no doubt agree. The foregoing provides one attempt at such, without parlance about "properties" or anything equally mysterious, and where 'ceasing to be the thing x is' is construed as 'x's being non-actual *quā* being such and such'. Also the notion of not yet applying seems needed. Even so, there is some approximation surely to what appears to be the Marcus view. Here, however, it is thought that "what x is" must be explicitly *specified* in order to be discussed intelligibly. An enduring entity x is many things, but can be said to come into being, to be actual, and pass out of being only *quā b* where b is some name or description of it.

Let us return for a moment to Socrates and his actuality. What *we* call 'Socrates' is actual at suitable e's under various predicate descriptions. He is actual at all e's during his lifetime under the predicate description 'identical with the living (468–399 B.C.) Socrates'. *We* might refer to his corpse, after his death, under this same description, but neither he nor it would then be actual as the living Socrates. We might go on to refer to the disintegrated corpse, to the logical sum of its atoms, molecules, and so on, under suitable predicate descriptions, but that logical sum would not then be actual as the living Socrates. What now are some *necessary* predicate descriptions of Socrates? First we must specify that we are referring to Socrates as taken under a suitable proper name (or description), say, 'the living Socrates', 'husband of Xantippe', or whatever, under which he is actual at some e. Then 'living' is necessary for Socrates taken under the description 'the living Socrates', because when 'living' ceases to apply to him, he is no longer actual *quā* 'the living Socrates'. But 'great Greek philosopher' is not necessary for x *quā* 'the living Socrates', for there is an e when Socrates was actual *quā* 'the living Socrates' but did not yet have 'great Greek philosopher' apply to him. And similarly for 'husband(s) of Xantippe'. It is not necessary for Socrates that he be a great Greek philosopher or that he be the husband of Xantippe; these are rather accidents of history. And similarly for other examples.

Note the need here for x to be taken *quā* some b. It is not the *thing* x but the concept (or quasi-concept) x *quā* b that is here regarded as having an objective modality, so to speak. The needed intensionality is gained by reference to x *quā* b rather than to just x. And similarly for the *predicate* a. Predicates are in effect intentional objects whereas the virtual classes (or relations) to which they refer are not. Note also that expressions are taken here as shapes or sign designs rather than as inscriptions or sign events. A more adequate theory would result if it were based on the latter, but a somewhat simpler notation is at hand if we use the former.

Note incidentally that 'PrNm' here is being taken as 'proper name or Russellian description of', as in III above.

We may now go on to introduce *objective possibility* and *objective contingency* in familiar fashion, by letting

'$a \, \mathrm{Psbl}_{\mathrm{Obj}} \, x,b$' abbreviate '$(\mathrm{PredConOne} \, a \cdot b \, \mathrm{PrNm} \, x \cdot (\mathrm{E}e)x \, \mathrm{Actl}_e \, b \cdot {\sim} \ulcorner -a \urcorner \mathrm{Nec}_{\mathrm{Obj}} \, x,b)$'

and

'$a \, \mathrm{Cntgnt}_{\mathrm{Obj}} \, x,b$' abbreviate '$(a \, \mathrm{Psbl}_{\mathrm{Obj}} \, x,b \cdot {\sim} a \, \mathrm{Nec}_{\mathrm{Obj}} \, x,b)$'.

To help make our ideas clear, the following principles characterizing 'Actl' would seem needed.

R1. $\vdash (x)(a)(e)(x \, \mathrm{Actl}_e \, a \supset \mathrm{PredConOne} \, a)$,

R2. $\vdash (a)(x)(e)((\mathrm{InCon} \, a \cdot x \, \mathrm{Actl}_e \, \ulcorner \{y \ni y = a\} \urcorner) \supset a \, \mathrm{Des}_{\mathrm{InCon}} \, x)$,

R3. $\vdash (a)(x)(e)(x \, \mathrm{Actl}_e \, a \supset a \, \mathrm{Den} \, x)$,

R4. $\vdash (x)(a)(e)((\mathrm{PredConOne} \, a \cdot {\sim} x = \mathrm{N} \cdot x \, \mathrm{Actl}_e \, a) \supset {\sim} x \, \mathrm{Actl}_e \, \ulcorner -a \urcorner)$,

R5. $\vdash (x)(a)(b)(e)((\mathrm{PredConOne} \, a \cdot \mathrm{PredConOne} \, b \cdot (x \, \mathrm{Actl}_e \, a \vee x \, \mathrm{Actl}_e \, a)) \supset x \, \mathrm{Actl}_e \, \ulcorner (a \cup b) \urcorner)$,

R6. $\vdash (x)(a)(b)(e)((\mathrm{PredConOne} \, a \cdot \mathrm{PredConOne} \, b) \supset (x \, \mathrm{Actl}_e \, \ulcorner (a \cap b) \urcorner \equiv (x \, \mathrm{Actl}_e \, a \cdot x \, \mathrm{Actl}_e \, b)))$.

Let now

'*a* Sub *b*' abbreviate '(PredConOne *a* · PredConOne *b* · LogThm ⌜(*y*)(*ay* ⊃ *by*)⌝)',

so that the definiendum expresses that *a* is subsumed in *b* in effect in the sense that it is a logical theorem that *b* denotes everything that *a* does. Then

'*a* Eq *b*' is short for '(*a* Sub *b* · *b* Sub *a*)'

and expresses that the one-place predicate constants are logically equivalent. Then, where V and Λ are the universal and null virtual classes, respectively,

R7.   ⊢ $(x)(e)(a)((\sim x = \text{N} \cdot a$ Eq 'V') ⊃ x Actl$_e$ $a)$,

R8.   ⊢ ∼ $(Ex)(Ee)(Ea)(a$ Eq 'Λ' · x Actl$_e$ $a)$,

R9.   ⊢ ∼ $(Ea)(Ee)(\text{PredConOne } a \cdot \text{N Actl}_e a)$,

R10.   ⊢ $(x)(a)(b)(e)((x$ Actl$_e$ $a \cdot a$ Sub b) ⊃ x Actl$_e$ $b)$.

R1 will be recognized as a principle of limitation, and *R2* and *R3* connect actuality with designation and denotation respectively. *R4, R5,* and *R6* are quasi-Boolean laws, connecting virtual-class negatives, sums, and products with truth-functional negation, disjunction, and conjunction respectively. *R7* is to the effect that every really real entity other than the null entity N is always actual *quā* really real, i.e., *quā* a member of the universal class V. *R8* states that nothing really real is ever actual *quā* a member of the null class Λ. And finally, *R9* assures us that the null entity N is never actual under any one-place predicate. *R10* is a principle of subsumption.

A few useful lemmas are as follows.

Lemma1.   ⊢ $(e)(e_1)(e_2)(x)(a)((\text{Mom } e_1 \cdot \text{Mom } e_2 \cdot e_1 \text{ Before }_{\text{Time}} e \cdot$ e_2 Before$_{\text{Time}}$ $e \cdot \sim (Ee_3)(e_1$ Before$_{\text{Time}}$ $e_3 \cdot e_3$ Before$_{\text{Time}}e) \cdot \sim (Ee_3)(e_2$ Before$_{\text{Time}}$ $e_3 \cdot e_3$ Before$_{\text{Time}}$ $e)$) ⊃ $(x$ Actl$_{e_1}$ $a \equiv x$ Actl$_{e_2}$ $a)$).

Lemma2.   ⊢ $(a)(b)(x)(e)(a$ Eq b ⊃ $((x$ Actl$_e$ $a \equiv x$ Actl$_e$ $b) \cdot (x$ Cease$_e$ $a \equiv x$ Cease$_e$ $b) \cdot (x$ NotYet$_e$ $a \equiv x$ NotYet$_e$ $b)))$,

Lemma3.   ⊢ $(a)(x)((a$ Eq 'V' · ∼ $x = $ N) ⊃ ∼ (Ee) x Cease$_e$ $a)$,

Lemma4.   ⊢ ∼ $(Ex)(Ee)(Ea)(Eb)(Ec)(b$ PrNm $x \cdot c$ PrNm $e \cdot x$ Actl$_e$ ⌜$\{y \ni (y = b \cdot \sim b$ Actl$_c$ $a)\}$⌝).

A few further important laws governing these notions are as follows.

R11. $\vdash (x)(a)(b)(e)((x \, \text{Cease}_e \, a \cdot b \, \text{Sub} \, a) \supset x \, \text{Cease}_e \, b)$,

R12. $\vdash (x)(a)(e)(x \, \text{Cease}_e \, a \supset \, \sim x \, \text{Cease}_e \, \ulcorner\text{-}a\urcorner)$,

R13. $\vdash (x)(a)(b)(e)((\text{PredConOne} \, a \cdot \text{PredConOne} \, b \cdot (x \, \text{Cease}_e \, a$ v $x \, \text{Cease}_e \, b)) \supset x \, \text{Cease}_e \, \ulcorner(a \cap b)\urcorner)$,

R14. $\vdash (x)(a)(b)(e)((\text{PredConOne} \, a \cdot \text{PredConOne} \, b) \supset (x \, \text{Cease}_e$ $\ulcorner(a \cup b)\urcorner \equiv (x \, \text{Cease}_e \, a \cdot x \, \text{Cease}_e \, b))$,

with analogous laws concerning 'Not Yet'. Also

R15. $\vdash (a)(x)(b)(a \, \text{Nec}_{\text{Obj}} \, x,b \supset a \, \text{Psbl}_{\text{obj}} \, x,b)$,

R16. $\vdash (a) \, (x) \, (b) \, (c) \, ((\text{PredConOne} \quad a \, \cdot \, \text{PredConOne} \quad b \, \cdot$ $\text{PredConOne} \, c) \supset (a \, \text{Nec}_{\text{Obj}} \, x,c \cdot b \, \text{Nec}_{\text{Obj}} \, x,c) \equiv \ulcorner(a \cap b)\urcorner \, \text{Nec}_{\text{Obj}}$ $x,c))$,

R17. $\vdash (a) \, (x) \, (b) \, (c) \, ((\text{PredConOne} \quad a \, \cdot \, \text{PredConOne} \quad b \, \cdot$ $\text{PredConOne} \, c \cdot (a \, \text{Nec}_{\text{Obj}} \, x,c \, \text{v} \, b \, \text{Nec}_{\text{Obj}} \, x,c)) \supset \ulcorner(a \cup b)\urcorner \, \text{Nec}_{\text{Obj}} \, x,c)$,

R18. $\vdash (a)(b)(x)(c)((\text{PredConOne} \, a \cdot \text{PredConOne} \, b \cdot c \, \text{PrNm} \, x \cdot$ $(\text{E}e)x \, \text{Actl}_e \, c \cdot \ulcorner(a \cap b)\urcorner \, \text{Psbl}_{\text{Obj}} \, x,c) \supset (a \, \text{Psbl}_{\text{Obj}} \, x,c \cdot b \, \text{Psbl}_{\text{Obj}} \, x,c))$,

R19. $\vdash (a)(b)(x)(c)((\text{PredConOne} \, a \cdot \text{PredConOne} \, b \cdot c \, \text{PrNm} \, x \cdot$ $(\text{E}e)x \, \text{Actl}_e \, c) \supset (\ulcorner(a \cup b)\urcorner \, \text{Psbl}_{\text{Obj}} \, x,c \equiv (a \, \text{Psbl}_{\text{Obj}} \, x,c \, \text{v} \, b \, \text{Psbl}_{\text{Obj}}$ $x,c)))$.

It is interesting to observe that the forms '$a \, \text{Nec}_{\text{Obj}} \, x,b$' and so on contain '$\text{Nec}_{\text{Obj}}$' and so on as *relational* terms. Modalities are thus handled relationally rather than as operations. Of course one could write — if we disregard for the moment the parameter 'b' — '$\text{Nec}_{\text{Obj}} \, ax$' equally well, or even '$\text{Nec}_{\text{Obj}} \, \ulcorner ax\urcorner$', and then, by disquotation where a is the shape, say 'F',

'$\text{Nec}_{\text{Obj}} \, \text{F}x$'.

Of course the form '$a \, \text{Nec}_{\text{Obj}} \, x$' would be significant for *variable* 'a' and for variable 'x', whereas any result of disquotation, '$\text{Nec}_{\text{Obj}}\text{F}x$', would be significant only for *constant* 'F'. It is also interesting to note that the purported forms '$a \, \text{Nec}_{\text{Obj}} \, x$', and so on, would be significant with quantifiers on 'x'. '$(x) \, a \, \text{Nec}_{\text{Obj}} \, x$' would be significant, and also even '(x) $\text{Nec}_{\text{Obj}} \, \text{F}x$' by disquotation. But because 'Nec_{Obj}' is a relational term, '$\text{Nec}_{\text{Obj}} \, (x)\text{F}x$' is of course meaningless. Thus there is no need of a Carnap-Barcan-like formula to the effect that

$(x)\text{Nec}_{\text{Obj}} \, \text{F}x \equiv \, \text{Nec}_{\text{Obj}} \, (x)\text{F}x$.

Also the modal notions here cannot be iterated. '$\text{Nec}_{\text{Obj}} \, \text{Nec}_{\text{Obj}} \, ax$' would

37

be as meaningless as 'a Nec$_{\text{Obj}}$ Nec$_{\text{Obj}}$ x' would be. And hence there is no need of a meaningless reducibility formula, to the effect that

$$\text{Nec}_{\text{Obj}} \, \text{Nec}_{\text{Obj}} \, ax \supset \text{Nec}_{\text{Obj}} \, ax$$

or of any formula of like kind. That all such formulae are meaningless is thought to be an advantage of the present notation. One is not then tempted to force more out of it than it is designed to deliver. Also the role of the parameter 'b' should not be disregarded. It is easy to see, however, how 'Nec$_{\text{Obj}}$' supplants the more familiar '$\square$' or 'N' for necessity, although the foregoing principles could be written in terms of them if desired.

Enough has been shown surely to see that a sufficient basis appears to be at hand for developing a rather extensive theory of objective modalities. Some interesting further notions are immediately definable. For example a restricted notion of *strict implication* may be introduced as follows. We let

'$(\ulcorner ax \urcorner <_c \ulcorner bx \urcorner)$' abbreviate '$\ulcorner \{ y \ni (ay \supset by) \} \urcorner$ Nec$_{\text{Obj}}$ x,c',

Of course here ' $<$ ' is defined here only in a context in which 'x' and 'c' appear as additional parameters.

Just as there are relational epistemic modalities, as in III above, so also are there *relational objective modalities*. And there are of course *objective essences* of various kinds depending upon restrictions on the various parameters.

Whether or not the suggested definitions provide an "immaculate conception" of the objective modalities must remain for further research. One thing is certain, however: namely, that such a conception will never take place short of explicitly bringing to light all of the "hidden" variables and predicates involved. It is the lack of clarity concerning these more than any other single factor, it would seem, that has blocked the road to inquiry into the fundamental syntax and semantics of the language needed for discussing the objective modalities. Among the hidden notions are those of being actual, of coming into being, of ceasing to be, and so on. It is unfortunate that the metaphysical theory of these notions seems not to have been looked at *logistice*. It is hoped that the foregoing comments, albeit highly tentative, will be useful as a first step in this direction. The material here is thus put forward more as a first sketch of a research proposal than as a statement of results achieved. If the going has been somewhat difficult, this is due in part to the nature of the subject matter, which has been under almost continual metaphysical discussion for well over two thousand years with little discernible progress.

CHAPTER V

On the Metaphysical Presuppositions of Logic

"Regard not then if wit be old or new,
   But blame the false, and value still the true."
                                            Pope

In his paper "The Metaphysical Presuppositions of Formal Logic,"
presented at the meeting of the Logic and Metaphysics Seminar of the
International Society for Metaphysics in 1980,[1] E. E. Harris commented
that "the suggestion that logic rests upon metaphysical presuppositions
is liable in these days to be rejected with scorn." The reasons for this
rejection seem, in Harris's view, to be threefold. "First, it will be said,"
he notes, "logic is a purely formal discipline abstracting entirely from
the material content of discourse and concerned solely with the form and
the formal relations of its expressions. . . . Further, it is widely held, the
logical structure of thought or its expression neither dictates nor is determined by metaphysical doctrine." And, thirdly, "criticism of metaphysical presuppositions is possible on logical grounds. . . . If logical principles were consequences of metaphysical presuppositions, such criticism
would be impossible and self-destructive."

If in fact there is scorn for the suggestion that logic rests upon metaphysical presuppositions, it would seem unlikely that it is for the reasons
Harris cites. Logic is not now regarded, it would seem, as "a purely formal discipline abstracting entirely from the material content of discourse
and concerned solely with the formal relations of its expressions." Logical *syntax* is the discipline concerned with such formal relations and logical *semantics* with material content, and logic is universally construed
nowadays as comprising both.[2] Secondly, the study of "the logical structure of thought or its expression" is now a part no doubt of *epistemic*
logic, the exact relations of which with metaphysics (howsoever conceived) remain to be examined. Of this more in a moment. Harris's third
reason, that criticism of metaphysics is possible on logical grounds, is
surely cogent, and actually appears to be an argument *against* his own
position. It invites also the related comment that criticism of logical presuppositions is possible on metaphysical grounds. Of this too, more in a
moment.

Harris rejects all three of these arguments on the grounds that they "presuppose, first, that form and content are unrelated and mutually independent, which is itself a metaphysical assumption. And secondly, validity in reasoning is what guarantees true conclusions from true premises, and that can be ensured on the ground of some real connection in the content. Principles of valid inference, therefore, can hardly be independent entirely of the nature of the subject matter, unless they are to be altogether trivial and ineffectual." It would surely seem incorrect, however, to contend that syntax and semantics, the modern prototypes of the study of "form" and "content," as used in the present context, are "unrelated and mutually independent." On the contrary, it would seem, the two go hand in hand, syntax being formulated in such a way that a semantics may be built upon its basis, and semantics being formulated in such wise as to incorporate the syntax within its inner structure. Is this interrelationship based on a metaphysical assumption? Perhaps, as we shall see later.

Harris wants "validity in reasoning" to be based on "some real connection in the content," and contends that the principles of validity are not "independent entirely of the nature of the subject matter." It is doubtful that anyone nowadays would disagree too much with the latter of these contentions if it is suitably construed. Valid rules of inference are such as always to lead from truths to truths, and 'truth' is now to be characterized in terms of the semantical relations the constituent expressions bear to items in the "subject matter." The former contention, however, that validity of reasoning is based on some real connection in the content, is rather vague, depending upon how the phrase 'real connection in the content' is to be construed. If construed in terms of truth, some appropriate meaning can very likely be given to this phrase. If it is construed in terms of *necessary* truth, however, a suitable rendition of that notion, not open to the objections usually launched against unanalyzed notions of necessity, should be provided.[3]

Harris goes on to suggest that inference "is an operation of thought" and that "few [logicians] would wish to deny that logic is concerned with concepts, with the relations between them, and between them and the entities of which they are the concepts." He goes on to construe 'concept' in a somewhat Fregean way, but succeeds no more than Frege did — or his followers have done — in making the notion clear or in formulating a suitable theory concerning it. It has frequently been urged, it will be recalled, that thoughts are best construed in terms of *acts of thinking* and concepts in terms of *acts of conceiving*. Logic is not ordinarily construed as comprising a theory of either of these, and most logicians would in fact deny that it should be. An *applied* logic, yes, but not logic in the standard sense of first-order quantification theory *cum* its syntax, semantics, and perhaps even its pragmatics.[4] Of this, too, more in a moment.

After presenting a purported critique of Frege's characterization of number, Harris comments that "the metaphysical background to this [Frege's] theory is, obviously, the conception of a pluralistic world of particular entities or 'objects' classifiable into sets. . . . The attributive relation between property and object remains undefined, but we may assume that it is a contingent relation. That [relation — what relation?] between objects is wholly external, depending only upon how they are collected together into classes or sets, and so likewise is the relation [which relation?] between sets. The appropriate metaphysical theory is Logical Atomism, as it was propounded by Bertrand Russell early in this century, and by Wittgenstein in his *Tractatus.*" Strictly, here, we should distinguish carefully among *Frege's* theory, reconstructions of it, and the ramified and simplified theories of types of Russell. To none of these, however, is Harris's comment applicable, if by 'the metaphysical background of a theory' one means its *ontology,* the domain of values for its variables. However, suitable emendations to Harris's comment could be given, each type of system having its own unique kind of ontology. Even so, by 'the metaphysical background of a theory' we should presumably mean more than just an ontology; we mean also some full metaphysical *theory* governing that ontology. The attributive relation in all of these theories may well be "contingent" in some sense to be characterized, 'contingent' not carrying its own meaning with it pellucidly on its sleeve. But to contend that all such theories are akin to Logical Atomism seems incorrect. None of them need be, but all of them can be made so. Logical Atomism is a theory about the world and about "facts," whatever these latter are.[5] One should be careful not to confuse here "atomic facts" with atomic, as opposed to molecular, *formulae.* This latter is a purely syntactical notion. The distinction between these two has been made much of in the relevant literature.

The next stage of Harris's argument — that what he calls 'formal logic' has metaphysical presuppositions that are inadequate because they are "not true of things as they really are in concrete fact" — is to the effect that "the fundamental laws of algebra," those of commutation, association, and distribution, do not hold "if . . . the units that make up a collection were internally related so that they affected one another in certain ways, or constituted one another by their mutual relations, if, in short, we were dealing with wholes and not with mere collections, . . ." The fundamental laws of algebra were never intended, by anyone ever, to be universally applicable. They are very special laws applicable only to given objects for which the constituent functors or operation-symbols are suitably defined. They *may* hold of some of Harris's wholes or they may not. This is a matter to be determined, not to be laid down *a priori*. And in any case, Leśniewski's mereology, or the calculus of individuals, an important but neglected adjunct to modern logic, is now available to help handle relations of part-to-whole. Unfortunately, most philosophers even today write as though Leśniewski, one of the very greatest of all logicians, had never written.

Harris comments that "logicians have been particularly careful to ensure that their manipulation of the *symbols* [italics added] which they employ shall conform to the three fundamental algebraic laws, and we now see that the condition for this is that these symbols should represent entities that are externally related or are composed of externally related elements." In the first part of this sentence, the *symbols* are under discussion, and in the latter the entities they "represent," and something or other about representation is said to be the "condition" for the conformity of the symbols to the fundamental algebraic laws. But this seems to be rather awry. In the first place, "the manipulation of symbols" is a syntactical affair, and syntax is based on an operation of *concatenation*.[6] Presumably it is some such operation as this that Harris thinks should be subject to the algebraic laws. Concatenation, however, has an "algebra" of its own, wherein commutative and distributive laws do not hold, although an associative one does. Thus where $(a \cap b)$ is the result of concatenating the expressions (shapes or sign designs) a and b in this order, we have that

$$((a \cap b) \cap c) = (a \cap (b \cap c)),$$

but also that

$$\sim a = b \supset \sim (a \cap b) = (b \cap a),$$

and

$$\sim (a \cap (b \cap c)) = ((a \cap b) \cap (a \cap c)).$$

This last concerns the non-distributivity of concatenation with respect to itself.

Semantics is the study of how symbols are related to the objects for which they stand. Individual constants are said to *designate* their objects and one-place predicates to *denote* the objects to which they apply. Algebraic laws are ordinarily construed as containing *free variables,* and variables neither designate nor denote, but instead have objects as their *values.* Expressions — single symbols and all concatenates of them — are the values for the variables 'a', 'b', and so on, of syntax. Whether the expressions are "internally" or "externally" related to each other, in some suitable sense, is quite beside the point that concatenation does not obey Harris's three fundamental laws; it was never intended by anyone that it should.

Are expressions, as construed in syntax — either as based on shapes or as based on inscriptions — externally or internally related to each other? One can, if one wishes, regard the axioms governing concatenation as *meaning postulates* in essentially Carnap's sense, so that all concatenational principles come to be regarded as analytic truths. Analytic truths are often construed as internally relating the objects they talk about. Or, one can take the axioms governing concatenation merely as metalinguistic axioms. Nothing very profound is at stake either way so far as regards "internal relations." The exact characterization of these relative to a given context — like that of 'necessity' itself — remains to be provided. (Again, recall III and IV.)

Harris contends that "symbols, if they are to be useful and if one is to be able to manipulate them algebraically, must represent identical and unchanging . . . entities." Such a contention seems much too strong and rules out all talk of changing entities. The phrase 'the pencil with which I am now writing' is a Russellian description for an entity under constant change — every letter written shortens the length of its lead. Even the very description itself, i.e., any physical *inscription* of it, is changing continually in time. Harris seems to have misstated his point here. Both symbols in the sense of physical inscriptions as well as the entities in the world they are taken to stand for in one way or another are temporal entities and thus are under constant change, whether these symbols be of a formal logical system or of a natural language. Harris's contention here is so strong as to rule out all possibility of an inscriptional notation for anything for which we would apply the term 'language'. He states also that "in a system in which the elements are internally related, so that any change in either part or whole is liable to affect any and every element in the system, symbols representing the elements would be unstable and algorithmic operations with them would break down." There seems to be confusion here between the use and mention of expressions. And, according to this, no language could ever talk about the very kinds of internally related elements intended. Harris's point here is so strong as to defeat its very purpose.

The next phase of the argument against formal logic is a repetition of familiar arguments against material implication. Harris does not seem to separate sufficiently material from formal or other kinds of implication and, again, ties the use of material implication to the doctrine of Logical Atomism. "It remains true, therefore," he writes, "that the doctrine of material implication makes sense only if the propositions to which it applies are all atomic and logically independent." This, however, seems not the case. Systems based upon material implication can handle all manner of the most intimate logical dependencies, and the "propositions to which it applies" can be expressed by all manner of molecular formulae of great internal complexity. Harris foists upon material implication here roles other than those for which it is intended and in isolation from the contexts to which it is "applicable"; also he takes no account of *quantifiers* or of the *inner vocabulary* of the formulae. Thus he writes that "the truth of 'Newton was a man' does not depend on that of 'The sun is hot', but must be known independently before we can write '⊃' between [all quotes added]." Now of course material implication is not intended in solitary splendor to capture a notion of "dependence," although it has often been construed to have been so intended. Also the notion of what must be *known* prior to such and such is a notion of *epistemic* logic and brings in a vast amount of theory over and above that required for the material conditional.

Harris insists upon reading the sign '⊃' for material implication in terms of the 'if . . . then . . .' of ordinary language. This is an error much to be lamented[7] and vitiates almost everything he says about it. The best reading of '$(p \supset q)$' is perhaps as 'not both p and $\sim q$' or 'p holds only if q does' (where 'holds' is a surrogate for 'is true' construed in Carnap's absolute sense, not in the semantical sense[8]). Harris confuses material implication not only with relations of dependence and with some epistemic ones, but even with causal relations, thereby enhancing the misunderstanding of what formal logic is and of its role in natural language and inquiry generally. Relations of dependence, epistemic ones, and so on, are all to be defined in terms of the full nonlogical vocabulary needed for them. It is a grave error to expect the poor little notion of material implication to bear the Herculean burden of all this.

In spite of these various points, Harris is one of the handful of metaphysicians who try at least to come to terms with modern logic. The more usual attitude is one of convenient disregard. 'Logica sunt, non leguntur' is the guiding maxim for most metaphysicians just as 'Metaphysica sunt, non leguntur' is for most logicians. Both attitudes, it will be recalled, were lamented by Frege.[9] Harris too seems to lament both attitudes, and this is very much to the good.

What Harris wants, as a surrogate for formal logic, is what he calls 'dialectical logic' in which what he calls 'internal relations' may be handled. Unfortunately he has told us very little about either of these, not enough anyhow to formulate laws concerning them with the kind of rigor now appropriate. Much work has been done since the days of Frege and Russell, of which note should be taken. In particular, the beginnings of a theory of intentionality are now available, in addition of course to the semantical theory of truth.[10] Both of these would be helpful to Harris in his attempt to formulate a "dialectical" logic. In addition, there is a theory of events, acts, states, and processes, including mental ones, that might be useful. In fact, there is the whole of *protometaphysics* as outlined in III above. These do not perhaps provide all of the resources Harris needs, but they would very likely help to get his enterprise off the ground, and in modern terms.

Another interesting — but more acceptable — discussion of the presuppositions of formal logic is that of Aron Gurwitsch, along Husserlian lines.[11] Gurwitsch makes essentially five points, as follows. (1) "The perceptual world as it presents itself in pre-predicative experience [prior to all categorical operation] appears as one of the fundamental presuppositions of logic" (p. 353). (2) Logic also presupposes (p. 356) "the constitutive consciousness of which the [perceptual] world is the intentional correlate." (3) "There is also (p. 357) the *ideal identity* of propositions — that is to say, there is the possibility of reverting to them, whenever one wishes to, as identically the same — and also the ideal possibility of reiterating logical operations." (4) "In speaking of the ideal identity of propositions, we contrast the *one* and identical proposition with the *multiplicity* of acts, real or possible, through which the proposition is grasped or may be grasped." And (5) there is (p. 358) "the principle of *phenomenological idealism* according to which whatever exists and has validity derives the sense of its existence and validity from conscious life and can find its ultimate clarification and final justification only by means of analyses of acts and of groups of acts in which it presents itself as existing and as valid." Some comments concerning these are now in order.

Gurwitsch is careful to note that by 'presupposition' one does not mean "a premise which one had simply forgotten to state . . . nor . . . an axiom which has a well-defined place within a deductive system and entails certain consequences, such that the change of the axiom in question would invalidate the consequences and entail different ones." What, then, precisely is a presupposition? It must be something *stated* or at least capable of being stated. Probably the best way of looking at the matter is to regard a presupposition as a *metalinguistic* statement concerning the system in question. Are all such statements presuppositions of that system? This might be thought too wide a construal. Not all such statements perhaps would appear to be "philosophical" or "metaphysical." On the other hand, it would be difficult to draw a sharp line between metalinguistic statements that would bear these labels and those that would not. Also much would depend upon the kind, and specific character, of metalanguage being spoken of. Some metalanguages might contain a theory of "perceptual experience," others not. Some might contain talk of the "constitutive consciousness," others not. Much here seems to depend upon the specificities of one's philosophical or metaphysical view. Usually metalanguages do *not* contain talk of these two types, the Husserl-Gurwitsch view being that they should do so, however, in order to handle the pertinent "presuppositions."

If we were to weaken Gurwitsch's item (1) to just a world of "objects" or "individuals," whether perceptual or not and whether "presented" in any particular kind of experience or not, we would have a requirement contained implicitly anyhow in practically all semantical metalanguages. There surely is no doubt but that there is both "perceptual" experience as well as pre-perceptual experience in some sense, but the "objects" considered might be wholly "abstract" or conceptual in some sense. However, in the formulation of a logical system, there must be some manipulative experience of its *symbols* and of the *concatenates* of such. Should we distinguish here acts of *formulating* a system from the system itself? Can the system "exist," in any reasonable sense, prior to or independent of its formulation? This is a delicate question that need not be decided here. A metalanguage might well contain a comprehensive theory of acts, mental ones as well as "pencil and paper" operations, including all kinds that would enter into the formulation of a logical system. (Cf. XI below.)

Gurwitsch's (2) would be rejected by most logicians as a presupposition of a logical system. The existence of a "constitutive consciousness" would, however, be needed if human *persons* figure among the values for variables of the system. All systems containing a pragmatics are of this kind, including those for intuitionistic logic and mathematics in which the "creative subject" is brought in as a separate factor. Although persons might not figure in the object language, they do so in the metalanguage. Their existence might thus well be regarded as a presupposition for a logical system, the *use* of whose statements in one form or another is under discussion — their being apprehended, known, asserted, or whatever.

In discussing (3), let us speak of statements, the interpreted declarative sentences of the system, in place of "propositions" — this latter being a highly ambiguous notion. The "ideal identity" of the statements is built into the very notation, so to speak, and is provided for by suitable pragmatical principles. Thus, where an inscription *a* is an eternal sentence and

$$\text{'}p \text{ Acpt } a,e\text{'}^{12}$$

expresses that person *p accepts* statement *a* during occasion *e*, and

$$\text{'}p \text{ Like } a,b,e\text{'}^{13}$$

expresses that *p* takes the inscriptions *a* and *b* during *e* to be typographically *alike* or of the *same shape*, then it clearly holds in the metalanguage that

$$(p)(a)(b)(e)((p \text{ Acpt } a,e \cdot p \text{ Like } a,b,e) \supset p \text{ Acpt } b,e).$$

And similarly for other pragmatical relations. Whatever one would want to say about ideal identity could be said in terms of the vast multiplicity of principles of this general kind, including of course some semantical ones. For the handling of noneternal or occasion sentences, additional factors must be brought in.

Gurwitsch's point (4) is also in effect built into the very notation. There is a multiplicity of noetic and epistemic acts in which one and the same statement can be grasped. And similarly for statements that bear the Like relation to each other. "These acts," Gurwitsch comments very appropriately, "can differ from one another in several ways. In the case of the repeated positing of the same proposition by the same subject, the acts of positing differ from one another at the least within phenomenal time by whatever follows from the difference in temporal placement. Furthermore, the same proposition may be posited by diverse subjects, in which case the acts of positing belong to different streams of consciousness. Besides the differences in temporal placement [and the subjects] there may be differences in what Husserl calls 'the quality of the act', when, for example, the same proposition is at one time simply posited, at another time doubted, questioned, subsequently reaffirmed, negated, etc., whether by the same person or by a plurality of subjects." All of these differences may readily be supplied in the pragmatics of the language, where

$$\text{'}\langle p,\text{Acpt},a,e\rangle e\text{''}$$

for example, expresses that *e'* is an act of *p*'s accepting *a* during *e*. Temporal differences are provided by the varying times during which *e'* can take place, differences in the subject by differences in the persons, and differences in the "quality of the act" by considering relations other than Acpt.

Phenomenological idealism, the point (5), likewise is provided by the pragmatic theory of acts, of individual acts, of virtual classes of them, and of mereological sums of them. The final justification of having a logical system at all is to be described in terms of what the users of it do with it, more particularly, do with its constituent sentences. All of

Gurwitsch's points thus seem legitimate ones, and we see that they may be provided for in full in terms of what is essentially the protometaphysics of III above. To say this, however, is not necessarily to subscribe *au pied de la lettre* to what Gurwitsch demands, so much as to record what would appear to be sameness of general intent. (Cf. again XI below.)

What now are we to conclude concerning the metaphysical presuppositions of logic and the logical presuppositions of metaphysics? A characterization of the latter is easier than for the former, although much must depend upon the particular character of the system involved. We must know what the metaphysical system is, at least roughly, before we can tell what its logical presuppositions are. Presumably it will be such as to presuppose at least the standard first-order quantification theory; even type and set theories can be construed as particular instances of such. The *specificia* of a given metaphysics are then handled by means of particular nonlogical constants taken as primitives. It is doubtful that any metaphysical system has ever been put forward that cannot be put into such a framework by a suitable choice of primitives.

What now are the metaphysical presuppositions of any system based upon first-order logic? Well, as already suggested, we would wish to include the syntax, semantics, and pragmatics of the full language of the given system. Thus presupposed is the full vocabulary of its semiotics, including the abbreviatory definitions within the semiotics, as well as its various principles. Among these principles, however, we do *not* include translations of the nonlogical axioms of the object language, but only the intrinsically semiotical principles, so to speak. These comprise, then, the logical truth-functional and quantificational principles, the principles of syntax, semantics (as based say on denotation), and pragmatics. Moreover, to handle Gurwitsch's *desiderata,* notions and principles of the theory of events also are to be available, including a form or forms of Leśniewski's mereology. All of this adds up to essentially the protometaphysics of III above.

The metaphysical presuppositions of logic are thus thought to be the notions and principles of the semiotics governing it and concern fundamental properties of the notation and of the way in which that notation relates to what it talks about, as well as fundamental properties concerning the human use of that notation. The metaphysical presuppositions of a logical system then are wholly contained, it would seem, within its protometaphysics. This latter might appear too narrow to be called a full-blown metaphysics. It is rather the antechamber, the interesting metaphysical problems coming only when we enter the edifice proper. We should strictly then speak hereafter only of the *proto*metaphysical presuppositions of logic.

The relation of being a presupposition of is presumably transitive, so that, metaphysics presupposing logic and logic presupposing protometaphysics, metaphysics presupposes protometaphysics. This seems precisely as it should be. Protometaphysics is of so completely general a nature as to be common to all clearly-articulated metaphysical systems. It is the antechamber over the gate of which is written: no one can approach the subject except ye who enter here. Once beyond the gate, however, one has enormous freedom of choice as to the kind of metaphysics he wishes. The principles of any full-blown system are always such as to be beyond the protometaphysical confines.

CHAPTER VI

On the Semantics of
Sommers' 'Some *S*'

"But when t'examine every part he came,
Nature and Homer were, he found, the same.
Convinc'd, amaz'd, he checks the bold design,
And rules as strict his labour'd work confine,
As if the Stagyrite o'orlook'd each line.
Learn hence for ancient rules a just esteem;
To copy Nature is to copy them."

Pope

That the English 'some *S'*, where '*S*' is a predicate, should be regarded as a term akin in some ways to singular terms, proper names, and definite descriptions, is a thesis that has been espoused by many logicians throughout history. It is a thesis that has some attractive features and that merits a close investigation. Fred Sommers, in his *The Logical Syntax of Natural Language*,[1] is one of the most recent writers to have espoused this thesis in a certain form. Sommers, as his title suggests, is concerned primarily with syntactical matters, the exact semantics of his theory thus remaining to be supplied. In this present paper, let us formulate a theory in accord with this thesis and akin to Sommer's work, and then go on to supply an exact semantics for it.

For the purposes here a good deal will depend upon the use of the theory of virtual classes and relations. Quine, in his *Set Theory and Its Logic*,[2] has made much of these, but only within the context of a set theory. It is curious that the multifarious uses of the virtual-class technique beyond the confines of set theory have not attracted him. These uses would seem by far the more important, however, mathematical set theory going its own way only in dealing with real classes, the virtual ones being merely ancillary. More depends on the use of virtual classes than one might suppose, however, the moment we step beyond set theory. And although virtual classes and relations are wholly eliminable, in all their philosophical uses, at the object language level, it is useful for semantical purposes to take expressions for them as primitives. Thus, although not eliminable as primitives in the semantics, all uses of them in the object-language part of the semantics, so to speak, are wholly eliminable as usual.[3]

Let us assume now that the truth-functional connectives are available in some familiar way, say in terms of ' ~ ' and 'v' as primitives with the Bernays axiom schemata characterizing them, essentially as in *Principia Mathematica*. Let us assume that the usual variables for individuals, '*x*', '*y*', etc., with or without accents or numerical subscripts, some proper names of individuals (optional), together with some nonlogical predicates, each of specified degree, are available as primitives. In addition we have as primitives virtual-class and -relation abstracts of the forms

$$\ulcorner \{x \ni \text{--}x\text{--}\} \urcorner, \ \ulcorner \{xy \ni \text{--}x\text{--}y\text{--}\} \urcorner,$$

and so on, where $\ulcorner \text{--}x\text{--} \urcorner$ and $\ulcorner \text{--}x\text{--}y\text{--} \urcorner$ are sentential forms. Here *x* may or may not occur freely in $\ulcorner \text{--}x\text{--} \urcorner$ and *x* and *y* may or may not occur freely in $\ulcorner \text{--}x\text{--}y\text{--} \urcorner$. Also these sentential forms are allowed to contain free occurrences of variables other than *x* or *y*. Let now '*F*', '*G*', and so on, by any virtual-class or -relation abstract, the degree of which will always be clear from the context. Also it is convenient to have ' = ' as a primitive as between variables or proper names. One more primitive and we are done, namely, 'some' in contexts $\ulcorner(\text{some } F)\urcorner$ where *F* is of degree 1.

We can make these various comments a bit more precise by the following syntactical stipulations by simultaneous recursion concerning 'formula', 'term' and 'abstract of degree *n*',

1. If *A* is a formula, so is $\ulcorner \sim A \urcorner$,

2. If *A* and *B* are formulae, so is $\ulcorner(A \text{ v } B)\urcorner$,

3. Any individual variable or primitive proper name is a term,

4. If $x_1, \ldots, x_n$ are individual variables and *A* a formula, then $\ulcorner\{x_1 \ldots x_n \ni A\}\urcorner$ is an abstract of degree *n*.

5. Where $\breve{P}$ is a primitive one-place predicate constant of degree 1, $\ulcorner(\text{some } P)\urcorner$ is a term.

6. Where *F* is an abstract of degree 1, $\ulcorner(\text{some } F)\urcorner$ is a term.

7. If *X* is a primitive nonlogical predicate of degree *n* and $x_1, \ldots, x_n$ are any proper names or variables, then $\ulcorner X \, x_1 \ldots x_n \urcorner$ is a formula.

8. If *F* and *G* are abstracts of degree 1 then $\ulcorner F(\text{some } G)\urcorner$ is a formula.

9. If *x* and *y* are variables or proper names, $\ulcorner x = y \urcorner$ is a formula.

These clauses do not strictly constitute a "definition," but are merely stipulations indicating how an exact metalinguistic definition could be given.

Clause 8 here is such, it should be observed, that $\ulcorner(\text{some } F)\urcorner$ is significant only in contexts of the form $\ulcorner G(\text{some } F)\urcorner$, where G is an *abstract* of degree 1, and not a one-place primitive constant. Thus strictly we must always write $\ulcorner \{x \ni --x--\}(\text{some } F)\urcorner$, but never $\ulcorner P(\text{some } F)\urcorner$ where 'P' is primitive and $\ulcorner --x--\urcorner$ molecular. No genuine limitation on the modes of expressiveness is imposed by this restriction, for we can always write $\ulcorner \{x \ni Px\}(\text{some } F)\urcorner$ in place of $\ulcorner P(\text{some } F)\urcorner$ for primitive 'P'. In insisting upon this way of writing, no conventions concerning scope are needed. Also there will be no danger of confusion between, say,

$$\ulcorner (\sim B \vee G(\text{some } F))\urcorner$$

and

$$\ulcorner \{x \ni (\sim B \vee Gx)\}(\text{some } F)\urcorner,$$

as there might be otherwise.[4]

As rules stipulating axioms concerning 'some' we have the following, stated entirely in terms of the primitives:

SR1. $\vdash \ulcorner (\{x \ni \sim A\}(\text{some } \{x \ni \sim A\}) \vee B)\urcorner$, where B differs from A only in containing free occurrences of a variable or proper name wherever there are free occurrences of x in A.[5]

SR2. $\vdash \ulcorner (\{x \ni \sim (A \vee B)\}(\text{some } \{x \ni \sim (A \vee B)\}) \vee (\sim \{x \ni \sim B\}(\text{some } \{x \ni \sim B\}) \vee A))\urcorner$, if there are no free occurrences of the variable x in A.

We have also one rule of inference, namely:

Inf.   If $\vdash A$, then $\vdash \ulcorner \sim \{x \ni \sim A\}(\text{some } \{x \ni \sim A\})\urcorner$.

The foregoing rules may be made more perspicuous as follows. First we may define in familiar fashion

$$\ulcorner (A \supset B)\urcorner \quad \text{as} \quad \ulcorner (\sim A \vee B)\urcorner,$$

$$\ulcorner (A \cdot B)\urcorner \quad \text{as} \quad \ulcorner \sim (\sim A \vee \sim B)\urcorner,$$

and

$$\ulcorner (A \equiv B)\urcorner \quad \text{as} \quad \ulcorner ((A \supset B) \cdot (B \supset A))\urcorner.$$

We may then define also

$$\ulcorner (Ex)(A \cdot B)\urcorner \quad \text{as} \quad \ulcorner \{x \ni A\}(\text{some } \{x \ni B\})\urcorner,$$

and then immediately

$$\ulcorner (Ex)A\urcorner \quad \text{as} \quad \ulcorner (Ex)(A \cdot A)\urcorner,$$

and then

$$\ulcorner(x)A\urcorner \text{ as } \ulcorner \sim (\text{E}x) \sim A\urcorner.$$

In this way we gain contextual definitions of the familiar notations for the existential and universal quantifiers within the system based on 'some'. And we can make the content of *SR1-SR2* clearer by noting, as logical consequences of them, the familiar principles that

$\vdash \ulcorner((x)A \supset B)\urcorner$, where *B* differs from *A* only in containing free occurrences of a term wherever there are free occurrences of *x* in *A*,

and

$\vdash \ulcorner((x)(A \lor B) \supset (A \lor (x)B))\urcorner$, if there are no free occurrences of *x* in *A*.

Similarly *Inf* is seen now, in view of the definitions, to be merely the familiar Rule of Generalization that

$$\text{If } \vdash A \text{ then } \vdash \ulcorner(x)A\urcorner.$$

It is well known that these principles, together with definitions, suffice for first-order quantification theory.

The following four principles are of especial interest in connection with 'some' and are easily proven. First there is the *Principle of Exchange*, let us call it, that

$$\vdash \ulcorner(F(\text{some } G) \equiv G(\text{some } F))\urcorner.$$

There are also the two *Principles of Extensionality*, that

$$\vdash \ulcorner(F = {}_{\text{VC}} G \supset (H(\text{some } F) \equiv H(\text{some } G)))\urcorner$$

and

$$\vdash \ulcorner(F = {}_{\text{VC}} G \supset (F(\text{some } H) \equiv G(\text{some } H)))\urcorner{}^{6}$$

And finally there is the *Principle of the Product*, that

$$\vdash \ulcorner(F(\text{some } G) \equiv (F \cap G)(\text{some V}))\urcorner,$$

where

$$\ulcorner(F \cap G)\urcorner \text{ is short for } \ulcorner\{x \ni (Fx \cdot Gx)\}\urcorner,{}^{7}$$

and

'V' for '$\{x \ni (Px \lor \sim Px)\}$' where 'P' is a primitive predicate of degree 1.

These last notations are for the logical product of any two virtual classes or class functions and for the universal virtual class. Similarly we may introduce

$$\ulcorner(F \cup G)\urcorner \text{ for } \ulcorner\{x \ni (Fx \vee Gx)\urcorner$$

and

$$\ulcorner-F\urcorner \text{ for } \ulcorner\{x \ni \sim Fx\}\urcorner,[8]$$

as expressions for the logical sum of two virtual classes or class functions and for the negation of one.

Because abstracts are taken as primitive expressions of the object language, suitable *Rules of Concretion and Abstraction* are to be added to the logical rules.[9] But only variables and proper names are allowed as arguments, due to the need for suitable scope restrictions for occurrences of expressions of the form $\ulcorner$(some $F)\urcorner$.

The problem remains of providing an exact semantics for the system based on 'some'. This may easily be gained, however, by a suitable adaptation of the familiar semantics based on 'Den' for multiple denotation.[10] Let 'a Den x' express that the object-language expression or shape a denotes the individual x. If now 'PrNm a' expresses that a is a primitive proper name, we may let

'a Des$_{PN}$ x' abbreviate '(PrNm $a \cdot \ulcorner\{x \ni x = a\}\urcorner$ Den x)'.

In this way a suitable notation for the designation of individuals by proper names (PN) may be introduced.[11]

The problem now is how to handle the designation, if such it be, of expressions of the form $\ulcorner$(some $F\urcorner$ or $\ulcorner$(some $a)\urcorner$ for appropriate a. For this purpose a slight extension must be made in the usual Rules of Denotation. Let us start from scratch, then, and formulate the rules as follows.

DenR1a. $\vdash \ulcorner(x)(u$ Den $x \equiv Px)\urcorner$, where P is a primitive predicate constant of degree 1 and a is its structural description,

DenR1b. $\vdash \ulcorner(x)(a$ Den $x \equiv$ --x--$)\urcorner$, where '--x--' is a sentential form containing 'x' as its only free variable if any and a is the structural description of the abstract '$\{x \ni$ --x--$\}$',

DenR2. $\vdash (a)(x)(a$ Den $x \supset$ PredConOne $a)$, where 'PredConOne a' expresses that a is a primitive predicate constant of degree 1 or an abstract of degree 1.

We now let

'$\ulcorner$(some $a)\urcorner$ Des$_S$ x' abbreviate '(PredConOne $a \cdot \ulcorner\{y \ni \{z \ni y = z\}($some $a)\}\urcorner$ Den x)', recognizing that this definition is akin to that for proper names given a moment back. The kind of designation it introduces is that appropriate for expressions of the form $\ulcorner$(some F)$\urcorner$. Our next rule now is that

$Den_SR.$ $\vdash (a)((Ex)a \text{ Den } x \supset (Ex)\ulcorner(\text{some } a)\urcorner \text{ Des}_S x).$

Note that, although this rule is a Rule of Denotation, it is stated partly in tems of 'Des$_S$'. Note also that it is a rule rather more special than the others in containing an existential quantifier. The rule does not tell us which entity any given 'some' expression designates, but only that there is such an entity satisfying such and such a nonnull condition.

A notion $\ulcorner$(all F)$\urcorner$ or $\ulcorner$(all a)$\urcorner$ may be introduced in context, in the object language, as follows. We let

$$\ulcorner G(\text{all } F)\urcorner \quad \text{abbreviate} \quad \ulcorner \sim \{x \ni \; \sim Gx\}(\text{some } F)\urcorner.$$

'(all F)', for any specific 'F', then becomes a denoting term along with 'F' itself. In fact, we may let "(all F)' Den x', or, more generally,

'$\ulcorner$(all a)$\urcorner$ Den$_A$ x', be merely an alternative notation for 'a Den x'.[12]

The appropriate semantical *Rule of Denotation for 'All'* is then merely that

$Den_AR.$ $\vdash (a)(x)(a \text{ Den } x \equiv \ulcorner(\text{all } a)\urcorner \text{ Den}_A x).$

And also the Russellian notion $\ulcorner$(the F)$\urcorner$ or $\ulcorner$(the a)$\urcorner$ is immediately forthcoming. We let

$$\ulcorner G(\text{the } F)\urcorner \quad \text{abbreviate} \quad \ulcorner G(\text{some } \{x \ni (Fx \cdot (y)(Fy \supset y = x))\})\urcorner.$$

A notion of designation appropriate to expressions of the form $\ulcorner$(the F)$\urcorner$ or $\ulcorner$(the a)$\urcorner$ is now as follows. We let

'$\ulcorner$(the a)$\urcorner$ Des$_T x$' abbreviate '(PredConOne $a \cdot \ulcorner\{y \ni ay \cdot (z)(az \supset z = y))\}\urcorner$ Den x)'.

The appropriate *Rule of Designation for 'the'* is then

$Des_TR.$ $\vdash (a)(x)((a \text{ Den } x \cdot (y)(a \text{ Den } y \supset y = x)) \supset \ulcorner(\text{the } a)\urcorner$ Des$_T x$).

One more relation of designation will be useful. Let

'a Des$_{\text{Ind}} x$' abbreviate '(a Des$_{\text{PN}} x$ v $\ulcorner$(the a)$\urcorner$ Des$_T x$)'.

This notion, designation of individuals, introduces nothing new.

The system based on 'some' provides a viable alternative formulation of quantification theory in line with Sommers' general approach. If we wish to concern ourselves now with the subtleties of natural language and to provide logical forms for all manner of its sentences, we would go on to extend the system in the directions indicated in *Semiotics and Linguistic Structure, Logico-Linguistic Papers*, and other previous publications. To simplify, however, a classical syntax and semantics based on shapes or sign designs is used here rather than one based on inscriptions or sign events.

At the very beginning Sommers contrasts two positions, the "constructionist" and the "naturalist," in what he calls 'logical syntax'. The former is regarded as that of Frege and the latter as that of Frege's predecessors, especially Aristotle and Leibniz. "The naturalist believes," Sommers writes, " . . . that logical syntax is implicit in the grammar of natural language and that the structure attributed by grammarians to sentences of natural language is in close correspondence to their logical form." This is not the occasion to press Sommers for an exact delineation of how he construes 'logical syntax' so much as to note that the spirit underlying the system above based on 'some' is to unify the two positions. The opposition Sommers draws is perhaps too sharp, especially if semantical considerations are added. From this somewhat wider point of view we are able to consolidate relevant features of the work of Aristotle and Leibniz with the essentials of the great tradition of Peirce, Leśniewski, Carnap, Tarski, and the newer logico-linguistics.

Rather than to comment on Sommers' main contentions one by one, let us rather cite logical forms for a few of the sentences he considers using the logico-linguistic devices referred to above.

Consider first the difference (p. 7) between 'Socrates is wise' and 'Socrates is unwise'. These sentences need not be regarded as negatives of each other, as Sommers rightly insists, but rather are to be construed in terms of a scale based on the relation of being-less-wise-than as confined to a predicate for human persons. To "represent" 'Socrates is wise', we have the form

'Socrates High Less-Wise-Than, 'HP'',

expressing that Socrates is high in the appropriate scale, for the comparative relation Less-Wise-Than as confined to the predicate for human persons. And 'Socrates is unwise' is represented by

'Socrates Low Less-Wise-Than, 'HP'',

that he is placed low in the scale. Thus the two are by no means contradictories of each other.[13] The theory of adjectives developed in terms of scales as based on certain comparative relations is in agreement with Sommers' kind of analysis of them.

The sentence (p. 13)

(1)   'If you've smelled one violet you have smelled them all'

should not be given the form

'Anyone is such that if there is a thing such that that thing is a violet and he or she smells it then anything is such that if it is a violet then he or she smells it'.

Clearly this latter is false, whereas (1) is intended to be true. Further, 'you' should not go over into 'he or she', and the tensed phrases should be taken seriously. Also the sentence is clearly an intensional one, albeit in a rather special sense. What we need rather is something like

'Anything you have done under the description of its being a smelling of one and only one violet is a doing under the description of its being a smelling of all violets'.

In logico-linguistic notation, this may be rendered as

(1')   '$(e)(e')((\langle$you,Do,$e\rangle e' \cdot e$ Under$_{e'}$ '$\{e'' \ni (\langle$Smell$\rangle e'' \cdot (Ex)(e''$ Of$_{Object}$ $x \cdot$ Violet $x \cdot (y)(e''$ Of$_{Object}$ $y \supset y = x))\}$') $\supset e$ Under$_{e'}$ '$\{e'' \ni (\langle$Smell$\rangle e'' \cdot (x)($Violet $x \supset e''$ Of$_{Object}$ $x))\}$')'.

The notations here are as in the various works referred to. To say '$\langle$you,Do,$e\rangle e''$ is to say that e' is a doing by you of e, i.e., '$(\langle$Do$\rangle e' \cdot e'$ By$_{Agent}$ you $\cdot e'$ Of$_{Object}$ $e)$', where By$_{Agent}$ is the by-relation of agency and Of$_{Object}$ is the of-relation of objectuality (or of being the object of). The sentential function 'e Under$_{e'}$ a' where a is a PredConOne expresses that e is taken in or during e' under the predicate description a. The relation Under is an intensional relation providing a way of capturing the essentials of Frege's *Art des Gegebenseins*. [14]

The sentence

(2)   'Some boy was admiring every girl'

is another interesting example of an intensional sentence that should not be given a simple quantificational form, say

(2')   '$(Ep)($Boy $p \cdot (q)($Girl $q \supset p$ Admired $q))$'.

Instead, 'admired' should be handled intensionally and the gerundive 'admiring' should be brought in explicitly. Let

$$\langle p, \text{Admire}, q \rangle e'''$$

express that e''' is an act of admiring q. Our sentence may then be given the form

(2″)   '(Ep)(Boy p · (Ee)(Ee')(Ea)($\langle p,$Do$,e\rangle e'$ · e Before$_{\text{Time}}$ now · a Des$_{\text{Ind}}p$ · e Under$_{e'}$ $\ulcorner\{e'' \ni (q)$(Girl $q \supset \langle a,$Admire$,q\rangle e'')\}\urcorner$))'.

Here 'e Before$_{\text{Time}}$ now' expresses that e took place before the now of any utterance or use of the formula in which it occurs. Also this formulation assumes that p has a proper name or definite description whether known to the speaker or not.

Let us presume that the original sentence (2) is intended to be true, so that (2′) also then should be true. Literally, however, (2′) cannot be true in any but a Pickwickian sense of 'Admires'. Presumably one cannot in any one act, or even state of mind, admire every girl, past, present, future, here, there, and everywhere. (2″), however, can be true, albeit in a somewhat extended sense, provided what the boy p does is taken under the given predicate description. The description may not truly apply to what he does, but it may truly be taken by the speaker to do so.

The sentence (p. 20)

(3)   'Everybody envies somebody'

becomes here, where 'Per p' expresses that p is a person, not

'(p)(Per $p \supset$ (Eq)(Per q · p Envies q))',

but rather, 'envy' also being intensional,

(3′)   '(p) (Per $p \supset$ (Ee) (Ee') (Ea) ($\langle p,$Do$,e\rangle e'$ · e Habitual p · a Des$_{\text{Ind}}$ p · e Under$_{e'}$ $\ulcorner\{e'' \ni$ (Eq)(Per q · $\langle a,$Envy$,q\rangle e'')\}\urcorner$))'.

To say that e Habitual p here is to say that e is the kind of act that is habitual to p. (3) is thus construed in the sense that it is habitual for each person to envy somebody (or other).

Although the forms (1′), (2′), and (3′) are cited in terms of the quantifiers, they could be equally well cited in primitive terms without quantifiers using only 'some'.

Sommers' comments concerning "indefinite" or "weak" reference (pp. 73ff.) may all be handled here in terms of the notions 'Des$_S$' and 'Den$_A$'. Also 'Des$_T$' and 'Des$_{\text{Ind}}$' are available where needed. It remains to consider cases of indefinite reference where there is nothing to be referred to, cases of null reference, as it were. Clearly,

(4)   'I see a ghost'

is not to be handled as

'(Ex)(Ghost x · I See x)',

but rather as

(4')   '(Ee)(Ee')(Ex)($\langle$I,Do,$e\rangle e'$ · e During now · $\langle$See$\rangle e$ · e Under$_{e'}$ '$\{e'' \ni$ (Ex)(Ghost x · e'' Of$_{\text{Object}}$ x)$\}$')'.

This form can of course be true just if I am truly doing a seeing under a description — my own presumably — of its being of a ghost. There need be no ghost for me to see, as is required by the simpler form. Similarly for sentences containing 'all ghosts' or 'the ghost', *mutatis mutandis*.

To handle pronominalization (Sommers' Chapter Four), we can in general where needed make use of a triadic relation of co- or cross-reference, CrRef, as in the work of Harris and Hiz. To illustrate, let us consider

(5)   'A man tried several times to reach you yesterday. He had a gravel voice'.

Here the 'he' is presumed, in the most natural reading, to cross-refer to the man who tried to reach you yesterday. To simplify and to "scratch only where it itches" at the moment, let

'(Ep)(Mp · Tp · GV He)'

abbreviate the form needed, for the "text" consisting of the two sentences, with the capital letters symbolizing the required predicates. To assure the requisite cross-reference of 'He' here, we add clauses to this effect. Thus

(5')   '(Ep)(Ea)(Mp · Tp · GV He · 'He' CrRef$_{\text{·GVHe·}}$ a · a Des$_{\text{Ind}}$ p)'

would be the desired form where the clause containing 'CrRef' expresses that 'He' as occuring in 'GV He' is cross-referential to some name or description of p. Alternatively, a triadic relation of pronomial direct reference could be introduced so that

''He' Ref$_{\text{·GVHe·}}$ p'

would express that 'He' as occuring in 'GV He' directly refers to p. (More adequate forms here would be in terms of inscriptions rather than shapes. Throughout, however, to simplify, as already remarked, the semantics used is a classical one based on the latter.) The triadic relations Ref and CrRef are taken here as *sui generis* and no attempt is made to reduce them to any of the semantical relations already introduced.

Incidentally, throughout the foregoing, there is the usual ambiguity in the use of 'some' in $\ulcorner$(some F)$\urcorner$ as between singular and plural. The usual reading is 'at least one' but for the plural reading 'at least two' is appropriate. Clearly we may let

$\ulcorner G(\text{some}_{\text{plural}}F,)\urcorner$ abbreviate $\ulcorner\{x \ni \{y \ni (Gx \cdot Gy \cdot \sim x = y)\}$ (some F)}(some F)$\urcorner$[15]

and

$\ulcorner G(\text{some}_{\text{singular}}F)\urcorner$ be an alternative notation for $\ulcorner G(\text{the } F)\urcorner$.

Using these notions, or their quantificational equivalents, we can handle the difference between the texts

(6)   'Some (one) man is at the door. Fred believes he is friendly'

and

(7)   'Some men are at the door. Fred believes they are friendly'.

The first text may be given the form

(6')   '({$p \ni (Ee)((\langle p, \text{At}_{\text{Location}},)(\text{the Door})\rangle e \cdot e$ During now)} (some$_{\text{singular}}$ M) $\cdot (Ee_1)(Ea)((\langle \text{Blv}\rangle e_1 \cdot e_1 \text{ By}_{\text{Agent}}$ Fred $\cdot e_1$ During now $\cdot e_1$ That$_{\text{Content}}$ $a \cdot$ 'he' Ref$_a$ (the $\{p \ni (Mp \cdot (Ee)(\langle p, \text{At}_{\text{Location}},(\text{the Door})\rangle e \cdot e$ During now)}) $\cdot a =$ 'he High Less-Friendly-Than, 'Per'))'.

Here 'That$_{\text{Content}}$' stands for the that-relation of giving the content of.

And similarly, *mutatis mutandis,* for the second. Note that the 'they' there should be construed collectively, rather than distributively. Presumably Fred believes that they as a whole are friendly and not necessarily that each and every one of them is friendly. The 'they' is thus to be handled in terms of the logical sum of persons who are at the door, logical sums of individuals being available from the calculus of individuals, which may now be presumed as incorporated in the system here.[16] A suitable form for (7) thus appears to be

(7')   '({$p \ni (Ee)$ ($\langle p, \text{At}_{\text{Location}},$ (the Door) $\rangle e \cdot e$ During now)}(some$_{\text{plural}}$ M) $\cdot (Ee_1)(Ea)((\langle \text{Blv}\rangle e_1 \cdot e_1 \text{ By}_{\text{Agent}}$ Fred $\cdot e_1$ During now $\cdot e_1$ That$_{\text{Content}}$ $a \cdot$ 'they' Ref$_a$ (Fu'$\{p \ni (Mp \cdot (Ee) (\langle p, \text{At-}_{\text{Location}},$ (the Door)$\rangle e \cdot e$ During now))}) $\cdot a =$ 'they High Less-Friendly- Than, 'SPer'))',

where (Fu'F) is the fusion of F in the sense of the calculus of individuals and 'SPer' is a predicate for being some logical sum of two or more human persons.

Some of these examples are interesting in showing that, in the strict sense, only whole "texts," not isolated sentences, are to be given logical forms — a point frequently emphasized by Harris and Hiz, as well as by Sommers.

There is much additional material in Sommers' book, and in its appendices, that merits commenting on in full. Here the concern has been only with foundational and semantical matters and with logical forms that are thought to be more perspicuous and closer in intent to their English originals than forms usually given.

CHAPTER VII

On Strawson's Subjects
and Predicates

"In every work regard the writer's end,
  Since none can compass more than they intend;
  And if the means be just, the conduct true,
  Applause, in spite of trivial faults, is due."

Pope

It is surely all to the good for Strawson to have observed that "logic, though it may dazzle us with the clarity of its structures, forms only one part — the first — of that modern *trivium* which now deservedly holds as central a place in liberal studies as ever its predecessor did. The other parts are general syntax-semantics and what, for want of a better word, may be called 'pragmatics'. There is no reason why that dazzling first part, as we have it, should dictate the course of the second, and clearly no possibility of its dictating the course of the third. Rather, for full, or philosophical comprehension, all three should be held, and viewed, in relation to each other and to investigations variously shared by, or apportioned between, metaphysics, epistemology, and philosophy of mind."[1]

Would that in fact it were true that logic in its newer developments had really dazzled with its structures at Oxford and elsewhere! Unfortunately little close attention has been paid to it and most writers, even Strawson himself, have paid little heed to its inner niceties, as we shall see. Would also that the modern *trivium* really did hold a "central place" in liberal studies! As a matter of fact, it seems for the most part to have no place at all, some facile or "faky, fluky" surrogate serving in its stead. Even so, it is splendid for Strawson to have called attention to syntax, semantics, and pragmatics and their relevance to metaphysics, epistemology, and the philosophy of mind, a relevance not sufficiently brought to the fore in most discussions of these various subjects.

Strawson groups syntax and semantics together and severs them rather sharply from pragmatics. Actually it is the *unification* of the three that seems to be of greatest philosophical significance and methodological relevance.[2] All three go hand in hand and should be "held" and "viewed" simultaneously as well as "in relation to each other." Syntax is of very little interest except in use and as a prelude to semantics, and pragmatics is so intimately interwoven with semantics as to be virtually inseparable from it.

Strawson seems unaware of the reasons why logic *simpliciter,* the dazzling first part of the trivium, "should dictate" the course of the second, and thinks that there is "no possibility of its dictating the third." The use of 'dictate' here is unfortunate. Logic does not dictate any more than it "regiments" or imposes a "straight-jacket" or anything of the kind. It guides with gentle firmness all who are sensitive to its call, leaving those who reject it to their own conceptual follies. And just as a matter of historical fact, exact syntax and semantics,[3] to say nothing of pragmatics,[4] were first developed on the basis of a very self-conscious use of formal logic. But for any such development, of course, a good deal of presystematic spadework must be at hand.

One of Strawson's fundamental concerns is (p. 3) with "a certain kind of combination — which ... [he calls] 'predication' — [that] has a fundamental position in our current logic." In order to "keep our logic closer to natural language" than it would otherwise be, he refrains from allowing complete sentences to contain quantification. Thus in writing the schemata 'Fx', 'Fxy', '$Fxyz$', etc., the lower case letters are in effect "name-letters" rather than variables. The 'F's are predicate terms, the 'x's, etc., are subject terms. In addition there are term connectives, '-', 'and', and 'or'. Note that '-' is used rather than 'not', but 'and' and 'or' rather than '·' (or '&') and 'v', respectively — as though '-' were an expression of natural language, which of course it is not. Further all three of these "connectives" are used ambiguously to form both compound predicates as well as compound subjects. Actually then these connectives become three-way ambiguous, significant in contexts, for example, '$-Fa$', '$\bar{F}a$', and '$F\bar{a}$', 'Fa and Ga', '$(F$ and $G)a$', and '$F(a$ and $b)$'. And similarly for 'or'. There is a long tradition that these three types of contexts be carefully distinguished *ab initio* — Leśniewski was perhaps the first to have seen the differences here clearly. It is not that Strawson fails to see them; it is that he misleadingly considers these connectives as unambiguous, where the ambiguities shine forth very clearly in the given symbolizations.

The examples Strawson cites,

(1)   'Either Tom or William both rides and drinks'

and

(2)   'Both Tom and William are either mad or lying',

fail to bring out, in the way he wishes, the (p. 8) "distinction between a truly compound term and a merely apparent compounding of terms which, from the logical point of view, simply abbreviates a compound sentence and yields no genuine term." Strawson purports to draw this distinction in terms of 'and' and 'or' but actually these examples make fundamental use also of 'either' and 'both'. In the two examples the 'or' and 'and' connectives do not occur, but rather the 'either . . . or' one and the 'both . . . and' ones. Without the use of 'either' and 'both', we can form examples with the same grammatical structure in which '*a* or *b*' is a genuine compound mereological term and '*F* or *G*' a genuinely compound predicate. Then, in place of (2), we could have

(3) 'Carter and Mondale are winning the election or are being defeated,'

as spoken, say, on 4 November 1980 early in the day. Here it is not Carter who is said to be winning or being defeated, nor is it Mondale; it is rather the mereological (or collective) sum of the two, represented by the genuinely compound subject '(Carter and Mondale)'. Strawson seems not to recognize that there are such genuinely compound subject terms in English.

Also there is here a mutual "relevance" between the components of the compound predicate in (3). But let us consider a case of a compound predicate without such relevance between its components, and where the sentence is not reducible to a truth-functional compound, say

'Carter and Mondale are winning the election and will (therefore) remain in office',
or

'They got married and (then) had a child'.

Neither of these uses of 'and' here is reducible to the truth-functional 'and' *tout court*.[5]

In speaking of 'true of' (pp. 9–11), it is noted that "no one at all fastidious would allow ''swims' is true of Socrates' as tolerable English. But is ''bald'' is true of Socrates' any better? Or ''man' is true of Socrates'? No, surely. 'True' is a predicate of statements, in the proper sense of the semantical truth predicate. Strawson seems unwilling to admit this predicate in its modern setting, in spite of his giving status to semantics in the desirable *trivium*. His conception of semantics remains thus rather indefinite. Very well, suppose we accept 'true' as characterized in some proper semantical way, perhaps in terms of 'Den' for denotation. Can we never then introduce 'true of' by definition, say? Well, there is the use of 'of' here in one of its many uses, the of-relation of being true of. We could define this by letting

'*a* Of$_{Tr}$ *x*' abbreviate '(PredConOne *a* · *a* Den *x*)'.

adding therewith one more of-relation to the galaxy of such.[5] The problem as to how we "read" this in English is quite beside the point. Strawson thinks that "'swims' is true of Socrates' is not fastidious English, but he nowhere offers an appropriate analysis of 'swims', say, as opposed to 'bald'. Full analyses of both are urgently needed. Strawson comments that

'It is true of Socrates that he swims'

and

'It is true of Socrates that Socrates swims'

are "perfectly allowable," but he does not specify the appropriate that-relation needed in order to substantiate this claim. This last sentence seems well "represented," to use the technical term of transformational grammer, by

'$(Ea)(Eb)(a$ Of$_{Tr}$ Socrates $\cdot$ a That$_{Content}$ b $\cdot$ 'Socrates swims' $b)$',

within an inscriptional semantics. Here 'That$_{Content}$' represents the that-relation of content, so that 'a That$_{Content}b$' expresses that the inscription a has whatever b expresses as its content where b is of the shape 'Socrates swims'.[7] Here 'Socrates swims' is left unanalyzed and is ambiguous as among 'Socrates swims habitually', 'Socrates is able to swim', 'Socrates is (now) swimming', and so on.

Strawson is quite correct, it would seem, in emphasizing the Englishry of such sentences as

(4)   'It is true of swimming that Socrates swims'.

To represent this properly we should worry about both the logical representation of 'Socrates swims' and of the gerundive 'swimming'. Let '$\langle Swim \rangle e$' express that e is an act of swimming during some time period, where '$\langle Swim \rangle$' is an event-descriptive predicate. To say that Socrates swims in the sense that he is now swimming is to say that

$(Ee)(e$ By$_{Agent}$ Socrates $\cdot$ $\langle Swim \rangle e$ $\cdot$ e During now).

Swimming itself, $\langle Swim \rangle$, is merely the virtual class of all acts of swimming, $\{e \ni \langle Swim \rangle e\}$. To represent (4) we need another true-of relation. Let 'a Tr$_{Of}$ $\langle F \rangle$' be defined to express that the one-place, second-order predicate a be true of $\langle F \rangle$, where '$\langle F \rangle$' is an event-descriptive predicate. (A one-place, second-order predicate is such as to stand for virtual classes of virtual classes.) The exact definition requires some technicalities — all, however, within the bounds of first-order logic — that need not be given here.[8] To represent (4), then, we have

'$(Ea)(Eb)(a \operatorname{Tr}_{Of} \langle \operatorname{Swim} \rangle \cdot a \operatorname{That}_{Content} b \cdot \{ F \ni (Ee)(e \operatorname{By}_{Agent}$
Socrates $\cdot \langle F \rangle e \cdot e$ During now) $\} 'b)$'.

It is easy to show, on these renditions, that (4) is a logical consequence of 'Socrates swims' (in the sense that he is now swimming). In a proof of such, some properties of the semantical truth-concept of course are needed fundamentally, as well as suitable rules of transformation.[9]

In a somewhat similar fashion, it can be shown that 'Socrates does something' is a logical consequence of 'Socrates swims'. For this purpose a meaning postulate to the effect that

$$(e)(\langle \operatorname{Swim} \rangle e \supset \langle \operatorname{Do} \rangle e),$$

that every swimming is a doing, is needed.

The example concerning 'Socrates is brave' is somewhat more complicated, for the handling of which a considerable foray into the theory of adjectives is needed, more particularly, into the theory of the finite number of comparative adjectives applicable to adult human males (of the Periclean period).[10] However, this can be done in such a way that 'Socrates is something' — a somewhat dubious sentence at best — or, better, 'Socrates exhibits some human quality' is a logical consequence of 'Socrates is brave'.

One can agree, then, with Strawson's view that the theory of commitment by noun but not by verb is implausible. To show this in detail requires a considerable development of the logic of natural language, one extending far beyond anything envisaged at Oxford. As Strawson himself notes, not all subject terms specify spatio-temporal particulars. There are also such things (p. 38) as "numbers or words or literary compositions" and presumably much more. Also there are in effect second-order notions — Strawson does not use this term — and, presumably also, notions of still higher order. We do have "propositions," we are told, such as '7 is prime', '7 is greater than 5', 'Green is soothing', 'Green is a more soothing colour than orange', 'This sonnet is Petrarchan', 'Monotheistic' has five syllables'," and so on. "These are all of the form 'Fa' or 'Fab'." Well, not quite. There is an enormous gap between what we have previously been told and what remains to be told concerning the forms needed to handle these types of sentences. For one thing, adjectives such as 'soothing' are not to be handled in the simple way suggested. Similarly for 'more soothing than' as between colors. The use of the demonstrative 'this' requires special care. Forms for syntactic sentences require a good deal of special theory. In all of these, forms of the kind 'Fa', 'Fab', and so on, are needed, but there are many other kinds of forms needed also — forms containing event-descriptive predicates, forms containing expressions of higher order having expressions for both "particulars" and expressions for "concepts" as arguments, many kinds of rather complex forms containing semantic ingredients, quotations within quotations, together with much else. An even approximative list of all the kinds of basic forms needed for the logical analysis of a natural language such as English seems never to have been given. Such a list may well be in the offing before too long. In any event, Strawson's inventory of forms seems too simple; it brings too much together under too gross a rubric.

We now come to the real nitty-gritty (p. 13) of Strawson's logico-metaphysical view, to which the foregoing "formal" considerations are a mere prelude. "We must be prepared," he tells us, "to use a richer vocabulary, a range of notions which fall outside these formal limits." This would seem to be in rough agreement with the contention of the preceding paragraph above. But wait! "We assume that the subject-predicate duality, and hence the difference [between subject and predicate] so far remarked on, reflect some fundamental features of our thought about the world." The main terms or phrases of this "richer vocabulary" are 'general concept' and 'spatio-temporal particular' (together with paraphrases of them), and the notion of an expression's "specifying" a particular. The discussion of these "richer" notions is perhaps a bit calorific, it is to be feared, and such as not to provide the nutritive value it is supposed to have. The point of the excursus concerning concepts and particulars in that our thought about the world (p. 20) "involves, at a level which, if not the most primitive of all, is yet primitive enough, the duality" of these two. This duality is thought to "justify" in some sense that of subject term and predicate term.

Strawson thinks to defend himself against the charge that the very notions of spatio-temporal particular and of concept are themselves less clear than those of subject term and predicate term. He even goes so far as to question the principle (p. 37) that "in philosophy, as elsewhere, ... what is less clear should be explained in terms of what is clearer, and hence that explanation of thoughts [or of language] should not rest upon a notion as obscure as the phenomenon to be explained." He seems to admit that 'concept' and 'spatio-temporal particular' are less clear than 'subject term' and 'predicate term'. His defense for attempting to "justify" the latter in terms of the former is that "philosophical explanation is not a steady, reductive movement in the direction of the intrinsically clear, but rather an exhibition of connections and relations between notions none of which is immediately transparent to philosophical understanding. The clarity is in the connections." One can agree with this contention, in principle anyhow, without accepting it as a defense of

Strawson's method. This contention could be used equally well as a defense the other way around, that is, as a defense of trying to "justify" 'concept' and 'spatio-temporal particular' in terms of 'predicate term' and 'subject term'. Strawson's real argument is rather that defenders of starting with the linguistic items abjure (p. 39) "any allusion to the semantic character" of them and do not inquire into "the sort of *sense,* or sort of *function* in sentences, or both, which the terms in question have, which accounts for the range of formal features the sentences present." Strawson then comments that "it is . . . precisely this question which I have attempted to answer . . . , making free use of 'expressions specifying concepts' and 'expressions specifying particulars'."

There are two grave misunderstandings here to which attention should be called. The first is a point stressed by Bocheński, that "in the whole history of logic, formal or otherwise, there is no known case of any serious study which has not been carried out on the basis of discourse. It is true that some philosophers (especially since Descartes [and *a fortiori* Kant]) have talked about the study of concepts "in themselves"; however, logicians have always dealt with concepts as expressed by words, that is, with discourse. This tradition started with Plato and is still absolutely general. There seems to have been two principal reasons for adopting this method. (1) Concepts do not subsist in themselves (as against Cartesian mythology) but are meanings of terms; therefore they should be studied through the terms, that is, through discourse. (2) Written (or spoken) terms are material things (or events) — and it is a basic methodological principle that, whenever possible, we should start with such things (or events), because they are much easier to study than mental entities. This does not mean, of course, that the logician is concerned with discourse only. On the contrary, his interest is directed toward meaningful discourse, and not toward the material things alone. But in practice he always deals with discourse."[11] In accord with this, it would seem advisable for Strawson *qua* logician to start with the linguistic factors and work his way up to concepts and spatio-temporal particulars. And working one's way up here is no easy matter. The notion of a spatio-temporal particular involves fundamentally a theory of space-time, or a theory of space together with one of time. Any such theory in turn will rest upon a prior logic with a well-articulated structure given to its sentences — perhaps the very kind of subject-predicate structure Strawson extolls. And likewise for the articulation of concepts, for which a rather considerable use of semantics is required, this semantics in turn being firmly based on a prior logic.[12]

The second point of misunderstanding is that there has been a tremendous development in recent years of logical semantics, both extensional and intensional, of which Strawson takes no notice. He speaks of *senses* in a pre-Fregean sense, and of the *function* of terms in sentences as though none of the work in structural linguistics has in any way contributed to the study of such. Defenders of the linguistic starting point need not, and indeed do not, abjure study of the semantical and functional character of terms.

Strawson's free use of 'expressions specifying concepts' and of 'expressions specifying particulars' is in disguise a use of various semantical relations, the character of which he does not inquire into. One may be skeptical of such relations until a suitable theory of them has been formulated. Skepticism concerning these notions, Strawson thinks, is "overstretched." Yes, surely, but not for the reason he adduces. He tells us (p. 40) that "we can ... see how very strange is the persistent illusion that to talk of words or expressions is to take one's stand on firm ground [in the manner of Frege, Leśniewski, Carnap, Tarski, Bocheński, *et al.*] instead of trusting oneself to the bogs and swamps of universals, concepts and the rest. For even as sign-design, the same word must be identified in different occurrences, or different inscriptions identified as inscriptions of the same word. So grasp of the identity of a word involves grasp of a principle of grouping inscriptions or utterances. How odd to think that one could escape acknowledgment of such principles by retreating to the ground of words! What a compounding of oddities indeed, given that another principle of grouping — the sense of the word — enters in fact into that very principle of grouping which we apply in identifying the word!"

There is much hidden confusion in this passage. Suppose we think that language is best and most thoroughly to be studied in terms of inscriptions or sign events rather than shapes or sign designs. The "principle of grouping" is then a relation of likeness or similarity between inscriptions, so that all like inscriptions can be grouped together. In inscriptional syntax and semantics fundamental use is made of a relation of likeness, Like, as well as of specific shape-descriptive predicates. Let '*a* Like *b*' express that inscription *a* is appropriately like inscription *b*, and let 'Vee *a*'' express that *a* is a vee- or 'v'-shaped inscription. A fundamental syntactical law is then that

$$\vdash (a)(b)((\text{Vee } a \cdot b \text{ Like } a) \supset \text{Vee } b).$$

And indeed Vee itself, the shape, can then be identified as the virtual class of all Vee's. This and allied principles constitute the "firm ground" of starting with words and expressions regarded as sign events. Thus one does not "escape acknowledgment of such principles by retreating to the ground of words." No one in the whole history of the subject has ever done so or even purported to have done so — a rather recent history, be it said, involving primarily only Goodman, Quine (in one of his moods), the present author, Fred Rickey, and a few others.

One may or may not take the further step of introducing a theory of senses or *Sinne*, à la Frege, say. But there is no "compounding of oddities" if one does *not* do so. The real oddity here is to proceed philosophically as though a theory of senses or of intensions, however embryonic, were available prior even to attempting to formulate it upon the basis of a well-articulated logic. In any such attempt one must of course pass through "bogs and swamps" to dry ground in order to rid oneself of the clinging mud of older conceptions and theories crying out for suitable cleansing in modern terms.

Strawson throughout thinks of logic as somehow "simple"; he speaks (p. 58) of "some relatively simple paradigm or framework, such as that provided by our logic." This is contrasted with "the complex phenomena of our discourse, all that is done, and the background of what is done, when we talk to each other. . . ." The problem is the delicate adjustment of one to the other, "of arranging for the facts to live in the frame of logic." As already suggested, Strawson's conception of logic seems rather narrow. On his view, it is reasonable to think, as he does, that (p. 66) "there is no wholly realistic way of fitting *all* the facts [concerning language] into the framework of logic." "There is nothing to deplore in this," he continues. "To think that there was, to resist this conclusion *à l'outrance,* would be to misunderstand the character of both logic and common discourse. The lack of perfect fit between them is not an imperfection in either." Quite, but the fit can be made much more perfect than Strawson supposes, as the newer work in logico-linguistics is showing more and more day after day.

Strawson's strength is not in getting the exact *logical* measure of ordinary sentences — in any narrow sense of 'logical' — so much as in calling attention to the varying pragmatic ambiences in which they are uttered, questioned, commanded, or whatever. Consider, for example, his comments (pp. 110–111) concerning the occasions of using 'a so-and-so' as contrasted with 'some so-and-so'. Consider

(5a)   'A policeman has been shot'

as contrasted with

(5b)   'Some $\left\{ \begin{array}{c} \text{general} \\ \text{cabinet minister} \\ \text{V.I.P.} \end{array} \right\}$ has been shot',

and

(6a)   'I've been stung by some insect',

(6b)   'I've been stung by a wasp',

and

(6c)   'I've been stung by some wasp'.

Strawson suggests that, in such sentences, we use 'some' rather than 'a' when we acknowledge or recognize that we are not identifying (for the hearer) the intended object as adequately as we might wish. Perhaps we are unable to do better in this regard, either concerning the individual or the kind of individual under discussion. "Thus there is more likely in general to be an individual-identification question asked in the case of a cabinet minister (general, V.I.P.) than in the case of a policeman; and more point, therefore, in acknowledging the question, as it were, even while exclaiming the ability to answer it."

It would be more pertinent, perhaps, to contrast (5a) with

(5c)   'Some policeman has been shot'.

(5a) would not ordinarily give rise to the question 'Who?' or 'Which one?', whereas (5c) would. Thus utterance of (5c) does seem to reveal greater identificatory willingness, so to speak, on the part of the speaker, than utterance of (5a). Is this difference a sufficiently significant one to incorporate into the respective logical forms? In the form for (5a) should we incorporate a clause, say, (roughly) that I do not know who or which one? And in the form for (5c) a clause (again, roughly) that I think I know which one?

The question is a moot one as to just where one draws the line between clauses in the logical forms that bring out essential *structural* features of the sentence and those that pertain only to *context,* more particularly, to the nonlinguistic context. Some linguists wish to have no commerce with the nonlinguistic context, but the number of them seems to be diminishing. Pure structural linguistics might well ignore the difference between (5a) and (5c), but for certain psycho-linguistic or socio-linguistic purposes, the difference would be crucial. In a court of law, for example, the difference between a witness uttering (5a) or (5c) might be crucial, for just the reason Strawson mentions.

Precisely similar remarks, it would seem, pertain to (5b) and its variants with 'A' replacing 'Some'. Surely there would be relevant situations in which 'A' would be more appropriate and others in which 'Some' would be. Also policemen can be V.I.P.'s on some occasions, so that the difference between (5a) and (5b) does not appear to be precisely as

Strawson claims it to be.

The examples (6a)–(6c) are concerned with the identification of a kind, insect or wasp, rather than of an individual. (6a) naturally invites the question 'What kind (of insect)?' whereas (6b) does not. In uttering (6a) I probably do not know what kind of an insect it was that bit me. Again, the contrast here might be of sufficient import to be incorporated in the respective logical forms. Strawson points out that (6c), "with its suggestion of a possible individual-identification of the wasp in question, seems absurd." Not absurd perhaps, but rather unlikely to occur; and if it does occur, perhaps only with derogatory intent, as though 'some wasp' in the context here were short for 'some blasted wasp' or something of the kind.

There is much additional material in Strawson's work that merits comment. Enough has been shown, however, to see that a viable theory of language does not seem to emerge from it. Nonetheless, along the way many useful and penetrating *aperçus* are put forward that can be of real help to the logico-linguistic when he settles down to the serious study of nonlinguistic context.

CHAPTER VIII

On Quine's
"Predicates, Terms, and Classes"

"'Tis with our judgments as our watches, none
  Go just alike, yet each believes his own.
  In poets as true genius is but rare,
  True taste as seldom is the critics's share;
  Both must from Heaven derive their light,
  Those born to judge, as well as those to write.
  Let such teach others as themselves excel,
  And censure freely who have written well.
  Authors are partial to their wit, 'tis true,
  But are not critics to their judgment too?"

Pope

A methodological axiom at work at the very beginning of Quine's paper[1] is: *Distinguer pour mieux unir.* The items of the title are distinguished in terms of three "kinds of expressions" that have been somewhat confused in the literature: predicates, general terms, and class names. Later in the paper some moves are taken that tend "to merge them again, though without confusion." In general, it would seem, it is good to make distinctions of relevance wherever possible, if only for the conceptual clarity — sometimes even exhilaration — that results. Some distinctions may of course be "unprofitable," as the Kneales point out in their history of logic. It is rare, however, that a distinction with a difference is not profitable for some purpose however minor. In any case, a good many fine distinctions will have to be made in discussing the niceties of the paper under review.

The point of Quine's distinguishing sharply predicates, general terms, and class names here is to help prepare the way for a specific formulation of first-order logic as a predicate-functor logic that has what are regarded as certain attractive features. These are to provide, so we are told, "full analysis and elimination of the relative clause, or abstract, and its variables." And predication disappears as well. But this is achieved, of course, only at the going price that must be paid for it.

Before attempting to evaluate these features, let us reflect first upon a few minor points. It is remarked that "the general term ... is a sign or a continuous string of signs. It may be a verb or verb phrase, a noun or noun phrase, an adjective or adjective phrase; these distinctions are immaterial to logic." To *pure* logic in the sense of first-order quantification theory, perhaps. But pure logic is a rather dull affair, a little baby mathematics — to use Murray Gell-Mann's phrase — and that is about all. Its importance arises in its applications. It is an instrument or tool, not a subject matter. *Quā* instrument in applications to language, the distinctions between or among verb, noun, and adjective phrase are of the highest concern. Logic as a tool has much to contribute to their analysis and clarification. In saying this, of course, nothing is being said with which Quine need disagree, for his concern is wholly with the applied logic of quantification theory.

In the third paragraph, it is emphasized that "a class name is not a general term ... and not a predicate. It is a singular term, simple or complex, *designating* a single abstract object, a class. The corresponding general term *denotes* any number of objects, each member of the class." It is good to see here that 'designates' is used correctly, in essentially the senses of Frege and Carnap, rather than some vague phrase such as 'refers to' in current use. Quine's use of 'denotes' here also is in accord with a good English tradition, that "common names" or general terms denote severally the objects to which they apply.

Quine makes fundamental use of the schematic or predicate letters '*F*', '*G*', and so on, in contexts '*Fx*', '*Gxy*', and so on. These latter are sentence forms, or "open" sentences containing free occurrences of '*x*', or of '*x*' and '*y*', however "numerous and scattered" these occurrences may be. Class names and general terms, as we have just noted, have a clear semantics attached to them. Class names designate their respective classes and denote severally their respective members. And general terms, according to Quine, denote the members of the corresponding classes. How now, do the corresponding schematic or predicate letters behave *semantically*? They do not designate nor do they denote — they neither toil nor do they spin. Individuals or sequences of such are sometimes said to *satisfy* the contexts containing them or not, as the case may be. Such talk, however, fails to give the schematic or predicate letters themselves any direct relatedness to something presumed to have a proper ontic status in the world, so to speak. It fails to interrelate the predicate expressions vis-à-vis nonlinguistic entities; it fails to interrelate word and object — to use a felicitous phrase of which Quine has made much elsewhere.

Of course one might contend that 'denotes' also fails to interrelate word and object. But in terms of 'Den' for 'denotes', we can immediately define *virtual-class designation*. We can let

(1)   '$a \operatorname{Des}_{VC} \{x \ni \text{--}x\text{--}\}$' abbreviate '$(\operatorname{PredConOne} a \cdot (x)(a \operatorname{Den} x \equiv \text{--}x\text{--}))$',

where '$--x--$' is a sentential form or "open" sentence containing 'x' as its only free variable and 'PredConOne a' expresses that a is one-place primitive predicate constant or a one-place abstract containing no free variable.[2]

In some such way as this we can always answer the question: What are the designata or denotata of predicate terms and of class names? We can answer: the predicate terms designate virtual classes and class names designate either virtual or real classes. A very natural question to ask now is: What are the denotata or designata of the schematic letters? Let us not speak of propositional *functions* here, for their ontic status is as vague as that of propositions. Those hoary notions, propositions and propositional functions, it is to be feared, were conceived in sin, along with much else, due in part to the failure to distinguish clearly between use and mention. Instead of introducing propositional functions, then, let us separate uses of the schematic letters for primitive predicates from uses of them for compound or defined ones. The former, the primitive ones, can be handled easily enough in terms of Den. A predicate that is a primitive sign can be said to denote severally the objects to which it applies. 'Dog' denotes severally Marni, Fido, Rover, and so on. Thus the problem here is of import only for compound or defined predicates, and these may be handled by means of virtual-class designation, as introduced by (1). Because the schematic letters as used for compound predicates have no semantic role to play, but only an adscititious syntactical one, it seems best to abjure them altogether, or at least to distinguish sharply the two uses made of them.

Already mention has been made of virtual classes and Peano's '$\ni$' with braces has been used to symbolize them. Quine uses rather '$\{x:Fx\}$' where 'F' is a schematic letter for either real or virtual classes. Strictly, if 'Fx' contains some free variable or variables other than 'x', '$\{x:Fx\}$' can no longer symbolize a real or virtual class but rather what we might call a real or virtual-class function. Strictly, then, we should speak throughout of both real and virtual classes and of real and virtual-class functions rather than, as Quine does, of merely real and virtual classes.

In the paper under review, Quine regards the abstracts '$\{x:Fx\}$' as "unpretentious relative clauses" rather than as presumably pretentious "simulated classes." The reason he thinks they are "simulated" is because of the use made of them in *Set Theory and Its Logic,* where virtual classes were embedded within a set theory.[3] Viewed properly, however, it would seem, virtual classes are never simulated classes in any reasonable sense. They are pure logical fictions resulting from a mere *manière de parler,* that and nothing else. It would seem best to keep virtual classes quite separate from simulated real ones. Virtual classes are of technical interest and utility even when not embedded within a set theory, and their salient characteristics can be given quite independently. Again, this is a point with which Quine need not disagree.

Curiously, Quine wishes to have no truck, here in the paper under discussion, with either virtual or real classes. He uses the set-theoretic notation '$\{x:Fx\}$' for the "innocent relative clause, and 'ϵ' correspondingly for the innocent copula 'is an' that is the inverse of 'such that'," and suggests that "we then simply deny that we are referring to classes." In what sense now are relative clauses "innocent"? Only, it would seem, if there is some well-developed and -authenticated background theory, presumably of a grammatical kind, in which they are characterized — in some paradigmatic logistic, or even set-theoretic way. Unfortunately, there is no such theory to which Quine can appeal, none in traditional grammar (which is highly suspect from a logical point of view anyhow) and none in any of the literature to which he makes reference. In short, the notion awaits characterization and should not be appealed to to justify use of the notation '$\{x:Fx\}$'. Also it should be asked in what sense the "innocent" 'ϵ' for 'is a' is the "inverse" of 'such that'? At best this is inept terminolgy. We might read '$x \epsilon G$' as 'x is a G'. The converse, we might write, following Finsler, '$G \beta x$' and read this as 'G has x as a member' or in some similar vein. Peano's '$\ni$', as used above, is the typographical inverse of 'ϵ', but Quine uses rather '$:$', reading it 'such that'! Now of course 'such that' is not the inverse of 'is a' nor is '$\ni$' an inverse of '$:$'. Is the notion or concept *is a* an inverse of the notion or concept *such that*? If so, it remains to be explained how and why within a clear theory and ontology of concepts.

Quine speaks of "the ontological innocence of the 'such that' idiom" and notes that once we appreciate it "we can admit it with equanimity to the language of elementary logic." As embodied in the theory of *virtual* classes and relations, yes, as urged elsewhere.[4] But what precisely is meant here by 'with equanimity'? There is a choice as to whether the notations for virtual classes and relations be *defined* or taken as *primitive*. It might seem that not much would hinge on this difference, and little does at the object-language level. When we turn to semantics, however, some subtle differences emerge, but not enough perhaps to upset us in any substantive way.[5]

A disturbing feature about Quine's talk of "general" and "singular terms," and even of "predicates" — here and in most of his writings on the philosophy of language — is that he thinks he knows what they are and that we should all follow suit. Also it is not clear whether he speaks of these relative to a natural language or relative to some well-articulated logical system. He does not seem to wish these points even to be raised, as though natural languages and logical systems were the same, and as though certain expressions wear their labels 'general term', 'singular term', and 'predicate' on their sleeves. The fact is, however, that they do not and that most of what we wish to say about a natural language, *ab initio* anyhow, we will not wish to say about a logical system. The notions of general and singular term, and of predicate, as used relative to a natural language, are much too vague and amorphous to be used without qualms of logical conscience. They are mere remnants of a traditional grammar to which no appeal should be made at the present stage of research. As Russell, Reichenbach, Carnap, and others have strongly urged, they need to be overhauled completely in the light of a logistic grammar, in the light of what more and more is now being called 'logico-linguistics'.

Quine wishes to admit the 'such that' idiom in the form of expressions such as '$\{x:Fx\}$' but "simply deny that we are referring to classes" in using this notation. Very well. Let us think of them as referring to virtual classes then. But no, Quine sees them "no longer in terms of virtual classes. The abstracts are now seen as unpretentious relative clauses, some of which may also be class names and some not." There would seem to be no clear reason, however, why they should not be regarded as referring to virtual classes, which are surely less "pretentious" than unanalyzed relative clauses. We lack a background theory incorporating these latter, as already observed. And since there are no such things as virtual classes or relations anyhow, talk of them being a mere *manière de parler,* the notations embodying them are as unpretentious as they could possibly be.

Another reason for doubting the innocence and unpretentiousness of the 'such that' idiom is that its unrestricted use gives rise to intensional contexts. The sentence

'The morning was (a morning) such that I wanted to fly my spaceship to the Morning Star'

contains a double intensionality, so to speak. Thus in general Quine's '$\{x:Fx\}$' cannot always be replaced by '$\{x:Gx\}$' just because

$$(x)(Fx \equiv Gx).$$

Let us get on now to the real nitty-gritty of Quine's reformulation of elementary logic, rewording it slightly here and there. As primitives we have 'Excl' — it seems better to capitalize the 'e' here — for the relation or copula of *exclusion* as between virtual classes or virtual class-functions. In addition there are four "predicate functors" symbolizing Schönfinkel–Curry-like operators: 'Inv' for *major inversion,* 'inv' for *minor inversion*, 'Pad' for *padding*, and 'Ref' for *reflection*. In addition a two-place predicate functor '‖' is introduced for *divergence*. The logical behavior of these functors is explained in the paper. It turns out that 'Excl' is definable in terms of divergence, and that both major and minor inversion may be defined in terms of a suitable predicate functor for *permutation*. We end up then with — ostensibly — just three one-place predicate functors, 'Perm', 'Pad', and 'Ref', and one two-place one, '‖', as primitives. Further reduction is perhaps possible.

It is well-known that the notion of a variable may be eliminated from the fundamental ideas of logic.[6] The real novelty here then, in this present paper, is to combine the elimination of the variable with the special two-place functor for divergence, in terms of which exclusion may be introduced by definition. However, it is a mistake to think that we have really gotten very far until suitable *axioms* and *rules* — or at least some basic principles — governing and interrelating the various primitives have been given. What would these axioms and principles look like? Some of them no doubt would be akin to those of Paul Bernays in his formulation of a somewhat allied system presented at the Amsterdam Colloquium on Constructivity in Mathematics in 1957.[7] Likewise exact *definitions* must be given, the definitions, axioms, and rules "interanimating" each other in most fundamental ways. Quine gives us neither definitions in any strict sense nor axioms or rules, but merely informal "explanations." Such explanations of course are of expository value. We must go on, however, to provide definitions step by step, to list axioms and rules, and then to show that the axioms-and-rules-cum-the-given-definitions suffice for the intended purposes.

What are the intended purposes here? There are several, it seems, separate though closely interrelated. The first, as already suggested, is to provide for quantification theory as usually formulated, on the basis of the axioms and rules for predicate functors to be given. There is the converse problem also, of developing the theory of 'Perm', 'Pad', 'Ref', and '‖' in terms of some suitable formulation of quantification theory. For this purpose Quine's "explanations" of these functors — in particular, his very last formula on p. 172, the two last formulae on p. 170, and formula (2) on p. 171 — could no doubt be transformed into abbreviative definitions. The problem would then remain of studying whether *all* the axioms and rules governing these functors would be forthcoming from the usual quantificational principles. If this should turn out to be the case, the system of predicate functors here would be shown to provide merely a deductively equivalent formulation of quantificational theory in a very exact sense. However, as already remarked, this has not yet been accomplished, and hence the exact interrelation between the two systems is merely one of conjecture.

Note, incidentally, that Quine's formulation, like some standard one needed for the proof of equivalence, is of an *applied* theory of quantification, not of a "pure" one. The availability of at least one nonlogical predicate constant is needed. (A pure theory, on the other hand, in accord with the distinction as drawn by Alonzo Church, would presumably have to contain instead variables for propositions and propositional functions with quantification upon them.) The need for at least one nonlogical constant is all to the good, in accord with the conception of logic as a tool or instrument, as suggested above, rather than a doctrine or subject matter.

Suppose the only nonlogical predicate constant admitted is 'ϵ' for set membership, say, as in the Zermelo-Skolem set theory or in one of Quine's own reworkings of it. The axioms and axiom schemata are now recast in terms of the predicate functors, and all goes well in the statement of the set-theoretic axioms and in the peroration of the theory. And similarly for any axiomatization of some domain of physics, biology, or other natural science.

How, now, are we to handle the *semantics*, the formalized semantics, of Quine's predicate-functor formulation? And how are we to construe its ontic commitment? And its ontic *involvement,* that is, the ontic commitment of the metalanguage? Quine seems not to have concerned himself with these questions. Let us consider the first first. In what sense must the semantical metalanguage be "essentially richer" than the object language? The usual method of providing this, that of Tarski, is to introduce in the metalanguage variables of type at least one higher than those of the object language. Here, however, the object language contains no variables, but only the four predicate functors and at least one nonlogical predicate constant.

We might be tempted to say that if a designation relation were available in the metalanguage, perhaps as a primitive, a kind of semantics would be forthcoming by postulating semantical rules to the effect that the functor 'Perm' designates the *function* Perm, and so on for the others. Such rules would be a bit dull and uninformative and would provide only a *homomorphic,* not an *explicative* semantics.[8] Such rules would be reminiscent of Carnap's principle that 'Chicago' designates Chicago. Even so, such a semantics would give a respectable interpretation for the primitive functors and the nonlogical primitive predicate or predicates, if we assume that direct translations of them are already available and understood in the metalanguage.

This temptation, however, should be resisted for the following reason. Quine's '*F*' and '*G*', remember, are only schematic and are not to be taken as referring to virtual classes or relations. The danger of using the syntactical schematic letters is that we are liable to read more into them than we should, as already suggested. If we use them only syntactically and always remember that '*Fx*' is mere shorthand for some "open" sentence or sentential function of the form '--*x*--*x*--', with one or more occurrences of '*x*' as a free variable and where the blanks are appropriately filled in, no harm can arise. The difficulty with the semantics hypothetically sketched in the preceding paragraph, however, is that although 'Perm' is regarded as a functor, there is no *function* Perm for it to designate and nothing for it to be an *argument* of. In fact 'Perm' is significant only in the way in which the truth-functional connectives are. Thus

(2)   '(Perm F^n)$x_1 \ldots x_n$'

is better written as

(3)   'Perm $F^n x_1 \ldots x_n$' or 'Perm ($F^n x_1 \ldots x_n$)',

and in a special case as

'Perm --x_1-- $\ldots x_n$--'.

It is thus not without reason that Quine speaks of a predicate-*functor* logic, and not of a propositional-function one, loathe as he would be presumably to posit propositional functions as real entities, as values for variables.

What kind of a semantics is appropriate, then, to Quine's formalism if we are careful not surreptitiously to reify the predicate letters, i.e., somehow to assign designata to them? One way would be to reconstrue the hypothetical semantics mentioned above in terms of virtual classes. We merely construe the schematic letters in the contexts (2) and (3), and elsewhere as needed, as standing for virtual classes or relations. '(Perm F^n)' becomes reconstrued as

'(Perm $\{y_1 \ldots y_n \ni$ --y_1-- $\ldots$ --y_n--$\})$',

and similarly for the others. No violation is done in this procedure to Quine's intent, the virtual-class notation being more innocent and unpretentious than use of the unanalyzed relative clauses and the 'such that' idiom. The kind of hypothetical, homomorphic semantics sketched can now be carried through without further ado.

We can do better than this, however, by interpreting the system within an explicative semantics. This latter we may assume formulated in the usual way in terms of some standard version of applied quantification theory, plus a formalized syntax, of course, plus semantical notions for denotation and designation. Let us consider first the functor 'Perm', which is to designate some function. What function? Well, let F^n and G^n

be real n-adic relations, and let

'$G^n \, Q^{(n)} \, F^n$' abbreviate '$(x_1)\ldots(x_n)(G^n x_1 x_3 \ldots x_n x_2 \equiv F^n x_1 \ldots x_n)$', for $n \geq 3$.

The familiar 'λ' of functional abstraction, in the form in which we now need it, is significant in the context '$(\lambda F^n \cdot (Q^{(n)} \, {}'F^n))$', where $Q^{(n)}$ is a one-many relation between n-adic relations, and where $n \geq 3$. We can then state semantical rules, Rules of Designation, that

$$\text{'Perm}^{(n)}\text{' Des } (\lambda F^n \cdot (Q^{(n)} \, {}'F^n))$$

for $n \geq 3$. And similarly now for 'Pad' and 'Ref', with $n \geq 1$ and $n \geq 2$, respectively.

Before we consider divergence, which must be handled a bit differently, two items should be noted. For one thing, we need n primitive functors, 'Perm$^{(n)}$', not just one, in the method here. How many? Presumably an *infinity*. And similarly for 'Pad' and 'Ref'. Suitable devices must thus be available for generating a single functor 'Perm' from the multiplicity 'Perm$^{(n)}$'. Further, to assure that $Q^{(n)}$ is a one-many relation in the appropriate sense, quantifiers upon 'F^n' and 'G^n' are needed. Thus first-order quantification theory will not suffice; we need some higher-order quantifiers fundamentally. The semantical metalanguage needed for these various purposes must thus be of higher order, with all the complexities thereunto appertaining.[9]

To provide for divergence, we have semantical rules to the effect that

(4)   '$\|^{n+1}$' Des $\{F^n G^n x_2 \ldots x_n : (x_1)(F^n x_1 \ldots x_n \mid G^n x_1 \ldots x_n)\}$, for $n \geq 1$,

and an instance of the Adequacy Principle that

$$\vdash \text{Tr } \ulcorner(A \,\|^2\, B)\urcorner \equiv (A \mid B),$$

where 'A' and 'B' are any sentences of which 'A' and 'B' are the shape-descriptions. Here '$\mid$' is the Sheffer stroke sign, as in Quine's paper. Here too we must work to define '$\|$' in terms of the multiplicity of '$\|^{n+1}$'s. For the nonlogical primitive predicate constants of the object language we have Carnap-like rules that 'B' Des the dyadic relation bites, 'F' Des the triadic relation of being farther than, and 'D' Des the class of dogs, to speak only of the three predicates Quine considers in "Variables Explained Away."[10]

What, now, about ontic commitment and involvement? The ontic commitment and ontic involvement are the same, in the homomorphic treatment, and consist of the real functions, relations, and/or classes designated by the primitives, plus no doubt all further functions, relations, and/or classes that can be introduced definitionally. If we are ontically committed to the class of dogs and to the relation of biting, it would be odd if were were to withhold commitment to the class of dogs who bite or who are bitten.

In the explicative semantics — the only kind really worthy of the name, perhaps, in which the functors and class and relational expressions are really analyzed in other terms presumed already available — the situation is very different. The ontic commitment is as above, but the ontic involvement consists of the entire ontology required in the formulation of the higher-order quantification theory required. So vast an ontic involvement might be thought to be too high a price to pay for predicate-functor logic.

If variables are given up, the principle — if such it be — 'To be is to be the value of a variable' must be given up too. One might then just dispense with all talk of ontic commitment, and go ahead and do as the mathematicians do, namely, give the matter no heed. And as to ontic involvement, this is a notion Quine has given no lip-service at all. It is, however, a notion on a par in importance with that of ontic commitment, and in general it is highly desirable that the involvement of a language, the commitment of its metalanguage, should be no more extensive than that of its commitment.

Quine apparently always regards semantics as essentially Tarskian, in which the ontic involvement vastly exceeds the ontic commitment. He nowhere has shown interest in the progress in semantics made since Tarski's work of almost a half century back, in particular, in weaker forms in which the ontic involvement and the ontic commitment are the same. The principle that to be is to be the value of a (bound) variable is then apparently to be given up as applied to the predicate-functor object language, for it contains no variables at all. How then, are we to think of its ontic commitment? Presumably, Quine would say, as the entities (or sequences of such) of which the nonlogical primitive predicates are true or false.[11] This explanation is unacceptable, however, on three scores. The very statement of it utilizes the phrases 'true of' and 'false of', which are definable in terms of the semantical predicate for truth. The very statement thus commits Quine to the vast Tarskian ontology. Secondly, the explanation is arbitrarily restricted to just the nonlogical primitives. Heretofore all talk of being as being the values for variables has not been restricted in this way. The restriction here is merely *ad hoc*, the resulting explanation giving us what Quine wishes the ontic commitment to be rather than what it should be as the result of some prior principle. Quine seems not to have enunciated the general principle that would justify this *ad hoc* restriction and the abandonment of the requirement that to be is to be the value of a variable. Thirdly, no answers are forth-coming to the questions: What are the primitive predicate *functors* true or false of? Why should the primitive predicates be regarded as true or false of something and the primitive functors not?

Quine has stated his position clearly. "When a theory is given the usual quantificational form," he writes (*loc. cit.*), "the things that the theory accepts as existing are indeed the things that it accepts as the values of its variables of quantification. If a theory is given another form, moreover, there is no sense in asking what the theory accepts as existing except as we are in a position to say how to *translate* [italics added] the theory into the usual quantificational form. I have long urged these points, and I continue to." But why, now, we may ask, is there "no sense" in asking what a theory accepts as the values of its variables of quantification other than to be in a position to say how to "translate" it into quantificational form? Indeed, there does seem to be sense in asking this question. Quine prohibits it by edict. It is a question we often wish to ask about theories which seem to resist — at first blush anyhow — translation into the usual quantificational form, such as intuitionistic logics, many-valued logics, modal logics, and so on. Also it seems reasonable to ask for the ontic commitment of Schönfinkel-Curry-like logics themselves, which — again, at first blush anyhow — seem to resist the desired kind of transla-tion.

Even if one were to give up the notions of ontic commitment and involvement, there remain the interesting notions of *conceptual* commit-ment and involvement. Suppose we think of mathematics as dealing, not with entities, but with *concepts* in some clear sense that we would try to get at in terms of *acts of conceiving.* Mathematicians do perform certain conceptual acts, it might be contended — as indeed it has been in effect by intuitionists such as Kreisel, Troelstra, van Dalen, and Myhill, for example. To prove a theorem is to perform a certain kind of act on the part of a "creative subject." Likewise to "construct" a mathematical object, in the sense of intuitionism, is to perform a creative act. What is it now to have a mathematical *conception*, say, of the Perm function or, more or less *pari passu,* of the 'Perm' functor? (Here we may assume that the multiplicity of the 'Perm^n's have been suitably unified.) It is, by way of answer, to take that functor under a given *Art Des Gegebenseins* — to use Frege's famous phrase. It is to regard that functor as character-ized by a certain metamathematical (or epimathematical) structure.[12] Let '(Ax1 · ... · Rk)' be the conjunction of all the translational axioms and of the rules needed for Quine's theory concerning Perm, Pad, Ref, and divergence. And let

(5) $'\{\alpha\beta\gamma\delta:(--\alpha--\beta--\gamma--\delta--)\}'$

be a four-place abstract of appropriate order, where

$$'(--\alpha--\beta--\gamma--\delta--)'$$

differs from '$(\text{Ax}1 \cdot \ldots \cdot \text{R}k)$' only in containing free occurrences respectively of 'α', 'β', 'γ', and 'δ' wherever 'Perm', 'Pad', 'Ref', and '$\|$' respectively occur in '$(\text{Ax}1 \cdot \ldots \cdot \text{R}k)$'. (The Greek letters here of course are being used as variables of appropriate order.) The abstract (5) then represents a certain structure. The axioms are such of course as to "interanimate" the primitives, so that we do not have a conception of one of them in isolation, but only of all of them simultaneously. Let 'Cncv' abbreviate 'conceives' in the present sense, and let

(6) 'p Cncv 'Perm', 'Pad', 'Ref', '$\|$', '$\{\alpha \ \beta \ \gamma \ \delta : (--\alpha--\beta--\gamma--\delta--)\}$'"

express that person or "creative subject" p conceives the given functors simultaneously as having the structure spelled out by the given higher-order abstract. In other words, the creative subject conceives these functors as being committed to the given structure — or, in still another way of speaking, the creative subject is conceptually committed to taking these functors simultaneously to be characterized by the given structure.

Ontic commitment thus goes by the wayside along with variables, and conceptual commitment comes in to take its place. Mathematicians fond of abstract structures will tell us that this has been the more important notion all along. Philosophers with a hankering for the real world, however, for what is "really real" in some ultimate metaphysical sense, will feel that something important has been lost. They can welcome the notion of conceptual commitment as a useful tool with which to help describe mathematical behavior, but they may also lament the lack of all direct reference to the entities of the real world.

Is there an interesting way of holding on to a reasonable notion of ontic commitment vis-à-vis Quine's kind of system without the ontic extravagance of the explicative semantics it requires? In other words, could we "virtualize" that semantics, so to speak, by making virtual classes and relations somehow carry the burden of the real classes and relations there? Perhaps we can, by extending still further the handling of virtual-class designation. Let us reflect for a moment on the salient points needed for this.

Heretofore, an expression for virtual-class designation has either been introduced by definition in terms of 'Den' as above, or taken as a primitive along with virtual-class abstracts themselves. We need now a still more powerful theory of virtual-class designation, of virtual-class *rela-*

tions, and even of virtual relations with two of their arguments as virtual relations of higher order. It will be recalled that we can form expressions for virtual classes and relations of higher order without introducing any variables other than those for individuals — but of course without introducing quantifiers over them and hence without increasing the ontic commitment. Let us now attempt to provide a semantics for such expressions in terms of virtual-relation designation, without increasing the ontic involvement.

Let us regard 'Perm', 'Ref', and 'Pad', now, not as functors strictly in the sense that they are names of functions, but as operators which, when combined with an n-place predicate form a new predicate. In other words, we consider '(Perm F^n)', and the like, in context. Let us suppose that

$$(7)\text{'}a \text{ Des}_{VR} \{G_1^n \ldots G_m^n x_1 \ldots x_n \ni (--G_1^n -----G_m^n ----x_1--\ldots--x_n--)\}\text{'}$$

is significant primitively now in the metalanguage to express that a designates uniquely the $(m+n)$-adic virtual relation among $G_1^n, \ldots, G_m^n, x_1, \ldots, x_n$ such that $(--G_1^n--\ldots--G_m^n--x_1--\ldots--x_n--)$. Here '$G_1^n$', $\ldots$, 'G_m^n' are any m distinct n-place virtual-relation abstracts containing no free variables and of course 'x_1', $\ldots$, 'x_n' are variables distinct from one another.

Concerning this relation Des_{VR} semantical rules must be given stipulating the required properties. Let 'Γ_1', 'Γ_2', etc., be any $(m+n)$-adic abstracts of the kind appearing in (7) and let 'PredCon $(m+n)$ a' express in the formalized syntax, where $n \geq 1$, that a is such an abstract where $m \geq 1$ or a primitive nonlogical predicate of degree n where $m = 0$. The Rules of Designation are then:

DesR1. $\vdash (a) (a \text{ Des}_{VR} \Gamma_1 \supset \text{PredCon } (m+n) \ a)$, for $m \geq 0$ and $n \geq 1$.

DesR2. $\vdash (a)((a \text{ Des}_{VR} \Gamma_1 \cdot a \text{ Des}_{VR} \Gamma_2) \supset \Gamma_1 = \Gamma_2)$.[13]

DesR3. $\vdash \ulcorner a \text{ Des}_{VR} \Gamma_1 \urcorner$, where in place of '$a$' the structural description of Γ_1 is inserted.

DesR1 is the *Principle of Limitation, DesR2* the *Principle of Unicity,* and *DesR3* the *Principle of Specificity.* These rules are of a familiar kind in any semantics based upon designation.[14]

Let us now define Quine's predicate functors as follows.

'(Perm F^n)' abbreviates '$\{G^n x_1 x_3 \ldots x_n x_2 \ni (G^n x_1 x_3 \ldots x_n x_2 \equiv F^n x_1 \ldots x_n)\}$', for each $n \geq 3$,

And similarly for '(Pad F^n)' and '(Ref F^n)'. And for '$\|^{n+1}$' we transform the rule (5) above into a definition, but with ' $\ni$ ' replacing ':' — a small syntactical change resulting in a mighty semantical one!

From *DesR3* precisely what we wish now immediately follows, namely that

'(Perm F^n)' Des_{VR} $\{G^n x_1 x_3 \ldots x_n x_2 \ni G^n x_1 x_3 \ldots x_n x_2 \equiv F^n x_1 \ldots x_n)\}$, for appropriate n,

and similarly for '(Pad F^n)', '(Ref F^n)' and '$\|^{n+1}$'. These expressions are thus fully explicated in being shown to designate the appropriate virtual relations.

What now is the ontic commitment of Quine's formulation as thus interpreted? The best way to view it would be no doubt to regard it as precisely its ontic involvement minus the values of the syntactical variables. In other words, it is the normal commitment of quantification theory as applied to whatever it is here applied to. This would appear to be precisely what one would wish it to be. An applied predicate-functor logic, of Quinean type, as thus interpreted, neither adds to nor subtracts from what one would otherwise regard as its commitment in standard quantificational formulation.

Can the notion of conceptual commitment be reconstrued with the semantics based on Des_{VC}? Yes, by speaking only of the functors and not of the respective functions and by virtualizing the notion of a structure. Thus now (6) above with ' $\ni$ ' in place of ':' can express that person p is conceptually committed by the various functors to a certain structure determined by the axioms and rules.

Quine speaks of predicate-functor logic as "reminiscent of the combinatory logic of Schönfinkel and Curry. Theirs, however, had the whole of higher set theory as its domain; the present scheme stays within the bounds of predicate logic."[15] The use of 'reminiscent' here seems too weak. Predicate-functor logic *is* combinatory logic within certain bounds. Although these bounds appear to be those of predicate logic, at the object-language level, they are not really so when looked at semantically. A type-theoretic structure is involved in place of the set-theoretic one of Schönfinkel and Curry, albeit at the metalinguistic level. As we have seen, the metalanguage may take the Tarskian form or that based on higher-order virtual relations with 'Des_{VR}' appropriately construed.

It is interesting to note, incidentally, that the notion of conceptual commitment, suggested above in two ways, is not metalinguistic in the same sense that the notion of ontic involvement is. For the characterization of conceptual commitment one needs the object-language (or translation of such) jointly with its syntax. Such a metalanguage is like Curry's λ-language, in not being a *semantical* metalanguage at all.[16] It should be noted also that the foregoing considerations are not intended to apply without further consideration to systems allied to predicate-functor logic such as Tarski's cylindrical algebra, Bernay's "natural extension of the calculus of relations," or Halmos' algebraic logic.

A final comment — concerning naturalness, fruitfulness, economy, simplicity, and the like. How does Quine's predicate-functor formulation of logic without variables come out with respect to these, relative to the usual kind of formulation with them? As to naturalness, probably not very well. Whitehead noted on one occasion that the discovery of the variable was one of the greatest steps forward in the history of mathematics. And likewise in logic, no doubt. The long history of these subjects attests also to the fruitfullness of the wholesale use of variables. As to economy and simplicity, no adequate comparison can be made until suitable axioms and rules for predicate-functor logic are forthcoming. It is to these primarily that measures of economy and simplicity are applicable. Meanwhile, one may well wonder whether predicate-functor logic is perhaps a mere *cul-de-sac,* a technical *jeu d'espirit.* Such wonder, however, does not entail a similar wonder about the Schönfinkel-Curry work itself, which is of great mathematical interest, involving as it does (and as Quine has pointed out) the high conceptual reaches of set theory. Quine's own work in set theory has been concerned with its lower reaches, but only the high reaches are of any deep interest to the mathematician.

The philosopher, in contrast to the mathematician, is interested in logic as an instrument of clarification, in *logica utens.* It is thus appropriate to ask: in what way or ways is predicate-functor logic of help to the philosopher? This, again, is a question Quine seems not to have considered. The answer remains in doubt until it is shown that predicate-functor logic provides a better or more appropriate approach to the needs of philosophic discourse — to say nothing of the analysis of natural language — than the usual formulation in quantification terms does.

A final point. Nothing said here precludes the possibility of developing a semantics for predicate-functor logic of a kind quite different from those considered above — e.g., one based on disquotation[17] or nontranslationality.[18]

CHAPTER IX

On the Algebra of Relations and Their Affiliates

(Logic without Connectives, Variables, or Quantifiers)

"True wit is nature to advantage dress'd,
  What oft was thought, but ne'er so well express'd;
  Something whose truth convinc'd we find,
  That gives us back the image of our mind."

Pope

Of all areas of modern logic, one of the most useful, but least used for philosophical and metaphysical purposes, is that of the theory of relations. Philosophers, even logically sophisticated ones and even those concerned with the language(s) of the sciences, often speak of relations in various guises but rarely tarry to consider in any exact way their *relata* (the entities the relations relate), their *degree* (the number of places a relation term significantly takes), the various *kinds* of relations to be distinguished, and the various underlying *principles* needed to characterize these kinds and to distinguish them one from another. A good example are relations connected with causality, so-called causal relations. Writers who speak of such relations, in the plural, rarely tell us the intended relata and intended properties these relations are supposed to have in a sufficiently clear way so that they could be easily symbolized. And yet, it would seem, one cannot get very far in studying causality in any exact way without doing precisely this. And similarly for almost any relation of which the metaphysician or theologian or analytic philosopher (in whatsoever domain) speaks or wishes to make use of. In short, the logic of relations is an almost indispensable *vademecum* to the philosopher for almost everything he wishes to say. Philosophical logicians, however, have given it little heed, turning their attention to areas of much less direct helpfulness, such as recursive function theory, modal logic, set theory, possible-worlds theory, and the like.

Let us reflect upon the general logic of relations in what would appear to be an especially simple and natural way, in terms of the theory of *virtual* relations somewhat in the manner in which it is developed in *Semiotics and Linguistic Structure*.[1] And to begin with let us speak of *dyadic* or two-place relations as a prelude to the general theory.

Let

(1) $$\text{`}\{xy \ni --x--y--\}\text{'}$$

be a two-place abstract, where '--x--y--' is a sentential form containing the distinct variables 'x' and 'y' as its only free variables. This sentential form is presumed constructed wholly out of the atomic formulae of the language (containing only the nonlogical *primitive* predicate constants) by means of ' ~ ', 'v', and universal quantification in the usual way. Let '*A*', '*B*', etc., be used for any such sentential forms and '*R*' and '*S*' for any such abstracts. These abstracts stand for (or designate) virtual dyadic relations. The *logical sum* of two virtual classes may be introduced now as follows.

(2) $\ulcorner(R \cup S)\urcorner$ abbreviates $\ulcorner\{xy \ni (Rxy \text{ v } Sxy)\}\urcorner$.

And similarly for the logical *product* and *negation*.

(3) $\ulcorner(R \cap S)\urcorner$ for $\ulcorner\{xy \ni (Rxy \cdot Sxy)\}\urcorner$

and

(4) $\ulcorner(-R\urcorner$ for $\ulcorner\{xy \ni \ \sim Rxy\}\urcorner$.

Likewise the *universal* dyadic virtual relation term

(5) 'V' is now short for '$\{xy \ni (x = x \cdot y = y)\}$'[2]

and the term for the *null* dyadic virtual relation

(6) 'Λ' is short for ' $-$V'.

The identity of virtual relations is also symbolized by ' = ', so that this overworked little symbol will be ambiguous. We let

(7) $\ulcorner R = S\urcorner$ abbreviate $\ulcorner(x)(y)(Rxy \equiv Sxy)\urcorner$.

The foregoing constitute the basic notions of the Boolean algebra of dyadic virtual relations.

Two interesting notions are immediately available the moment we step beyond the Boolean notions. The first is the notion of the *converse*.

(8) $\ulcorner\cup R\urcorner$ abbreviates $\ulcorner\{xy \ni Ryx\}\urcorner$.

The other two are the notions of the *domain* and *counter-* or *converse domain* of a virtual relation. Let

(9) $\ulcorner D_1 R\urcorner$ abbreviate $\ulcorner\{x \ni (Ey)Rxy\}\urcorner$

and

(10) $\ulcorner D_2 R\urcorner$ abbreviate $\ulcorner\{y \ni (Ex)Rxy\}\urcorner$.

These notations give us, respectively, the virtual class of all entities that bear a relation to something, and the virtual class of all entities to which something bears the relation. In dealing with any relation it is obviously of the highest concern to determine or stipulate its domains as precisely as possible.

Relation theory is of course not confined to dyadic relations, for there are triadic ones, quadratic ones, and so on, to be considered. This could be done stepwise, but one may as well move on directly to the general theory. The various notations (1) and those introduced in the definitions (2)–(7) can now be extended immediately to n-adic virtual relations in general. The extensions of (8) allow of several varieties, as do those of (9)–(10). We need then a general notation. Also *monadic* virtual relations, i.e., virtual *classes*, may be included. In place of (1), we need now the general case of an n-place abstract

(11) $\qquad\qquad$ '$\{x_1 \ldots x_n \ni$ ---x_1--- $\ldots x_n$---$\}$'

for any $n \geq 1$. Here of course 'x_1', $\ldots$, 'x_n' are distinct variables occurring (freely) in '---x_1--- $\ldots$ ---x_n---', this latter being a sentential form containing no other variables and no predicates other than the primitive ones. Let 'R_n', 'S_n', and so on, stand for any n-place abstract (containing of course no free variables). The definitions (2)–(7) may then be given for any n. The signs '$\cup$', '$\cap$', '$-$', and '$=$', thus become ambiguous, but all ambiguity is removed when they are properly embedded in context. Thus '$\cup$' as occurring in $\ulcorner(R_3 \cup S_3)_3\urcorner$ — the final subscript being added for perspicuity — is the sign for the sum of triadic virtual relations, which sum in turn is triadic. Let 'V_1', 'V_2', and so on, now be the signs for the universal virtual class, the universal dyadic virtual relation, and so on. And similarly for 'Λ_1', 'Λ_2', and so on, for the null virtual class, the null dyadic virtual relation, and so on.

Let us reflect now upon the generalizations needed for (9) and (10). In place of $\ulcorner D_1 R\urcorner$ and $\ulcorner D_2 R\urcorner$ above we now have several notations to distinguish depending upon the degree of R. Thus for an R_n, we now let

$\qquad \ulcorner(D_1 R_n)_1\urcorner$ abbreviate $\ulcorner\{x_1 \ni (Ex_2)\ldots(Ex_n)R_n \, x_1 \ldots x_n\}\urcorner$,
$\qquad \ulcorner(D_2 R_n)_1\urcorner$ abbreviate $\ulcorner\{x_2 \ni (Ex_1)(Ex_3)\ldots(Ex_n)R_n \, x_1 \ldots x_n\}\urcorner$,

and so on. These are the *simple* or *monadic* or one-place domains. In addition, where $n \geq 3$, we have *relational domains* to consider. Thus, for example,

$\qquad \ulcorner(D_{12} R_n)_2\urcorner$ abbreviates $\ulcorner\{x_1 x_2 \ni (Ex_3)\ldots(Ex_n) \, R_n x_1 \ldots x_n\}\urcorner$,

$\qquad \ulcorner(D_{24} R_n)_2\urcorner$ $\quad$ abbreviates $\quad \ulcorner\{x_2 x_4 \ni (Ex_1)(Ex_3)(Ex_5)\ldots(Ex_n)$ $R_n x_1 \ldots x_n\}\urcorner$ for $n \geq 5$, and so on. In general,

(12) $\ulcorner(D_{i\ldots k}R_n)_k\urcorner$ abbreviates $\ulcorner\{x_i\ldots x_k \ni (Ex_1)\ldots(Ex_{(i-1)})\ldots$
$(Ex_{(i+1)})\ldots(Ex_{(k-1)})(Ex_{(k+1)})\ldots(Ex_n)R_n x_1\ldots x_n\}\urcorner$, for $1 \leq i < \ldots$
$< k \leq n$ where the number of numbers $i, \ldots, k$ is $< n$.

We see, then, that given any R_n, there are many monadic domains, dyadic relational domains, triadic relational domains, and in general $(n-1)$-adic relational domains to be distinguished.

There is no reason why the various relational domains should be restricted, as in (12), to just those in the expressions for which the left-to-right order of the subscripts is taken in the order of increasing magnitude. We can also admit further relational domains by allowing

$\ulcorner(D_{42}R_n)_2\urcorner$ as short for $\ulcorner\{x_4 x_2 \ni (Ex_1)(Ex_3)(Ex_5)\ldots(Ex_n)R_n x_1\ldots$
$x_n\}\urcorner$,

and so on. In general

(13) $\ulcorner(D_{i\ldots k}R_n)_k\urcorner$ abbreviates $\ulcorner\{x_i\ldots x_k \ni (Ex_j)\ldots(Ex_m)$
$R_n x_1\ldots x_n\}\urcorner$, where each of the distinct variables 'x_i', $\ldots$, 'x_k',
'x_j', $\ldots$, 'x_m' is one of 'x_1', $\ldots$, 'x_n' and conversely.

We may also let

$\ulcorner(D_{1\ldots n}R_n)_n\urcorner$ abbreviate $\ulcorner\{x_1\ldots x_n \ni R_n x_1\ldots x_n\}\urcorner$,

if desired, so as to allow an n-adic relation itself to be one of its own relational domains. And similarly,

(14) $\ulcorner(D_{i\ldots k}R_n)_k\urcorner$ abbreviates $\ulcorner\{x_i\ldots x_k \ni Rx_1\ldots x_m\}\urcorner$, where
each 'x_i', $\ldots$, 'x_k' is one of 'x_1', $\ldots$, 'x_n' and conversely.

The notion of a relational domain seems a most natural extension of the notion of a simple domain and should play an important role in the theory of relations when we turn in a moment to consider that theory *sui generis* and independently of the theory of virtual classes and relations upon which it has been developed above.

Note that once relational domains are introduced, all manner of *converses* of an n-adic virtual relation may be introduced by definition. Thus

$\ulcorner(\cup R_2)_2\urcorner$ is now short for $\ulcorner(D_{21}R_2)_2\urcorner$·

But also, for triadic relations, we let[3]

$\ulcorner(C_{132}R_3)_3\urcorner$ be an alternative to $\ulcorner(D_{132}R_3)_3\urcorner$,

$\ulcorner(C_{213}R_3)_3\urcorner$ for $\ulcorner(D_{213}R_3)_3\urcorner$,

$$\ulcorner (C_{231}R_3)_3 \urcorner \text{ for } \ulcorner (D_{231}R_3)_3 \urcorner,$$

$$\ulcorner (C_{312}R_3)_3 \urcorner \text{ for } \ulcorner (D_{312}R_3)_3 \urcorner,$$

and

$$\ulcorner (C_{321}R_3)_3 \urcorner \text{ for } \ulcorner (D_{321}R_3)_3 \urcorner,$$

and so on for relations of any degree. And similarly for all relational domains. Given the generalized notion of relational domain, we see that the various notions of converse are automatically forthcoming.

A given n-adic relation together with all of its domains, relational domains, and converses, constitutes a family of closely *affiliated* relations. Consider, by way of an example, the triadic relation of giving. Let '$Gxyz$' express that person x gives object y to person z — taken in the tense of timelessness. There are in fact 15 relations affiliated with G, if we count G as one of its own affiliates. There are the 6 converses, 6 dyadic relational domains including their converses, and the 3 monadic domains. All of these can easily be expressed in ordinary language by the use of various nouns, the passive voice, various prepositions, and so on. The monadic domains for G are well expressed by 'givers', 'gifts', and 'persons given to'. The 6 dyadic relational domains are captured by 'gives the gift' without specification of the person to whom it is given, 'gives something to the person' without specification of the gift, 'is given to' without specification of the giver, and 'is given by', 'is given something by', and 'is given'. The 5 converses of G are captured by the sentential forms 'x gives to z the gift y', 'the gift y is given by x to z', 'y is given to z by x', 'z is given by x to y', and 'z is given to y by x'. It is interesting to note that for a quadratic relation, there are 64 affiliated relations, for a pentadic one, 325, and for hexadic ones, 1956! In general, it seems, for an n-adic relation the number of affiliated relations is

$$(n! + n! + (n \times (n-1) \times \ldots \times 3) + \ldots + (n \times (n-1)) + n), \text{ for}$$
$n \geq 2$.

All of the notions (1)–(14) can be defined within the theory of n-adic relations for any given fixed n, where $n \geq 2$, and of course the Boolean notions for classes may be defined within the theory of monadic relations (or virtual classes) where $n = 1$. The various notions of domain, however, for $n \geq 2$, make use also of the theories of k-adic relations for any $k < n$. Thus the D_1 of a dyadic relation is a virtual class, the D_{23} of a triadic one is a virtual dyadic relation, and so on. In short, the theory of relations of degree n is cumulative in the sense that it utilizes the notions of the theories of relations of all degrees k, where $1 \leq k < n$.

We now turn to a notion, that of a *Cartesian product*, in which the degree of the relation introduced in the definiendum is the sum of the degrees of the relations expressions for which occur in the definiens. The simplest example is to let

$$\ulcorner (R_1 \times S_1)_2 \urcorner \quad \text{abbreviate} \quad \ulcorner \{xy \ni (R_1 x \cdot S_1 y)\} \urcorner.$$

In general, we allow

(15) $\ulcorner (R_n \times S_m)_{(n+m)} \urcorner$ to abbreviate $\ulcorner \{x_1 \ldots x_n y_1 \ldots y_m \ni (R_n x_1 \ldots x_n \cdot S_m y_1 \ldots y_m)\} \urcorner$, for $n \geq 1$, $m \geq 1$.

This notion is of course significant only in the theory of $(n + m)$-adic relations.

For the full theory of n-adic relations, then, we need just the Boolean notions, the general notion of being an affiliated relation (a domain or relational domain or converse), and the general notion of the Cartesian product. The problem arises then of constructing a language system, with a set of axioms, based upon these notions taken as *primitives* and thus without presupposing in any way the theory of *virtual* classes and relations, as above, and hence also without the use of variables. What would such a system look like?

Well, first we specify the primitive nonlogical relational terms (or predicates); we then specify recursively the notion of a *relational term of such and such a degree* as follows.

(Def1)   i. Any primitive n-place relational term is a relational term of degree n.

ii. If R_n and S_n are relational terms of degree n, so are $\ulcorner (R_n \cup S_n)_n \urcorner$, $\ulcorner (R_n \cap S_n)_n \urcorner$, and $\ulcorner -R_n \urcorner$, for $n \geq 1$.

iii. 'V_n' and 'Λ'_n' are relational terms of degree n, for $n \geq 1$.

iv. If R_n is a relational term of degree n, then $\ulcorner (D_{i \ldots k} R_n)_j \urcorner$ is a relational term of degree j, where $j \leq n$ and $i, \ldots, k$ are j distinct numbers each $\leq n$ and taken in any order of magnitude, and where $n \geq 2$.

v. If R_n and S_m are relational terms of degree n and m respectively, then $\ulcorner (R_n \times S_m)_{(n+m)} \urcorner$ is a relational term of degree $(n + m)$, for $n \geq 1$, $m \geq 1$.

We need now also a recursive specification of the *formulae* admitted.

(Def2)   i. If R_n *and* S_n are relational terms of degree n then $\ulcorner R_n = S_n \urcorner$ is a formula.

ii. If A and B are formulae, so are $\ulcorner \sim A \urcorner$, $\ulcorner (A \vee B) \urcorner$, $\ulcorner (A \cdot B) \urcorner$, $\ulcorner (A \supset B) \urcorner$, and $\ulcorner (A \equiv B) \urcorner$.

The bold-face letters '$\boldsymbol{R}_n$', and so on, will be used hereafter for any relational terms of degree n.

No attempt need be made here to whittle down the array of primitives to a minimum. It is well known that

$\ulcorner (\boldsymbol{R}_n \cap \boldsymbol{S}_n)_n \urcorner$, for example, can be defined as $\ulcorner -(-\boldsymbol{R}_n \cup -\boldsymbol{S}_n)_n \urcorner$,

and similarly for 'V_n' *and* 'Λ_n' and for some of the truth-functional connectives. Also notions of domain simpler than those given can be made to suffice. No such niceties, however, will affect the overall philosophic character of the system, which is the main object of concern here.

Let us list a few fundamental principles governing these various notions.

Pr1. $\vdash \ulcorner \boldsymbol{R}_n = \boldsymbol{R}_n \urcorner$.

Pr2. $\vdash \ulcorner (\boldsymbol{R}_n = \boldsymbol{S}_n \cdot \boldsymbol{S}_n = \boldsymbol{T}_n) \supset \boldsymbol{R}_n = \boldsymbol{T}_n \urcorner$.

Pr3. $\vdash \ulcorner \boldsymbol{R}_n = \boldsymbol{S}_n \supset (\boldsymbol{R}_n \cup \boldsymbol{T}_n)_n = (\boldsymbol{S}_n \cup \boldsymbol{T}_n)_n \urcorner$.

Pr4. $\vdash \ulcorner \boldsymbol{R}_n = \boldsymbol{S}_n \supset (\boldsymbol{R}_n \cap \boldsymbol{T}_n)_n = (\boldsymbol{S}_n \cap \boldsymbol{T}_n)_n \urcorner$.

Pr5. $\vdash \ulcorner (\boldsymbol{R}_n \cup \boldsymbol{S}_n)_n = (\boldsymbol{S}_n \cup \boldsymbol{R}_n)_n \urcorner$.

Pr6. $\vdash \ulcorner (\boldsymbol{R}_n \cap \boldsymbol{S}_n)_n = (\boldsymbol{S}_n \cap \boldsymbol{R}_n)_n \urcorner$.

Pr7. $\vdash \ulcorner ((\boldsymbol{R}_n \cup \boldsymbol{S}_n)_n \cup \boldsymbol{T}_n)_n = (\boldsymbol{R}_n \cup (\boldsymbol{S}_n \cup \boldsymbol{T}_n)_n)_n \urcorner$.

Pr8. $\vdash \ulcorner ((\boldsymbol{R}_n \cap \boldsymbol{S}_n)_n \cap \boldsymbol{T}_n)_n = (\boldsymbol{R}_n \cap (\boldsymbol{S}_n \cap \boldsymbol{T}_n)_n)_n \urcorner$.

Pr9. $\vdash \ulcorner ((\boldsymbol{R}_n \cup \boldsymbol{S}_n)_n \cap \boldsymbol{T}_n)_n = ((\boldsymbol{R}_n \cap \boldsymbol{T}_n)_n \cup (\boldsymbol{S}_n \cap \boldsymbol{T}_n)_n)_n \urcorner$.

Pr10. $\vdash \ulcorner ((\boldsymbol{R}_n \cap \boldsymbol{S}_n)_n \cup \boldsymbol{T}_n)_n = ((\boldsymbol{R}_n \cup \boldsymbol{T}_n)_n \cap (\boldsymbol{S}_n \cup \boldsymbol{T}_n)_n)_n \urcorner$.

Pr11. $\vdash \ulcorner (\boldsymbol{R}_n \cup \Lambda_n) = \boldsymbol{R}_n \urcorner$.

Pr12. $\vdash \ulcorner (\boldsymbol{R}_n \cap V_n) = \boldsymbol{R}_n \urcorner$.

Pr13. $\vdash \ulcorner \boldsymbol{R}_n = \boldsymbol{S}_n \supset -\boldsymbol{R}_n = -\boldsymbol{S}_n \urcorner$.

Pr14. $\vdash \ulcorner \boldsymbol{R}_n = --\boldsymbol{R}_n \urcorner$.

Pr15. $\vdash \ulcorner (\boldsymbol{R}_n \cup -\boldsymbol{R}_n)_n = V_n \urcorner$.

Pr16. $\vdash \ulcorner (\boldsymbol{R}_n \cap -\boldsymbol{R}_n)_n = \Lambda_n \urcorner$.

Pr17. $\vdash \ulcorner (\boldsymbol{R}_n \cup \boldsymbol{S}_n)_n = -(-\boldsymbol{R}_n \cap -\boldsymbol{S}_n)_n \urcorner$.

Pr18. $\vdash \ulcorner (\boldsymbol{R}_n \cap \boldsymbol{S}_n)_n = -(-\boldsymbol{R}_n \cup -\boldsymbol{S}_n)_n \urcorner$.

Pr19. $\vdash \ulcorner \sim V_n = \Lambda_n \urcorner$.

Pr20. $\vdash \ulcorner R_n = S_n \supset (D_i \ldots {}_k R_n)_j = (D_i \ldots {}_k S_n)_j \urcorner$, where (as in *Def1* (iv)).

Pr21. $\vdash \ulcorner (D_i \ldots {}_k (D_k \ldots {}_i R_n)_j)_j = (D_i \ldots {}_k R_n)_j \urcorner$, where (as in *Def1* (iv)).

Pr22. $\vdash \ulcorner (D_i \ldots {}_k (R_n \cup S_n)_n)_j = ((D_i \ldots {}_k R_n)_j \cup (D_i \ldots {}_k S_n)_j)_j \urcorner$, where (as in *Def1* (iv)).

Pr23. $\vdash \ulcorner (D_i \ldots {}_k R_n)_k = V_k \equiv (D_j \ldots {}_m R_n)_k = V_k \urcorner$ where each of i, ..., k is one of j, ..., m and conversely.

Pr24. $\vdash \ulcorner \sim (D_i \ldots {}_k R_n)_j = \Lambda_j \supset \sim R_n = \Lambda_n \urcorner$ where (as in *Def1* (iv)).

Pr25. $\vdash \ulcorner \sim (D_i \ldots {}_k R_n)_j = \Lambda_j \supset \sim (D_{i'} \ldots {}_{k'} R_n)_{j'} = \Lambda_j \urcorner$, where i, ..., k, i', ..., k' are $(j+j')$ distinct numbers, each $\geq n$, $1 \geq$ each, $(j+j') = n$, and $n \geq 2$.

Pr26. $\vdash \ulcorner R_n = S_n \supset (R_n \times T_m)_{(n+m)} = (S_n \times T_m)_{(n+m)} \urcorner$.

Pr27. $\vdash \ulcorner R_n = S_n \supset (T_m \times R_n)_{(m+n)} = (T_m \times S_n)_{(m+n)} \urcorner$.

Pr28. $\vdash \ulcorner (R_n \times T_m)_{(n+m)} = (S_n \times T_m)_{(n+m)} \supset R_n = S_n \urcorner$.

Pr29. $\vdash \ulcorner (T_m \times R_n)_{(m+n)} = (T_m \times S_n)_{(m+n)} \supset R_n = S_n \urcorner$.

Pr30. $\vdash \ulcorner (R_n \times (S_m \times T_k)_{(m+k)})_{(n+m+k)} = ((R_n \times S_m)_{(n+m)} \times T_k)_{(n+m+k)} \urcorner$.

Pr31. $\vdash \ulcorner (T_m \times (R_n \cup S_n)_n)_{(m+n)} = ((T_m \times R_n)_{(m+n)} \cup (T_m \times S_n)_{(m+n)})_{(m+n)} \urcorner$.

Pr32. $\vdash \ulcorner ((R_n \cup S_n)_n \times T_m)_{(n+m)} = ((R_n \times T_m)_{(n+m)} \cup (S_n \times T_m)_{(n+m)})_{(n+m)} \urcorner$.

Pr33. $\vdash \ulcorner (T_m \times (R_n \cap S_n)_n)_{(m+n)} = ((T_m \times R_n)_{(m+n)} \cap (T_m \times S_n)_{(m+n)})_{(m+n)} \urcorner$.

Pr34. $\vdash \ulcorner ((R_n \cap S_n)_n \times T_m)_{(n+m)} = ((R_n \times T_m)_{(n+m)} \cap (S_n \times T_m)_{(n+m)})_{(n+m)} \urcorner$.

Pr35. $\vdash \ulcorner (-(T_m \times -R_n)_{(m+n)} \cup -(T_m \times R_n)_{(m+n)})_{(m+n)} = V_{(m+n)} \urcorner$.

Pr36. $\vdash \ulcorner (R_n \times S_m)_{(n+m)} = ((R_n \times V_m)_{(n+m)} \cap (V_n \times S_m)_{(n+m)})_{(n+m)} \urcorner$.

Pr37. $\vdash \ulcorner R_n = S_n \equiv ((-R_n \cup S_n)_n \cap (R_n \cup -S_n)_n)_n = V_n \urcorner$.

Pr38. $\vdash \ulcorner R_n = S_n \equiv ((-R_n \cap S_n)_n \cup (R_n \cap -S_n)_n)_n = V_n \urcorner$.

Pr39. $\vdash \ulcorner \sim R_n = \Lambda_n \equiv \sim -R_n = V_n \urcorner$.

Pr40. $\vdash \ulcorner \sim R_n = V_n \equiv (D_1(V_1 \times - R_n)_{(n+1)})_1 = V_1 \urcorner$.

Pr41. $\vdash \ulcorner (R_n \cap S_n)_n = V_n \equiv (R_n = V_n \cdot S_n = V_n) \urcorner$.

Pr42. $\vdash \ulcorner (D_1(V_1 \times - (R_n \cap S_n)_n)_{(n+1)})_1 = V_1 \equiv (R_n = V_n \vee S_n = V_n) \urcorner$.

Most of these laws are of a familiar kind and may be listed here without comment. A suitable subset of them would appear among the axioms, together with a rule of *Modus Ponens*. In addition suitable axioms governing the connectives are needed as well as nonlogical axioms governing whatever nonlogical relation terms are taken as primitives.

Nothing thus far has been said about the interesting notions of the *relative product* and the *relative sum* of two relations. For dyadic ones we can let

$\ulcorner (R_2 \ / \ S_2)_2 \urcorner$ be short for $\ulcorner (D_{12}(D_{132}((R_2 \times V_1)_3 \cap (V_1 \times (\cup S_2)_3)_3)_3)_2) \urcorner$

and

$\ulcorner (R_2 \ \# \ S_2)_2 \urcorner$ for $\ulcorner (- D_{12}(D_{132}((- R_2 \times V_1)_3 \cap (V_1 \times - (\cup S_2)_3)_3)_3)_2) \urcorner$

We are now in a position to observe that whatever can be expressed in the theory of virtual classes and relations, and thus in the usual quantification theory, can be expressed here. The only contexts we need consider are those conaining the primitive nonlogical predicate constants, and signs for conjunction and negation. But for the negation of any atomic formula, we can always negate the predicate instead, no matter how many argument places it takes. And for a conjunction of atomic formulae, we first unify the number of argument places each predicate occurring in it takes, using Cartesian products and the appropriate V_n's, then perform whatever conversions are needed to assure that the arguments occur in the same left to right order, and then form the logical sum. And so on for formulae of any complexity. All formulae being of finite length, this procedure must come to a stop in some n-adic predicate term. Likewise, in view of the prenex normal form theorem,[4] we know that all quantifiers of a formula may be initially placed. Thus we need consider our n-adic predicate term, say 'T_n', with its n arguments, only as occuring in some context with all the quantifiers, universal or existential, initially placed. More specifically, all our quantificational formulae can now be expressed in formulae of the form

$$\ulcorner (Qx_1)\ldots(Qx_n)T_n x_1 \ldots x_n \urcorner,$$

where each $\ulcorner(Qx_i)\urcorner$ is either $\ulcorner(x_i)\urcorner$ or $\ulcorner(\mathrm{E}x_i)\urcorner$. But all formulae of this form may now be expressed by saying that the relation T_n is universal, or that one or more of its domains or relational domains are universal. Thus

$$`(x)(y)(z)(\mathrm{E}u)T_4xyzu'$$

may be expressed by saying instead that

$$(\mathrm{D}_{123}T_4)_3 = \mathrm{V}_3.$$

Similarly

$$`(\mathrm{E}x)(u)(\mathrm{E}y)(z)T_4xuyz'$$

may be expressed as

$$`(\mathrm{D}_{24}T_4)_2 = \mathrm{V}_2'.$$

And so on.

We are left then with a *logic without variables or quantifiers*, comparable in this respect to Quine's predicate-functor logic, discussed in VIII above. Moreover, all the formulae are of the form $\ulcorner R_n = S_n\urcorner$ together with truth-functional compounds of such. Logic is thus seen to be a kind of *molecular equational algebra*, not, however, an algebra utilizing free variables but only the primitive nonlogical predicates together with the truth-functional connectives.

There are some alternatives to the formulation above that are worthy of note. Observe that, in view of *Pr37* and *Pr38*, any formula of the form $\ulcorner R_n = S_n\urcorner$ is equivalent to one of the form $\ulcorner T_n = \mathrm{V}_n\urcorner$. Thus all our formulae could be written in this latter form, with no loss of expressive power. Of course, to achieve this suitable alterations must be made in the formulation of the axioms and rules.

Moreover, in view of *Pr40*, the negation of a formula of the form $\ulcorner R_n = \mathrm{V}_n\urcorner$ is itself equivalent to one of the simple form $\ulcorner T_l = \mathrm{V}_l\urcorner$ and in view of *Pr41*, the conjunction of any two formulae of the forms $\ulcorner R_n = \mathrm{V}_n\urcorner$ and $\ulcorner S_n = \mathrm{V}_n\urcorner$ is equivalent to one of the form $\ulcorner T_n = \mathrm{V}_n\urcorner$. (And similarly for disjunction in view of *Pr42*.) Because all of the truth-functional connectives are expressible in terms of negation and conjunction (or negation and disjunction, or *a fortiori* in terms of all three), we see that the connectives themselves may be eliminated. In view of these considerations, we could formulate a *quasiatomic* equational algebra without connectives, where all the atomic and quasiatomic formulae are of the form $\ulcorner R_n = \mathrm{V}_n\urcorner$. Another possibility is to retain the formulae of the form $\ulcorner R_n = S_n\urcorner$, but eliminate the connectives, any formula of the form $\ulcorner T_n = \mathrm{V}_n\urcorner$ being a special case of one of the form $\ulcorner R_n = S_n\urcorner$. For all of these formulations, of course, suitable adjustments must be made in the axioms, and suitable rules of inference, especially rules of replacement, must be formulated. For example, a rule of replacement would be to the effect that if $\vdash \ulcorner R_n = S_n \urcorner$ then $\vdash \ulcorner (\text{--}R_n\text{--})_k = (\text{--}S_n\text{--})_k \urcorner$, where $\ulcorner (\text{--}S_n\text{--})_k \urcorner$ is a relation term containing S_n in one or more places where the relation term $\ulcorner (\text{--}R_n\text{--}) \urcorner$ contains R_n.

Still another possibility suggests itself by recalling again *Pr40* together with *Pr42*. Every formula of the form $\ulcorner R_n = V_n \urcorner$ can be expressed in terms of one of the form $\ulcorner T_1 = V_1 \urcorner$, and similarly for every disjunction or conjunction of such. We could then formulate a quasiatomic equational algebra without connectives and in which every equation is of the form $\ulcorner T_1 = V_1 \urcorner$. For this also suitable axioms and rules remain to be chosen.

Still another alternative is to take a notion of *n*-adic *inclusion*, symbolized by '$\subset$', as a primitive in place of '$=$'. This latter could then be introduced by letting, where connectives are available,

$$\ulcorner R_n = S_n \urcorner \text{ abbreviate } \ulcorner (R_n \subset S_n \cdot S_n \subset R_n) \urcorner,$$

or

$$\ulcorner R_n = V_n \urcorner \text{ for } \ulcorner V_n \subset R_n \urcorner,$$

where they are not — again, with appropriate reformulation of the axioms and rules. There are a number of further alternatives also.

All of these ways of eliminating variables, quantifiers and the truth-functional connectives contrast with the methods of Schönfinkel and Curry in taking relations as more fundamental than *functions*. On the relational view, functions are a special kind of relation, namely, one-many relations. We may let, where Id_2 is the identity relation,

$$\ulcorner \text{Func } R_n \urcorner \text{ abbreviate } \ulcorner ((-(D_{213\ldots(n+1)} (V_1 \times R_n)_{(n+1)})_{(n+1)}$$
$$\cup - (V_1 \times R_n)_{(n+1)})_{(n+1)} \cup (Id_2 \times V_{(n-1)})_{(n+1)})_{(n+1)} = V_{(n+1)} \urcorner.$$

All talk of functions thus naturally reduces itself to talk of suitable relations. From the present point of view relations are regarded as the more fundamental kind of entity. They are historically prior and are of greater generality. Functions are of interest primarily in numerical mathematics and its applications in the sciences, but relations are needed fundamentally wherever there is systematic thought of any kind. In particular, they have, and indeed do now, play an important role in metaphysics and theology,[5] to say nothing of the basic role they play in structural linguistics and hence in the philosophy of language.

Suppose now that among the nonlogical primitives there is 'E_2' for a (dyadic) set-theoretic relation of membership within some suitable rendition of set theory. Among the nonlogical axioms of the system above we should have then adaptations of the axioms of that theory. Suppose it is that of the famous Zermelo-Skolem system. The *Axiom of Pairs*, that for any two sets or *Urelemente* there exists a set whose only members are those two, can be expressed here as

$$\text{`}(D_{412}(((E_2 \times V_2)_4 \cap ((Id_2 \times V_1)_3 \cup (D_{132}(Id_2 \times V_1)_3)_3 \times V_1)_4)_4$$
$$\cup (-(E_2 \times V_2)_4 \cap -((Id_2 \times V_1)_3 \cup (D_{132}(Id_2 \times V_1)_3)_3 \times V_1)_4)_4)_4)_3$$
$$= V_3\text{'}.$$

Similarly, certain instances of the *Aussonderungsschema* may be expressed as

$$\ulcorner(D_{13}(((D_{132}(E_2 \times V_1)_3)_3 \cap ((E_2 \cap (V_1 \times R_1)_2)_2 \times V_1)_3)_3 \cup$$
$$(-(D_{132}(E_2 \times V_1)_3)_3 \cap -((E_2 \times (V_1 \times R_1)_2)_2 \times V_1)_3)_3)_3)_2$$
$$= V_2\urcorner.$$

This states, roughly, that given any monadic R_1 and any set x, there exists a set y the members of which are just the members z of x such that R_1z. And similarly for the other axioms.

In this way we see that the whole of set theory, and therewith such mathematics as can be incorporated in it, may be included here in the extended theory of relations. Further, all sentences of that theory may be expressed in the forms $\ulcorner R_n = S_n \urcorner$ or even $\ulcorner R_1 = V_1 \urcorner$, for constant R_m and S_n ($m = n$ or $m = 1$). No variables occur, so that we have a *mathematics without variables*. Also all truth-functional connectives may be eliminated if desired. If the algebraic theory of relations plus set theory is regarded as mathematical rather than logical in nature, then logic itself may be seen to be a branch of mathematics. If the theory of relations without set theory is regarded as constituting logic, then this latter likewise can be viewed as a branch of mathematics, more particularly, as a kind of algebra. However viewed, logic can then be regarded here as subservient to mathematics in ways contrary to the logistic thesis of Frege and of Whitehead and Russell.

Similar considerations apply if we consider a Russellian theory of types in place of a set theory, but with a good deal of technicalia needed by way of superscripts, say, for the indication of type level.

Proper names of individuals throughout have been presupposed as handled familiarly either in terms of Russellian descriptions or predicates applicable to just one entity. The use of parentheses likewise is merely ancillary and could be eliminated using the familiar devices of Lukasiewicz.

The technical handling of the material above is comparable in various respects to work by Bernays, Halmos, and Tarski *inter alios*.[6] There are some significant differences in detail, however, as well as in the general philosophical and methodological *ambiente*. In particular, the material here concerns relations only algebraically but not as values of variables, whereas the authors referred to deal with real relations — as values for variables — and presuppose a set theory by way of general mathematical background. No use of course is made of set theory here. In fact, the algebraic theory of relations is regarded here as a necessary background for the development of set theory, not the other way around as regards real relations, as is customary among mathematicians.

Let us reflect for a moment on the systematic semantics of the foregoing theory without variables. Let

$$\text{`}a \text{ Den } x_1 \ldots x_n\text{'}$$

express primitively, in the semantical metalanguage, in which of course variables occur, that the expression *a denotes* $x_1, \ldots, x_n$ in order. We might also say here that *a* denotes the ordered *n*-tuple consisting of x_1, $\ldots, x_n$ in this order, provided it is understood that this is a mere *manière de parler* and that *n*-tuples are not therewith recognized as values for variables. Let the usual quantifiers and connectives be available also. It is proposed now to show how the foregoing system can be "interpreted" within this metalanguage by postulating suitable *semantical rules*. These are as follows, where by 'predicate' one means of course the relation terms of the system. (In the system with variables and virtual relations one speaks of predicates, whereas in the system without variables 'relational term' seems more appropriate.)

DenR1. $\vdash \ulcorner (x_1) \ldots (x_n)(R_n \text{ Den } x_1 \ldots x_n \equiv R_n x_1 \ldots x_n)\urcorner$, where R_n is the shape description of 'R_n', 'R_n' being a primitive nonlogical *n*-adic predicate.[7]

DenR2a. $\vdash \ulcorner (x_1) \ldots (x_n)(\ulcorner R_n \cup S_n)_n\urcorner \text{ Den } x_1 \ldots x_n \equiv (R_n x_1 \ldots x_n$ v $S_n x_1 \ldots x_n))\urcorner$, where R_n and S_n are the shape descriptions of the primitive or defined *n*-adic predicates 'R_n' and 'S_n' respectively.

DenR2b. $\vdash \ulcorner (x_1) \ldots (x_n)(\ulcorner (R_n \cap S_n)_n\urcorner \text{Den} x_1 \ldots x_n \equiv (R_n x_1 \ldots x_n$ · $S_n x_1 \ldots x_n))\urcorner$, where (etc.)

DenR2c. $\vdash \ulcorner (x_1) \ldots (x_n)(\ulcorner - R_n\urcorner \text{ Den } x_1 \ldots x_n \equiv \sim R_n x_1 \ldots x_n)\urcorner$, where R_n is the shape description of the primitive or defined *n*-adic predicate 'R_n'.

DenR2d. $\vdash \ulcorner (x_1) \ldots (x_n)\text{'}V_n\text{' Den } x_1 \ldots x_n.$

DenR2e. $\vdash \sim (\text{E}x_1)\ldots(\text{E}x_n)\ulcorner\Lambda_n\urcorner\,\text{Den}\,x_1\ldots x_n.$

DenR3. $\vdash\ulcorner(x_i)\ldots(x_k)\,(\ulcorner\text{D}_i\ldots{}_k R_n)_k\urcorner\,\text{Den}\,x_i\ldots x_k \equiv (\text{E}x_j)\ldots$ $(\text{E}x_m)R_n x_1\ldots x_n)\urcorner$, where R_n is the shape description of 'R_n' and (etc., as in (13)).

DenR4. $\vdash\ulcorner(x_1)\ldots(x_n)(y_1)\ldots(y_m)(\ulcorner(R_n \times S_m)_{(n+m)}\urcorner\,\text{Den}$ $x_1\ldots x_n y_1\ldots y_m \equiv (R_n x_1\ldots x_n \cdot S_m y_1\ldots y_m))\urcorner$, where (as in DenR2a).

DenR5. $\vdash\ulcorner(x_1)\ldots(x_n)(a)(a\,\text{Den}\,x_1\ldots x_n \supset \text{RelTrm}(n)a)\urcorner$, where $\ulcorner\text{RelTrm}(n)\,a\urcorner$ expresses that a is an n-adic predicate term.

Note that these rules are framed in terms of 'Den'. We can also formulate them in terms of *designation,* Des, by defining

$\ulcorner a\,\text{Des}\,\{x_1\ldots x_n \ni R_n x_1\ldots x_n\}\urcorner$ as $\ulcorner(x_1)\ldots(x_n)(a\,\text{Den}\,x_1\ldots x_n \equiv R_n x_1\ldots x_n)\urcorner$.

The denotation rules above then could all be transformed into rules of *virtual-relation designation.*

A semantical notion of truth for the system is immediately forthcoming now by letting

'Tr a' abbreviate '(Sent $a \cdot (\text{E}b)(\text{Vbl}\,b \cdot \ulcorner\{b \ni a\}\urcorner\,\text{Des}\,\text{V}_1))$'.

And this predicate may readily be proved adequate in the sense that all formulae of the form

$$\ulcorner(\text{Tr}\,a \equiv A)\urcorner,$$

where in place of 'A' a sentence is inserted and in place of 'a' its shape description, are provable in the metalanguage.

No attempt has been made here to achieve the maximum of economy with regard either to the object-language primitives adopted or to the number of axioms, as already remarked. The aim has been rather to gain a smooth-running algebraic theory adequate for the intended purposes. One point of economy is perhaps worth mentioning, however: namely, that the only interchange of indices that need be allowed primitively in contexts of the form $\ulcorner(\text{D}_i\ldots{}_{m1}\ldots{}_k R_n)_j\urcorner$, as in Def1 (iv), are '1' with 'm', all others being then definable. Still further economy here is perhaps possible.

It remains now merely to note that the theory or theories here are not subject to most of the objections put forward in VIII above to Quine's formulation of predicate-functor logic. There is no reliance upon an unanalyzed notion of relative clause or upon a notion 'such that'. No illicit reification is made of whatever "schematic letters" are supposed to stand for. The bold-face letters here are used merely syntactically.

Some suggestions towards formulating axioms and rules of inference for the systems here are given, details being left open for future research. An explicative semantics of the systems may easily be given in terms of 'Den' and the usual quantification theory. The ontic commitment of the systems can be straightforwardly characterized as their ontic involvement (i.e., as the ontic commitment of the metalanguage). The entities to which the systems commit us are precisely the values for the variables of the semantical metalanguages in which the interpretations of the systems are given. Adequate semantical notions of truth for the systems are immediately forthcoming. The systems are of an especially simple kind, a "natural" extension of the calculus of relations, the fruitfulness of which is one of the greatest triumphs in the history of logic, as is now universally recognized. The use of variables, however, and such advantages as accrue therefrom, must of course be given up.

CHAPTER X

On the Logic of Psychoanalytic Language: Mental Actions

"Language is evidently one of the principal instruments or helps of thought; and any imperfection in the instrument, or in the mode of employing it, is confessedly liable, still more than in almost any other art, to confuse and impede the process, and to destroy all ground of confidence in the result."

J. S. Mill

In his provocative *A New Language for Psychoanalysis,*[1] Roy Schafer has suggested (p. 9) that we should "regard each psychological process, event, experience, or behavior as some kind of activity, henceforth to be called 'action', and . . . [should] designate each action by an active verb stating its nature and by an adverb (or adverbial locution), when applicable, stating the mode of this action." If we follow this suggestion, he continues, "we shall not use nouns and adjectives to refer to psychological processes, events, etc. In this, we should avoid substantive designations of actions as well as adjectival or traitlike designations of modes of actions. Thus, we should not use such phrases as 'a strong ego', 'the dynamic unconscious', 'the inner world', 'libidinal energy', 'rigid defense', 'an intense emotion', 'antonomous ego function', and 'instinctual drive'. This radical departure from accustomed designations is what it takes really to discontinue physicochemical and biological modes of psychological thinking. The essential referents of these designations will, however, be preserved in other terms." In other words, we should avoid the eclectic Freudian language of mechanism, force, structure, energy, cathexis, sublimation, drive, adaption, and the like, in favor of a new vocabulary.

The language rules governing the old vocabulary, it should be noted, were never very well formulated, and every effort should be made to supply them in full detail. And similarly for the language rules governing the new vocabulary. Only *after* such rules have been formulated for each, however, is it fruitful, or even possible, to compare and contrast them in any strict sense. Can rules adequate to the purposes at hand be formulated for either in a logically rigorous way? For reasons that will emerge, it will be easier to formulate them in a natural way for the new vocabulary than for the old. And if rules for the old are adequately formulable at all, it would seem, they will presuppose those for the new. Thus the various abstract terms constituting the old vocabulary, it seems, are best formulable, if at all, in actional terms.[2]

In this present paper, let us examine some of the requirements Schafer puts forward for the new vocabulary and its language, and subject them to a logical scrutiny and "rational reconstruction" in the light of recent work in contemporary symbolic logic.[3] This logic, briefly, consists of the usual first-order theory of *quantification* with identity, a form of Leśniewski's mereology or the calculus of *individuals,* a systematic *metalogic* or *semiotics* containing a syntax, semantics, and pragmatics, together with a systematic theory of *events, states, acts, and processes.* For this latter variables over a domain of events, including actions, are introduced, together with a special kind of predicate, the so-called *event-descriptive* ones. The events may be regarded as distinct from "things" or "concrete" or physical individuals, or as special cases of them, or the individuals may be regarded as constructs of some kind in terms of events. Which view here is taken is immaterial for present purposes. To be definite, however, to simplify, and to remain close to ordinary language, let us take *both* physical individuals and events, etc., as values for variables. In addition there are the *sign events* or inscriptions constituting the words and expressions of the language to be constructed, and there are the human beings, the *analysanda* of the practitioner as well as the practitioner himself, who are the *users* of the language. Strictly, then, we shall employ just four distinct types of variables, for individuals, for events and actions, for sign events, and for human beings. If desired, of course, these types of variables may easily be unified by purely technical means.

Let us get right at the heart of the new language by reflecting upon what appear to be the most important features that Schafer requires of it.

The first rule has already been stated, namely, that psychological processes should be spoken of primarily in terms of actions, and that verbs and adverbs provide the fundamental means of doing this. Problems arise, however, the moment we ask how verbs and adverbs are to be handled in a logically suitable way. One will hunt far and wide in the logical literature for an adequate account of them. Take the stock example of 'John loves Mary'. This is usually symbolized by, say, 'j L m', where 'L', we are told, stands for the relation *loves.* In similar fashion 'f F b', say, is taken to express that Frank is the father of Bill. An active verb 'loves' is symbolized in the same way as the substantive or sortal 'father'. But note the differences. 'Loves' is in the present tense, whereas the substantive 'father' has no tense. The English reading of 'f F b' requires the additional 'is the' (not 'is a', note) not required in the reading of 'j L m'. (Strictly 'f = (F'b)' should be taken as the reading of 'Frank is *the* father of Bill'.)[4] One might be tempted to read 'j L m' analogously to the reading of 'f F b', i.e., as 'John is the lover of Mary', but this of course differs drastically in meaning from 'John loves Mary'.

To get around these problems and for other reasons as well, let us introduce event-descriptive predicates. Let '⟨Love⟩' stand for all acts or states of *loving*, expressed gerundively. And let '⟨Love⟩e' express that e is such an act or state. Let 'Act e' express that e is an act and 'St e' that e is a state. Precisely how the two are differentiated is of little import for the present discussion. More important is the difference between action or event *types* and action or event *events*, so to speak. An action type is a general species, or a class or virtual class of action events.[5] Thus where '⟨Love⟩e' holds, ⟨Love⟩ is an action or state type and e is an action or state event. The difference is akin to the familiar one between types and tokens or between sign designs or sign events or shapes of expressions and particular inscriptions of them.[6]

The distinction between an action kind and an action event is an important one, but one that Schafer sometimes overlooks. Thus, in his very first "rule," it is stated that each psychological process should be regarded as some *kind* of activity. What is meant is presumably that each psychological process should be regarded as *of* some kind of activity, that each e under discussion be such as to have some suitable event-descriptive predicate applicable to it. Thus 'action' in Schafer's writing is often ambiguous as between the e's and the virtual classes of which they are taken to be members. Further, it will be recalled, Schafer suggests that we "shall designate each action by an active verb stating its nature and by an adverb (or adverbial locution), when applicable, stating the mode of this action." The statement of this suggestion is not quite accurate. What is intended is perhaps that any action event under discussion shall be *denoted*[7] by an event-descriptive predicate stating its nature and by an adverbial construction (where applicable) stating some mode. How are adverbs handled? The best way of reflecting upon this question is perhaps to consider an example.

Let us reflect upon Schafer's first example intended to illustrate the kind of verb-adverb formulation he advocates. Consider

(1)   'She resolutely strives to perceive her situation objectively'.

And in order not to get bogged down into details that are not of immediate relevance, let us follow the maxim to "scratch only where it itches," so to speak, even though in so doing we neglect important material. The relevant feature of (1) to be considered is her resolute striving and not in the details concerning how 'perceives' is to be handled.[8] Here '⟨Strive⟩' is short for 'strivings', and the final 's' in 'strives' may be taken to indicate the present tense.

Further it is she who is the *agent* of a striving, the one who *does* the striving. For her to do so resolutely — or rather for us to report or state that this is the case — is for her striving to be placed high on some scale of all actions of the same kind as human strivings graded with respect to their being less-resolute-than others.[9] The comparative relation of being *less-resolute-than* holds between acts or states of certain kinds, but here we restrict it just to strivings, or to strivings of a certain variety. To say that some striving is resolute is then to say that it is *high* on this scale, where the least resolute are placed low in it. Let

$$\text{'}e \text{ High Less-Resolute-Than, 'HS''}$$

express then that e is high in this scale. By definition, then,

$$\text{'Res.}_{HS}. \ e\text{'} \text{ is short for } \text{'}e \text{ High Less-Resolute-Than, 'HS''.}$$

Our sentence (1) now becomes

(1′)   '$(Ee)(Ea)(⟨\text{Strive}⟩e \cdot e$ During now $\cdot$ she Agent $e \cdot$ Res.$_{HS}$. $e \cdot e$ That $_{\text{Content}} a \cdot$ 'she perceives her situation objectively'$a)$',

where, however, we leave unanalyzed the material, within the pairs of inner single quotes.[10]

Note that there is considerable slack here in the use of 'Res', a considerable latitude among strivings said to be resolute. Some strivings might be more resolute than others, and yet we might call them all resolute. It would be desirable, perhaps, to have an exact measure of *degree of resoluteness* with respect to human strivings. Lacking this, we allow considerable slack in the looser idea of being resolute. Note that to be nonresolute, or irresolute, is not quite the same as not being resolute.[11] To be irresolute is to be low on the scale. Not to be resolute is to be somewhere in the middle. Note also that 'HS' ought to be taken not just for human strivings but for just human strivings of a certain kind, e.g., of the kind of which she is capable and that are of some pertinence perhaps to her psychoanalytic treatment.

Schafer seems essentially correct, then, in saying in his first rule, that an adverb is to be used where applicable to indicate a mode of action. Technically, however, we do not "designate" the mode by the adverb. It is rather that a certain event-descriptive predicate is applicable to the appropriate action event, or merely that the action event stands in such and such a position in an appropriate scale.

We are now in a position to reflect upon Schafer's rules, and their corollaries, more closely. As a corollary to the first rule, it is noted (p. 10), "we shall no longer refer to location, movement, direction, sheer quantity, and the like, for these terms are suitable only for things and thinglike entities." Well, not quite. Some of these notions might be relevant to mental actions.

'She desires it intensely'

suggests a considerable quantity or high degree of desire.

'Whenever she is in the country her thoughts take wings'

contains essential reference to a type of location. The key point here seems to be that "we shall not speak of internalization except in the sense of a person's imagining something. . . ." Uses of the abstract noun 'internalization' in general give way to use of the gerundive 'internaliz*ing*' or 'imagin*ing*', and the like. In fact a proper definition of the former probably requires fundamental reference to acts or states describable by means of the latter.

A second corollary (p. 11) is that "so far as possible, we shall not use the verb *to have* in relation to psychological activity, for, in using it, we should be implying that things and thinglike entities are the referents of psychological propositions. Thus it will no longer do to say that one *has* a feeling or an impulse or even a disposition; nor shall it be acceptable to speak of anyone's *having* symptoms, habits, or sublimations." To say that she is lethargic, is thus not to attribute a habit to her but rather to say that lethargic acts are habitual with her, or that she frequently or usually performs lethargic acts, or something of the sort. In any case, all uses of 'habit' within the psychoanalytic language may presumably be accommodated in terms of the adverb 'habitually' as applicable to actions or performances.

Another corollary is that "only the active voice and constructions that clarify activity and modes of activity shall be used. For whenever we use the passive voice or equivalent passive or indefinite constructions, we obscure the fact that we are speaking of actions performed by persons, . . ." Of course, the use of the clause 'she Agent *e*' in (1') assures that it is *she* who is the agent in question. Thus even if (1) were to be paraphrased in the passive voice, we would not be tempted to obscure her agency provided we remembered that (1') is the appropriate logical form. Similarly no harm could arise from

'That man appears to be odd'

if it is regarded as having the same form as

'That man appears to me to be odd',

all appearings being of something *to* someone.

The fourth corollary is that "we shall give up the idea that there are special classes of processes that prepare or propel mental activity, that is to say, classes that are qualitatively different from the mental activity they prepare or propel; for now everything is an action." To think consciously is thus an action, to intend to do such and such is one, and so on. To intend to make an omelette does no doubt, in some instances, "prepare or propel" one to make an omelette. Let '⟨Intd⟩*e*' express that *e* is an *intending*.

'I intend to make an omelette'

has a special intensional structure, due to the intentionality of 'intending'. Here use can be made of Frege's *Art des Gegebenseins* or mode of linguistic description.[12] 'I intend to make an omelette' becomes something like

'$(Ee)(Ea)(Eb)(I$ Agent $e \cdot \langle Intd \rangle \ e \cdot b$ Des I $\cdot e$ That$_{Content} a \cdot$
$\ulcorner (Ex)(Omelette \ x \cdot b$ Make $x)\urcorner a)$'.

The locution '$\ulcorner ---- \urcorner a$' here expresses that *a* is an inscription of such and such a shape. The content *a* of the intending *e* is in this way described by means of an inscription of such and such a shape.

To intend to make an omelette is just as good an act as making one, although of course it has a very different inner structure. On the other hand, and somewhat contrary to what Schafer says, there is a difference of kind — a "qualitative" one? — between intendings and makings of omelettes. We can easily get at the successive *parts* of the latter. The intending might be the first part, temporally speaking. Then there comes "getting eggs, getting a pan, starting a fire, and so on." These latter involve the physical manipulation of external objects, however, in ways that intendings never do. What are the successive "parts" of an intending, more particularly, of an intending to make an omelette? To intend to get eggs, to intend to get a pan, to intend to start a fire, and so on — perhaps. These intendings, however, might be instantaneous, and only when prompted would the respondent recognize the full content of what he intends. Further, these "parts," if such they be, are parts of the *content* of what is intended, not of the *intending* itself. We should not mistake parts of the content for parts of the intending. Perhaps acts or states of intending, like those of believing, knowing, desiring, and others, are to be taken as unique wholes, and not to be subdivided into parts other than in terms of their content in special instances. However, all of these contentions need a closer looking at than can be given them at present.

Schafer would have made his point here more forcefully if he had considered an example such as

'I intend to try to solve the equation'

or

'I intend to try to be more considerate of my colleagues'

or the like. Here the content of the intending is in turn intensional (or intentional) and thus of the same general kind as the original intending. For these examples, we would no longer say (as on Schafer's p. 13) that our conscious thinking, in this case intending, "requires preparation by a qualitatively different type of event such as preconscious or unconscious mental processes. For what could that preparation be but other thinking that is, in our new terms, other action, though action in another mode?" So far, so good. But is it the case that "if thinking consciously requires preparation, then thinking preconsciously or unconsciously requires preparation, too, and so *ad infinitum*"? Perhaps "unconscious thinking" is more statelike than actlike and is not the sort of thing that allows of preparation, in any ordinary sense anyhow. But no matter, Schafer's point is surely well taken, not to "resort to the notion of propulsive entities" such as "impulses or drives that must initiate, propel, sustain, and guide actions. . . . Whereas to wish is to perform an action of a certain sort, . . . *a wish*, in the sense of an autonomous dynamic agency, is now an inadmissible conception." There are no wishes other than as some actual wishing by someone or other in certain circumstances.

The second rule is that actions may be designated or denoted "in an indefinitely large number of ways, that is to say, there can be no one final and correct statement of the action in question." Many statements about an action could of course be correct without being "final." One and the same action *e* may be correctly described in many ways, and one and the same intentional action may even seem to involve action descriptions that are contradictory.

'He wishes to succeed but is not willing, and therefore does not wish, to flatter the powers that be'

is a good case in point, where it is known that flattery of the powers that be is necessary for the success wished for. Each mental action is thus a "manifold of possibilities." It may be described in this way or that, some ways of course being "more fitting, durable, and useful than others for purposes of psychoanalytic interpretation and personal transformation."

As we have noticed, some actions are *constituents* of, or successive parts of, as the example concerning making an omelette revealed. In general, here we seem to have a kind of law of *inverse variation* as between the inclusion of action types and the part-whole relation between action events. An instance is that if the action type of making an omelette is a subclass of the general action type of cooking with eggs, then any action event of making an omelette has a part (a temporal part) that is an action event of cooking eggs.[13]

The problem as to how action events, especially mental ones, are constituted is a good deal more complicated than Schafer indicates. There are surely *successive* parts of action events of some kinds, the totality of the parts constituting the full action. Here we have temporal succession as our guide. The very shortest action events would be those requiring the minimal stretch of time needed for an action event, or whatever types are under consideration in a given context, to occur. Once this shortest time stretch is determined, and some action events are said to take place during it, are there then *simultaneous* parts of it also to be recognized? This question is merely raised here, but no easy answer is forthcoming. Consider a perceiving of a flash of lightning at any split second. Can simultaneous parts of this perceiving be distinguished in any fruitful way? Probably not, and once we reach action events of *minimal perceptible duration*, we need not further subdivide unless compelled to do so for some given purpose.

With intentional phenomena such as wishing, whose content is given wholly propositionally, so to speak, rather than relative in part to some outer object or occurrence, the situation seems rather different. To use Schafer's example (p. 365), "one may describe one and the same action variously as a wishing, desiring, yearning, hoping, dreaming, daydreaming, or looking forward to eagerly or pleasurably." Such actions are perhaps best regarded as states, there being no significant change in them over the times during which they obtain. Here the successive parts are all alike, so to speak. Whatever we would wish to say of one of them — other than as concerns their temporality — we would no doubt wish to say of the others also.

Among mental actions and states, some may be said to be performed consciously, or preconsciously, or even unconsciously. These notions are to be handled adverbially and hence in terms of certain scales as based on the relations *less-conscious-than* and *less-preconscious-than*. And similarly for any classification depending upon whether the action is voluntary, involuntary, or neither.

To *refrain* from performing an action is itself to be recognized as an action. How is the logic of this notion to be handled? Let '⟨Rfrn⟩' be the event- or action-descriptive predicate for refrainings. Consider

(2)   'John refrained from smoking on that day'.

We cannot regard this as saying that there are acts of his smoking on that day from which John refrains, for this would be to state that there exist the very action events that he refrains to perform! There are two ways we can circumvent this situation. One way is to construe '⟨Rfrn⟩' as denoting acts of refraining-to-bring-it-about-that, and then use the That-relation of content. Thus our sentence would have the form

'$(Ee)(Ea)(j$ Agent $e \cdot$ ⟨Rfrn⟩ $e \cdot e$ Before$_{Time}$ now $\cdot e$ That$_{Content}$ a · 'John did not smoke on that day'a)'.

The other method of handling (2) is in terms of an adaptation of Leśniewski's null individual, *the one individual that does not exist.* Here we recognize also the *null event* or action, the one event or action event that does not take place. Let 'NE' designate this event, and let 'NE Under$_e$ a' express that NE is taken under the predicate description a relative to the intensional act e. (2) then has the form

(2′)   '$(Ee)(Ea)(j$ Agent $e \cdot$ ⟨Rfrn⟩ $e \cdot e$ Before$_{Time}$ now $\cdot e$ From$_{Object}$ NE $\cdot$ NE Under$_e$ $a \cdot$ '$\{e' \ni (⟨Smoke⟩e' \cdot j$ Agent $e' \cdot e'$ During (that day))$\}$'a)'.

Here '$\{e' \ni ----\}$' stands for the virtual class of all John's acts of smoking on that day. The refraining may of course be performed consciously, unconsciously, or preconsciously, and indeed in all manner of other ways also. (More will be said about the special relation Under in a moment.)[14]

Schafer shrewdly observes (p. 366) that "to designate refraining as an action is not to say that everything one does *not* do must likewise be designated an action; it would be absurd to say so. One must have grounds for speaking of the action of refraining." The notions of *doing* and of being an *act* are closely interwoven. Probably we have as a meaning postulate that

$$\vdash (e)(⟨Do⟩e \equiv \text{Act } e),$$

so that every doing is an act and conversely. It then also obtains that

$$\vdash (e)(\sim ⟨Do⟩e \equiv \sim \text{Act } e),$$

that every nondoing is a nonact and conversely. Thus strictly no nondoing should be designated an act. On the other hand, if one is doing such and such, then he is refraining from doing all manner of other things. If one is sitting, one is not standing, one is not walking, one is not swimming, and so on. Likewise, if one is swimming one is refraining from standing, walking, sitting, and so on, perhaps consciously so, perhaps unconsciously, but in any case of necessity in view of the meaning postulates that

$$\vdash (e)(\langle \text{Sit} \rangle e \supset \sim \langle \text{Stand} \rangle e),$$

$$\vdash (e)(\langle \text{Sit} \rangle e \supset \sim \langle \text{Walk} \rangle e),$$

and

$$\vdash (e)(\langle \text{Sit} \rangle e \supset \sim \langle \text{Swim} \rangle e),$$

The "grounds" for speaking of refraining here are that one is sitting.

Another species of action consists of the "conditional" ones, that is, "the things one continues [at a given time] to wish to do but refrains from doing. Should circumstances change . . . he or she would [might] then perform the action in question." The notion of a conditional action is relative to both a person and a time. An action type might be conditional for one analysand but not for another, and even conditional for one and the same analysand at one time but not at another. In general, then, we may let

$\ulcorner \langle F \rangle \text{ CndtlAct } p,e \urcorner$ abbreviate $\ulcorner(\text{E}e_1) \ (\text{E}e_2)(\text{E}a)(\text{E}b)(\langle \text{Wish} \rangle e_1$ $\cdot p \text{ Agent } e_1 \cdot \langle \text{Rfrn} \rangle e_2 \cdot p \text{ Agent } e_2 \cdot e_1 \text{ That }_{\text{Content}} a \cdot e_2 \text{ That}_{\text{Content}}$ $a \cdot b \text{ Des } p \cdot \ulcorner\{e' \ni (\langle F \rangle e' \cdot b \text{ Do } e')\}\urcorner a \cdot e_1 \text{ Continuous } p,e \cdot e_2$ $\text{Continuous } p,e)\urcorner$.

Here 'e_1 Continuous p,e' expresses that e_1 is a continuous state for p throughout the temporal duration of e.

The importance of conditional actions in psychoanalysis goes without saying. "Much wishing [p. 366], self-punishing, forgetting, and the like become understandable only upon one's defining [locating?] the conditional actions that are especially problematic to the person in question."

The contradictory character of some types of mental action has already been noted, and is seen best as expressed in terms of their content. "The complexity of actions [p. 367] often includes contradictory or paradoxical constituents, such as loving and hating, cooperating and defying, or fleeing and fighting." Loving and hating, for example, are intentional relations, and statements concerning them require an *Art des Gegebenseins*. One loves or hates something as described in such and such a way by means of such and such a predicate. Thus '*p* loves *x* as described by the predicate *a*'

is the kind of locution needed. And similarly for 'hates'. And of course one might both love and hate the same entity but under different, even contradictory, descriptions.

Let us reflect upon the Under relation a little more than above. We might dub it 'the Frege Under-relation', for it is more or less implicit in Frege's work although never actually symbolized there or characterized in any exact way. Let 'Int' for the moment stand for any intentional or mentalistic relation such as believing, knowing, hoping, loving, desiring, and so on — the very kinds of relations that play so central a role in the psychoanalytic vocabulary. And let '$\langle \text{Int} \rangle e$, express that *e* is an act or state of the kind Int. For such *e*,

$$\text{'}x \text{ Under}_e \ a\text{'},$$

the general form of which the form used above in (2') is a special case with 'NE' substituted for '*x*', expresses that *x* is taken under the predicate description *a* throughout or during *e*. We now wish to express that *p* bears the relation Int, relative to *e*, to *x* taken as *a*, or to *x quā a* — to use an old notion made much of by Aristotle. Thus we may define

'*p* Int$_e$ (*x quā a*)' as '(*p* Agent *e* · $\langle \text{Int} \rangle$ *e* · *e* Of$_{\text{Object}}$ *x* · *x* Under$_e$ *a*)'.

Particular instances of the definiendum would express that *p* loves (desires, knows, and so on) *x quā* such and such. In any extended treatment of this notion axioms or meaning postulates concerning this Under-relation must of course be given.

We see then that there is no contradiction between

$$\text{'}p \text{ Love(s)}_e \ x,a\text{'}$$

and

$$\text{'}p \text{ Hate(s)}_{e'} \ x,a\text{'},$$

where *e* and *e'* are distinct. But suppose they are the same. Can *p* both love and hate the same object simultaneously under precisely the same description? Under no circumstances would the analyst make an assertion to this effect without qualification. The qualification would ordinarily be to the effect that the predicates have a different *innuendo* at least, or a different aspect, or something of the sort. One may simultaneously love someone *quā* person who has been kind to him or her, but hate that person *quā* person who has committed such and such an unkind act to him or her. There would, in other words, be a difference, however slight, in the two cases in the modes of description *a*.

"It may be fitting in certain contexts," Schafer observes (p. 367), "to speak of several actions rather than of one complex action and to say of them that they are performed simultaneously and in a more or less coordinated or mutually contradictory fashion. At other times, it may be best to include all the referents under the designation of a complex action. . . ." There are several points to be made here. Consider again loving and hating the same thing simultaneously. This might be thought to be a complex action type, to be handled by a certain kind of logical product. The best way of handling the complexity in such a case is perhaps to consider the logical sum $(e \cup e')$ of the two respective action events of loving and hating the same thing under the same description. This complex event is both a loving and a hating. If *e* and *e'* are taken as temporally successive, so that $(e \cup e')$ is a so-called *successive* sum, we can let

$$`p \langle (L \cap H) \rangle_{(e \cup e')} x, a'$$

express this. If, however, *e* and *e'* are taken simultaneously, we must then have some clear way of separating the two, usually in terms of slight variation in the *a*'s involved. As noted above, there seems to be no clear way of doing this in any other way for intensional relations, which seem best regarded holistically — at least pending further study and clarification, especially as concerns the exact meaning of 'part of' as between simultaneous intensional action states or events.

Schafer notes (p. 367) that "in no case may any one constituent action or only one of the [relevant] group of simultaneous and contradictory actions be designated the 'real' action, where 'real' would be being used in the sense of the only genuine or significant meaning which is being referred to; for any action must be as real as any other (e.g., pretending is as real an action as behaving sincerely)." There is great richness in the modes of description available, and in the subtlety of differences amongst them, under which action events may be taken. As a result, the most delicate nuances in the description of the analysand's actions can be accommodated. All of them may be of relevance at some point in the analysis.

Underlying the theory of actions and action events is of course a theory of time flow of some elementary kind, in terms of which the temporal locutions needed are definable. We have already met with the notion of a continuous action type or event. Noncontinuous ones are such that (p. 368) "a person need not be performing it continuously in the sense of doing it every moment of the stretch of time in question." Also "there need be no fixed moment marking either the initiation or the termination of an action" — although of course there may be.

Schafer makes much of the contention that actions are to be discussed in terms of their "reasons, that is, the personal meanings of doing them, what they are about, their point, the goals they imply." Causal talk, on the other hand, is thought to be more appropriate in the physical sciences and "in the behavioristic approach to people." Not too much should be made of this distinction, however, as Michael Scriven has noted.[15] "We normally say," according to him, "that it is the *state of believing* (or *having*), or perception of . . . [such and such a] fact that constitutes a certain reason that is the cause of (other) behavior or states of belief, rather than the reason *simpliciter.*" Thus presumably an adequate definition of 'is a reason for' may be given in terms of a suitable intensional relation for causality. In any case, the two are so closely interrelated that neither should be considered in isolation from the other. Talk of reasons seems to be a special case, albeit a most significant one, of talk about causation.

Schafer's tenth rule is that "the idea of a person serves only as a pointer. The person specifies the originator [or agent] of the actions and modes of action in question and nothing more than that; . . ." In the foregoing formulae, the only role of the person parameter 'p' is as the agent of actions. All the actions under discussion in a particular instance are those of the agent or agents. But we could not dispense with the person parameters, or some equivalent, without loss. Both analyst and analysand may wish to report another person's actions by way of comparison, so that some mode of distinguishing whose actions are being referred to must be at hand. One could, of course, take a person as a class, or better, as a logical sum of events *genidentical* to some given event. But the notion of genidentity poses as many philosophical problems as personhood does, so we may as well retain the person parameters throughout.

Nothing in the foregoing has been said about tone of voice, emphasis, rising tone, falling tone, expressive gestures and "other non-verbal communicative actions," and so on. But, as we all know, such items are sometimes of the highest import in communication and often reveal more than what is being said. "A language does not depend for its existence on words or words alone [— perhaps we should say here rather 'for its communicativeness' —] although to a considerable extent our world [of psychoanalytic talk] is a world of words." What role do these extralinguistic items play in logical form? As much as is deemed relevant or indicative of anything significant in a given context. In any event, technical means should be at hand for handling them.[16]

Schafer's last "rule" would seem to be his least satisfactory. "As a set of rules for saying things, a language is not subject to tests of truth or falsity." Not the language as a whole, certainly not. But how about some of its individual sentences? Surely Schafer does not intend by this rule to exclude the applicability of the semantical truth concept from all discussion of language. No; what he is calling attention to rather would seem to be that truth should not be dogmatically ascribed to the psychoanalyst's reports nor to those of the analysand *sans phrase*. All of the analyst's reports are presumably intentional statements involving an 'I think', an 'I surmise', an 'I believe', an 'It seems to me on the basis of the evidence', and so on. The analysand's reports are taken by the analyst not at face value but as indications of inner states of mind, feeling, and so on. To say that these latter are true or false would be to say too much. Likewise the contents of the analyst's reports are not to be taken at face value. Again, this would be to ascribe too much, more than the evidence and situation would ordinarily warrant. As Schafer comments (p. 369), "psychoanalytic interpretation of subjective experience can . . . only be the [analyst's] interpretations of the analysand's interpretations; for it never deals directly with experience unmediated by some personal construction of it."

In place of truth and falsity Schafer suggests that "it is always a question of whether one is following the rules consistently so as always to be constructing facts of the same kind and interrelating them in an orderly and enlightening fashion." Having stated a surmise with such and such a content, the analyst goes on to test it, to see if it coheres with other contents already surmised or accepted, to explore its logical consequences, and so on. All this is done in a rough and ready way, but the more strictly one adheres to the "rules of the language," the better.

What are the rules of the psychoanalytic language, when looked at from the logical point of view? They comprise the usual kind of formation rules, stipulating the primitive vocabulary and the kinds of sentences taken as meaningful, and of course appropriate rules of logic. As nonlogical axioms we need many meaning postulates characterizing the primitive predicates chosen. We should not glide over the difficulties in choosing primitives or in framing meaning postulates. Most of the work concerning these lies ahead. For the present, we must be content, as here, with only a partially formalized language[17] built around such terms for mental actions as we know to be indispensable.

As Whitehead put it well: We cannot know too much about notions and principles we are always using. We are always using implicitly in our psychoanalytic talk, if not precisely the logical material discussed above, then at least something similar, so that any step forward in trying to get at the exact logic underlying it should surely be welcome.

Schafer's work has not been used here as a paragon or final statement of what "the native tongue of psychoanalysis" is, but rather as a guide to the inner vocabulary of the practitioner and as calling attention to important items that have to some extent been overlooked in the literature. At best the exact characterization of the "native tongue" is still in its infancy, an important new field in the application of modern logic crying for competent workers.

CHAPTER XI

A Prolegomenon to
Husserl's *Prolegomena*

"Je prend mon bien où je le trouve."

At the very beginning (p. 53) of the Introduction to his *Logische Untersuchungen*[1], Husserl calls our attention to J. S. Mill's comment that "there is ... as much difference of opinion in regard to the definition of logic as there is in the treatment of the science itself." Many decades have passed by since the days of Mill, and indeed since those of Husserl also, and yet "even today [in 1900 as well as in 1983] these sentences could serve as a suitable expression of the state of logical science, even today we are very far from complete agreement as to the definition of logic and the content of its essential doctrines." The logic known to Husserl in 1900, of course, "wears quite a different face from the logic of the mid-[nineteenth]-century," as indeed does that of 1982 from that at the time Husserl wrote. And even the logic of which Husserl took account does not represent sufficiently the most advanced work of the time — DeMorgan, Boole, Frege, Schröder, and Peirce had after all already made notable contributions. Husserl's song, however, is a different one, concerning what (p. 60) he thought to be "the field for a new, and, as we shall see, complex discipline, whose peculiarity it is to be the science of science, and which could therefore be most pointedly called *Wissenschaftslehre* or theory of science" — "a normative and practical discipline relating to the Idea of science."

Let us attempt, in this present paper, to get the measure of some of the basic notions of this new discipline in modern terms, i.e., in terms of what we now know about syntax, semantics, pragmatics, event logic, and the epistemic study of mental acts. All the significant works of the past are to be read in terms contemporary to that of the reader — although of course this is not the only way of reading them — and it is often remarkable how well they hold their own. The *Prolegomena* to the *Logische Untersuchungen* is a case in point, and Husserl himself would surely wish us to do no less than to subject it to a searching, sympathetic examination in the light of what we now know.

The aim here is thus not to follow Husserl literally, but rather to show how some of his key notions anticipate, some of them to a remarkable degree, notions and techniques that have been coming into their own, so to speak, only quite recently. If we are to understand Husserl now in modern terms, it would seem that we can no longer disregard these technical developments. And to be sure that we do not misrepresent Husserl himself, ample use will be made of direct quotation in what follows.

We are told straightaway (p. 60) that "science is concerned ... with knowing [Wissen]," but "this does not mean that it itself consists [merely] of a tissue [eine Summe oder ein Gewebe] of acts of knowing [Wissensakten]." Husserl calls attention immediately to the study of such *acts*, which study is to play a central role in the "science of science." "Science aims at knowledge," we are told, and the gaining of knowledge takes place by means of certain kinds of human acts. We will do well to take cognizance of this fact immediately by letting

(1) $\qquad\qquad$ '$\langle$ Know $\rangle e$',

where '$\langle$ Know $\rangle$' is an event-descriptive predicate, express that e is an act of knowing. The use of a form such as (1) would seem indispensable for present purposes.[2]

"In knowledge, however, we preserve truth, ... truth as the object of a correct judgment." The notion of truth has received a far-reaching analysis in modern formalized semantics. We should therefore no doubt add the semantical truth predicate 'Tr' to the list of the basic notions needed. Let

(2) $\qquad\qquad$ '$Tr_S\ a$'

express that the sentence a is true in the system S. If one objects to the use of 'sentence' here in place of 'proposition', one can easily introduce

'Tr_S -----' as an abbreviation for $\ulcorner Tr_S\ a \urcorner$, where a is the shape description of the sentence '----' of S.[3]

This is in effect a definition by means of *disquotation*, providing for "propositions" as arguments of 'Tr' in certain contexts.

Notions for truth and knowledge are "not enough," however (pp. 60–61), "since not every correct judgment, every affirmation or rejection of a state of affairs that accords with truth, represents *knowledge* of the being or non-being of this state of affairs. Rather we may say that, if it is to be called 'knowledge' in the narrowest, strictest sense, it requires to be *evident* [italics added], to have the luminous certainty that what we have acknowledged *is*, that what we have rejected *is not*. . . ." Knowledge must thus be distinguished from "baseless opinion" by means of "inward evidence" as "an immediate intimation of truth itself." When this is lacking the inward evidence is rather "for a higher or lower degree of probability for our state of affairs, with which, if probability levels become high enough, a firm judgment is usually associated." We are not, however, to think of probability here in the sense of some *a priori* assignment of confirmation values to a sentence *solo* or in isolation, but only comparatively. "The inward evidence of the probability of a state of affairs ... will serve to ground those comparative, inwardly evident value-assessments, through which, in accordance with positive or negative probability-values, we can distinguish the reasonable from the unreasonable, the better-founded from the worse-founded assumptions, opinions, and surmises. Ultimately, therefore, all genuine, and, in particular, scientific knowledge, rests on inner evidence. ..." of one of the two kinds.

The use here of several notions of pragmatics is to be noted straightaway. There is *judgment, affirmation, rejection,* and *being evident to.* Let us take 'judgment' here in essentially the sense of Frege, i.e., as the recognition of the truth of a thought[4] — or, as we may say equally well, as the *acceptance* of the sentence expressing that thought. Husserl does not explicitly refer to the *person* whose judgments, affirmations, and so on, are under consideration. His pragmatical concerns, unlike those of Frege, are completely general in the sense of not being relativized to the person. Thus we may let

(3) $'\langle \text{Acpt} \rangle e'$

express that *e* is an act of accepting, leaving open who it is that does the accepting and even what it is that is accepted. Similarly, let

(4) $'\langle \text{Affrm} \rangle e'$,

(5) $'\langle \text{Rjct} \rangle e'$,

and

(6) $'\langle \text{Evid} \rangle e'$

express that *e* is an act of affirming, of rejecting, and of evidencing, respectively. If *e* is an evidencing of a sentence *a,* then *a* is taken as wholly evident in the act *e.* Thus we could define

$$'e \text{ Evid}_e a' \text{ as } '(\langle \text{Evid} \rangle e \cdot e \text{ Of}_{\text{Object}} a)',$$

where $\text{Of}_{\text{Object}}$ is the prepositional of-relation of being-the-object-of.[5] And similarly for the others.

How now are we to handle the probability values? It seems clear that Husserl is not concerned here with probability in the sense of the limit of relative frequencies in the long run (von Mises, Reichenbach) or in the sense of a measure of subjective degree or strength of belief (de Finetti, Savage), but rather in the sense of *degree of evidential support* or *confirmation* (Carnap). Let

(7)   '*a* Cnfrm *b*'

express, in some theory, that the sentence *a* confirms the sentence *b* to a sufficiently high degree depending on *a* and *b*. It is very likely the case that no adequate theory of confirmation has yet been formulated, so that the invocation of such here by use of the form (7) is more of a hope than a reality — a mere promissory note. (In place of (7) a more refined form containing a real-number variable could be introduced, but this is not needed for present purposes.)

Among noetic acts, *noeses,* knowledge acts are of especial import for the science of science. But there are many others, acts of assuming, of opining, of surmising, of believing, of guessing, and so on and on. All such acts are of course intentional in a suitable sense. We may let

'$\langle R \rangle e$'

express that *e* is an act of the kind R, where '$\langle R \rangle$' is the event- or act-descriptive predicate for one of these kinds. In this way expressions for all modes of intentional acts may be suitably introduced.

A few ancillary predicates that will be needed in what follows are: 'Utt' for utterance, 'LogThm' for the logical theorems (as based on the first-order theory of quantification), 'Before$_{Time}$' for the relation of occurring (wholly) before in time, 'During' for the relation of occurring during in time, and 'Sent' for the sentences of the language.[6]

Some properties of and interrelations between or among the kinds of intentional acts distinguished may be stipulated by the following tentative principles.

Pr1. $\vdash (e)(a)(((\langle \text{Evid} \rangle e \cdot e \text{ Of}_{\text{Object}} a) \supset \text{Sent } a),$

Pr2. $\vdash (e)((\langle \text{Evid} \rangle e \supset \langle \text{Know} \rangle e),$

Pr3. $\vdash (e)(a)(((\langle \text{Know} \rangle e \cdot e \text{ Of}_{\text{Object}} a) \supset \text{Tr}_S a),$

Pr4. $\vdash (e)((\langle \text{Know} \rangle e \supset \langle \text{Acpt} \rangle e),$

Pr5. $\vdash (e)(a)(((\langle \text{Affrm} \rangle e \cdot e \text{ Of}_{\text{Object}} a) \equiv ((\langle \text{Utt} \rangle e \cdot \langle \text{Acpt} \rangle e \cdot e \text{ Of}_{\text{Object}} a)),$

Pr6. $\vdash (e)(a)(((\langle \text{Rjct} \rangle e \cdot e \text{ Of}_{\text{Object}} a) \supset (\text{Sent } a \cdot \sim ((\langle \text{Acpt} \rangle e \cdot e \text{ Of}_{\text{Object}} \ulcorner \sim a \urcorner))),$

Pr7. $\vdash (e)(((\langle \text{Acpt} \rangle e \lor \langle \text{Affrm} \rangle e \lor \langle \text{Rjct} \rangle e \lor \langle \text{Evid} \rangle e \lor$

$\langle$Know$\rangle e) \supset (\mathrm{E}a)e \, \mathrm{Of}_{\mathrm{Object}} \, a)$,

Pr8. $\vdash(a)(b)(a \, \mathrm{Cnfrm} \, b \supset (\mathrm{Sent} \, a \cdot \mathrm{Sent} \, b))$,

Pr9. $\vdash(e)(b)(c)(((\langle$Know$\rangle e \cdot e \, \mathrm{Of}_{\mathrm{Object}} \, \ulcorner b \, \mathrm{Cnfrm} \, c \urcorner) \supset (\langle$Evid$\rangle e \cdot e \, \mathrm{Of}_{\mathrm{Object}} \, \ulcorner b \, \mathrm{Cnfrm} \, c \urcorner))$,

Pr10. $\vdash(e)(a)(((\langle$Know$\rangle e \cdot e \, \mathrm{Of}_{\mathrm{Object}} \, a \cdot \mathrm{LogThm} \, a) \supset (\langle$Evid$\rangle e \cdot e \, \mathrm{Of}_{\mathrm{Object}} \, a))$.

These principles together with others to be given, are more or less self-explanatory and would seem to hold on the basis of the interpretation given to the event-descriptive predicates occurring. They are not intended to provide an exhaustive list but merely a few samples of the kinds of laws that should obtain. All of them are to be thought of, not as empirical generalizations of observed regularities, or anything of the sort, but as *meaning postulates* in essentially the sense of Carnap.[7] Note that *Pr9* is at the metametalinguistic level.

Also we have the following principles concerning negations, disjunctions, and conjunctions.

Pr11. $\vdash(e)(a)(((\langle$Know$\rangle e \cdot e \, \mathrm{Of}_{\mathrm{Object}} \, a) \supset \sim e \, \mathrm{Of}_{\mathrm{Object}} \, \ulcorner \sim a \urcorner)$,

Pr12. $\vdash(e)(a)(b)(((\langle$Know$\rangle e \cdot (e \, \mathrm{Of}_{\mathrm{Object}} \, a) \, \mathrm{v} \, e \, \mathrm{Of}_{\mathrm{Object}} \, b)) \supset e \, \mathrm{Of}_{\mathrm{Object}} \, \ulcorner(a \, \mathrm{v} \, b)\urcorner)$,

Pr13. $\vdash(e)(a)(b)(\langle$Know$\rangle e \supset ((e \, \mathrm{Of}_{\mathrm{Object}} \, a \cdot e \, \mathrm{Of}_{\mathrm{Object}} \, b) \equiv e \, \mathrm{Of}_{\mathrm{Object}} \, \ulcorner(a \cdot b)\urcorner))$.

It is interesting to note that the would-be converses of *Pr11* and *Pr12* do not hold. A disjunction (e.g., $\ulcorner(a \, \mathrm{v} \sim a)\urcorner$ may be known without either of its disjuncts being known, and it may be the case that neither a sentence nor its negation are known. It is very important here of course to distinguish not knowing that a holds from knowing that $\ulcorner \sim a \urcorner$ does.

In view of the probability values (pp. 61–62), "there is . . . a remaining duality in the concept of knowledge. Knowledge in the narrrowest sense of the word is being inwardly evident that a certain state of affairs is or is not . . . If it is evident that it is probable to this or that degree, then we have knowledge in the strictest sense of such a probability, but in regard to the being of the state of affairs, and not of its probability, we have only knowledge in a wider, modified sense. It is in this latter sense, with an eye to degrees of probability, that one speaks of a greater or lesser degree of knowledge. Knowledge in the pregnant [full] sense — its being quite evident that S is P — then counts as the absolutely fixed, ideal limit which the graded probabilities for the being-P of S approach asymptotically."

This passage is not without its difficulties, but we may explicate it to some extent by distinguishing three kinds of acts of knowing, again at the metametalinguistic level. We can let

'$\langle \text{Know} \rangle_1 e$' abbreviate '$(Ea)(\langle \text{Evid} \rangle e \cdot e \text{ Of}_{\text{Object}} \ulcorner \text{Tr}_S a \urcorner)$',

'$\langle \text{Know} \rangle_2 e$' abbreviate '$(Eb)(Ec)(\langle \text{Evid} \rangle e \cdot e \text{ Of}_{\text{Object}} \ulcorner b \text{ Cnfrm } c \urcorner)$',

and

'$\langle \text{Know} \rangle_3 e$' abbreviate '$(Eb)(Ec)(Ee')(\langle \text{Evid} \rangle e \cdot e \text{ Of}_{\text{Object}} \ulcorner b \text{ Cnfrm } c \urcorner \cdot \langle \text{Acpt} \rangle e' \cdot e' \text{ Of}_{\text{Object}} b \cdot (e' \text{ Before}_{\text{Time}} e \text{ v } e' \text{ During } e))$'.

Knowings$_1$ are thus acts in which truths of the language are fully evidenced as such, and knowings$_2$ are those in which suitable statements of probability are fully evidenced. A knowing$_3$, however, is an evidencing e of a sentence a to the effect that some sentence c is confirmed by some sentence b accepted before or during e. Acts of knowing$_1$ constitute knowledge "in the narrowest sense of the word" whereas knowings$_2$ constitute "knowledge in the strictest sense of a probability." It is in knowings$_3$ that "we have knowledge only in a wider, modified sense" and in which "one speaks of a greater or less degree of knowledge." That knowledge in the sense of knowings$_1$ is the "ideal limit which the graded probabilities" of knowings$_3$ "approach asymptotically," however, is a special thesis that needs careful examination. Husserl uses it here without further comment. The theories governing 'Tr' and 'Cnfrm' have a very complex inner structure, and truths need not always come out as those having the highest confirmation values on the given evidence.

Husserl notes that more is required of a science than mere knowledge, however (p. 62), namely, "*systematic coherence in the theoretical sense,* which means finding grounds for one's knowledge, and suitably combining and arranging the sequence of such groundings." One aspect of systematic coherence is no doubt the kind of unity a theory or logical system or formalized language system has. Husserl himself does not emphasize this point with sufficient clarity, perhaps, but it is eminently Husserlian to do so. There must be a specified vocabulary, with suitable definitions of 'term', 'sentence', 'axiom', 'proof', 'theorem', and so on. Hence the presence of 'S' in the form (2) above to indicate a specific system. But there is also systematic coherence in the "system of grounded validation" itself, i.e., in the system built *inter alia* around the notions (1)–(7), and so on, above. The "science of sciences" or *Wissenschaftslehre* is in turn a science, a theory, and hence must also have the unity or systematicity of any such. The system of grounded validation is a metasystem — even a metametasystem — incorporating fundamental semantical and pragmatical or epistemic features, as well as a basic underlying logic.

In addition to (1)–(7), a notion of acts of *ideating* or forming the Idea of is needed. Let

(8) $\qquad\qquad\qquad$ '$\langle$Idea$\rangle e$'

express that e as an ideating, in a sense to be understood fully only as we go on. And still another notion is that of being a *law,* so that

(9) $\qquad\qquad\qquad$ 'Law a'

is to express that the sentence a is a law, secientific or otherwise. "The realm of truth is ... no disordered chaos but is dominated and unified by law." Further "the system peculiar to science," with the laws and acts entering into it, "is not its own invention, but is present in things, where we simply find or discover it." Husserl's ontology of what is "present in things" thus presumably consists not only of the objects with which the sciences themselves deal, but also of the appropriate noetic acts of grounded validation (*Begründungen*) and — to accommodate the existence of language — of the whole vocabulary needed for stating laws.

What specifically, is a *Begründung*? Well, presumably any act of the kinds describable by (1), (3)–(6), and (8), together with such further ones as are to be distinguished or introduced definitionally. Certain significant features of such acts, or of the linguistic expressions designating them, are as follows (pp. 64–65). "They have ... the character of a fixed structure in relation to their content." The forms (1), (3), and so on, are such as to contain *variables,* the values for which vary from context to context. The "fixed structure" is given by the event-descriptive predicates, the "content" then being given by additional clauses as needed in a given context. For example, if

(10) $\qquad\qquad$ ($\langle$Know$\rangle e \cdot e$ Of$_{\text{Object}}$ a),

the content of the knowing is given by the sentence a, but the structure of a noetic act e relative to a is always that given in (10).

Secondly, the interrelations among *Begründungsakten* "are not governed by caprice or chance, but by reason and order, i.e. by regulative laws." Hence there must be explicit metalaws concerning (1), (3), and so on, most of them in the form of meaning postulates, as already observed above.

Husserl seems to have in mind, however, not the points just made, so much as the temporally ordered *sequence of acts* required for, say, the evidence for the Pythagorean theorem "to burst forth genuinely" and for the "validation [of it] to be a genuine validation." A *proof,* say, of the theorem, i.e., a proof in actual praxis, will consist of an ordered sequence of acts, each consisting of the *Begründung* of an axiom or of other accepted sentences in preceding acts in the sequence. Similarly in carrying out an argument of the "syllogistic" form

(11)   'Every *A* is *B*, *X* is *A,* so *X* is *B*',

we note successively that where 'Every *A* is *B*' is properly grounded, as well as '*X* is *A*', then '*X* is *B*' is so also. There is a succession here of three acts in accord with the logical law (11).

Strictly we should distinguish the notion of a *proof* in the syntactic sense from the corresponding praxiological notion. In the strict syntactical sense, a proof is an ordered sequence of formulae, each of which is either an axiom (of the system in question) or follows from preceding items in the sequence by use of one or more of the rules of inference. Praxiologically regarded, a proof is — ideally — an ordered sequence of *Begründungsakten*, each item of which corresponds with an item in a syntactical proof. Thus if 'C' is the *n*-th item in the syntactical proof, some formula such as

$$\text{'}(\langle \text{Evid}\rangle e_n \cdot e_n \text{ Of}_{\text{Object}} \text{ 'C'})\text{'}$$

might be the corresponding item in the praxiological proof. There are many kinds of praxiological proofs, depending upon the character of each of the *n* steps. Thus '⟨Know⟩' might replace '⟨Evid⟩' in some of them. And similarly for other of the epistemic act-descriptive predicates. The stupendous variety of acceptable praxiological "proofs" ought to be classified and reflected upon one by one.

Let us consider some "proof" — merely one out of many — of the Pythagorean theorem in a little more detail, merely for purposes of clarification. Let 'Pyth' be short for a suitable formulation of it within an appropriately axiomatized Euclidean geometry, and let

$$\text{'}A_1\ldots,A_n \vdash \text{Pyth'}$$

express that 'Pyth' is provable from 'A_1', ..., 'A_n', these latter being either axioms or previously proved theorems. Each 'A_i' will be established in some appropriate epistemic act. Let us presume these to be acts of acceptance. There is also the general logical law that

$$\vdash \text{'}((A_1 \cdot \ldots \cdot A_n) \supset \text{Pyth})\text{'},$$

that is brought in in an act of evidencing. And finally there is an act of accepting 'Pyth' itself. We may distinguish, then, acts $e_1, \ldots, e_{n+2}$, taken in some temporal order, such that

$$(\langle \text{Acpt} \rangle e_1 \cdot e_1 \text{ Of}_{\text{Object}} \text{ 'A}_1\text{'} \cdot \langle \text{Acpt} \rangle e_2 \cdot e_2 \text{ Of}_{\text{Object}} \text{ 'A}_2\text{'} \cdot \ldots \cdot \langle \text{Acpt} \rangle e_n$$
$$\cdot e_n \text{ Of}_{\text{Object}} \text{ 'A}_n\text{'} \cdot \langle \text{Evid} \rangle e_{n+1} \cdot e_{n+1} \text{ Of}_{\text{Object}} \text{ '}((A_1 \cdot \ldots \cdot A_n) \supset \text{Pyth})\text{'} \cdot$$
$$\langle \text{Acpt} \rangle e_{n+2} \cdot e_{n+2} \text{ Of}_{\text{Object}} \text{ 'Pyth'}).$$

The $e_1 \ldots, e_{n+2}$ here then constitute a type of praxiological "proof" of 'Pyth'. Many further ones can be distinguished by noting that other types of epistemic acts may occur rather than acceptances, including of course ones based on confirmation. And in turn an act establishing any one of the 'A_i's may itself have a complex structure. Also the temporality of the e_i's may vary in all manner of ways. In some cases, the e_{n+2} might even come before any of the others. The person proving 'Pyth' might well accept it *ab initio* but still go on to convince himself, or others, as to just why. By noting different temporal patterns among the e_i's, we see that some proofs will be merely proofs of justification, so to speak, others, proofs of discovery, and still others, of still further kinds.

Husserl makes an important point concerning the content-neutrality of the *Begründungsakten*. Several "arguments" can have the *same form*. "There is an *a priori* law," he notes (p. 64), "making any putative validation that follows this form also actually a correct one, provided, that is, that it proceeds from correct premises." "This holds in general," he goes on. "Whenever we ascend by an establishing argument from given pieces of knowledge to new ones, a certain form resides in our modes of validation, which is common to countless other validating arguments, and which stands in a certain relation to a general law that allows us to justify these single validations all at once." The "certain relation" here is the kind of correspondence pointed out between the syntactical and praxiological senses of 'proof', or between a general logical law such as (11) and a succession of validating acts in accord with it.

A third characteristic of validating acts, closely akin to the second, is that the forms of validation are the same for all "territories of knowledge." All the sciences are alike in this regard, that the general logical laws obtain and that sequences of *Begründungsakten* take place in accord with them. Logic itself as well as the theory of epistemic acts is thus *subject-matter neutral* — in a happy phrase frequently used by Gilbert Ryle. "There is no science where laws are not applicable to individual cases. . . ."

These properties of our *Begründungsakten*, Husserl notes (p. 66), "whose remarkable character escapes us since we are all too little disposed to turn everyday matters into problems, are . . . related to the *possibility of a science* and, further, of a *theory of science*." Our *Begründungsakten* are subject to rule, to exact law, and rational thought in all its ramifications "falls under laws and forms." Husserl here comes out squarely against those who do not wish to see in logic and its applications the guiding principles for the rational conduct of the mind. Further, a theory of the science of science has significant ramifications beyond science itself in any narrow sense. Although the theory of the *Begründungsakten* does "not exhaust the notion of methodical procedure" in general, such acts do seem to play a "central significance" in all rational thought. "One can in fact say [p. 68] that all scientific methods which do not themselves have the character of actual validating arguments . . . are, on the one hand, *abbreviations* and *substitutes* for such validating arguments, used to economize thought. . . ." Or "they may, on the other hand, represent more or less complex *auxiliary devices*. . . ." The full study of such abbreviations, substitutes, and auxiliary devices seems never to have been undertaken with even a modicum of sensitivity to the varying scientific and other contexts in which they occur.

Another of Husserl's remarkable observations (pp. 68–69) concerns the ambiguities inherent in natural languages. It is, he notes, "an important prerequisite for securing one's validations that one's thoughts are adequately expressed by readily distinguishable, unambiguous signs. [Ordinary] language . . . represents a most imperfect aid toward strict research. The pernicious influence of ambiguities on the validity of syllogistic [and other forms of] inferences are familiar. The careful thinker will not therefore use language without artificial precautions; to the extent that the terms he uses are not unambiguous and lack sharp meaning, he must define them. . . . The same is true of *nomenclature*. Brief, charactistic symbols for the more important, recurrent concepts [such as those of (1) *et seq.* above] are . . . indispensable wherever the expression of such concepts . . . would be unduly circumstantial" and hence cumbrous and involved. The advantages of the use of characteristic symbols for extra-logical or -mathematical notions are akin to the use of special symbols for root notions in logic or mathematics themselves. Such use does not shackle thought; on the contrary it gives it wings. These remarkable observations of Husserl show that, in spirit if not in achievement, he is already on the side of those moderns who see in logical symbolism the necessary propaedeutic for getting ahead with the methodological and philosophical tasks at hand.

This is not the occasion to discuss Husserl's arguments against psychologism. We shall note, however, that the science of science as sketched above makes significant distinctions that cut psychologism in any pernicious sense at its very roots. There are "certain ready confusions" (p. 102) that have "opened the way to psychologist errors." In particular, attention is drawn to three of them. "Logical laws have been confused with the judgments, in the sense of acts of judgment, in which we may know them: the laws, as '*contents of judgment*' have been confused with the *judgments themselves*. The latter are real events, having causes and effects." The distinction between these is explicitly brought out in the notation here. A *judging* is an e such that $\langle \text{Judg} \rangle e$, the content of which in a given context is an a where $e \, \text{Of}_{\text{Object}} \, a$ (or, alternatively, $e \, \text{That}_{\text{Content}} \, a$) .[8] The second confusion is that "of a law as a *term in causation with a law as a rule of causation*." "If the law is confused with the judgment or knowledge of the law, the ideal with the real, the law appears as a *governing power* in our train of thought. . . ." Reasons are thus to be distinguished suitably from causes. The third confusion is that "if the laws of logic have their epistemological source in psychological matter of fact, if . . . they are normative transformations of such facts, they must themselves be psychological in content. . . . This is palpably false. No logical law implies a 'matter of fact', not even the existence of presentations or judgments or other phenomena of knowledge. No logical law, properly understood, is a law for the facticities of mental life. . . ." Husserl's contention here is closely akin to that of Russell, Carnap, and others, to the effect that pure logical laws contain no factual "content."

Some readers will object to the use in the foregoing of the variable 'a' as taking linguistic shapes as values. They will think the Husserlian "ideal meaning-units," propositions or judgments in the logical sense, cannot be adequately handled in such terms. Thus '$e \, \text{Of}_{\text{Object}} \, a$' or '$e \, \text{That}_{\text{Content}} \, a$' might be thought to be too linguistically oriented — too dependent on the language for whose expressions 'a' is a metalinguistic variable — to capture *meaning*. Such an objection would seem ill-founded, however. A meaning in any technical sense must be captured by means of a sentence; it must somehow be expressed in some articulate way. There seems to be little if any use for condoning unexpressible meanings. Of course there might well be meanings that are never in fact expressed, but the range of the variable 'a' is all the possible sentences of the language, not just those that are overtly exhibited in some concrete sense. Further, the relevant intentional acts e are such that they always hold of paraphrastic sentences. Let '$a \, \text{Prphrs} \, b$' express that the sentences a and b are paraphrases of each other in the language S. Then, where R is a suitable intentional relation, it obtains that

Pr14. $\vdash (e)(a)(b)((\langle \text{R} \rangle e \cdot a \, \text{Prphrs} \, b) \supset (e \, \text{Of}_{\text{Object}} \, a \equiv e \, \text{Of}_{\text{Object}} \, b))$

and

Pr15. $\vdash (e)(a)(b)((\langle \text{R} \rangle e \cdot a \, \text{Prphrs} \, b) \supset (e \, \text{That}_{\text{Content}} \, a \equiv$

e That$_{Content}$ b)).

Similar laws obtain for relations of synonymy, sameness of sense, and so on. By means of these laws all the subtlety that is usually thought packed into the notion of a proposition in the semantical sense seems to be captured.

It might be objected also to the foregoing that logic, in the narrow sense of modern quantification theory, is taken here as in some sense *prior* to the theory of noetic acts. Husserl comments that he hopes to have "made plain that a correct grasp of the essence of pure logic, and its unique position in relation to all other sciences, is one of the most important questions in the whole of epistemology. If this is plain, it is likewise of vital interest to this fundamental philosophical science, that pure logic should be fully expounded in purity and independence." Such an exposition should presumably be of the usual kind that has now become commonplace: an exact specification of formation and transformation rules (in the terminology of Carnap). It is much clearer now than at the time Husserl wrote, that the notions of modern logic permeate our everyday language in very deep and subtle ways, and hence that any attempt to be clear about the language needed in which the theory of noetic acts can be discussed must presuppose these notions fundamentally. In any case, such a presupposition, being made explicit in the material of this paper, is in no way contrary of Husserl's intent.

The notion of *law* is so significant for Husserl that it is surprising that he did not see that much of his effort in grounding the new science of sciences should be to try to enunciate its fundamental laws. Nothing can take the place of this, and nothing should. The laws of a given discipline are determinative of it in the sense that they are necessary for that discipline to be what it is. "Scientific knowledge [p. 227] is, as such, *grounded knowledge*. To know the ground of anything means to see the necessity of its being so and so. Necessity as an objective predicate of a truth (which is then called a *necessary truth* [italics added]) is tantamount to the law-governed validity of the state of affairs in question. To see *a state of affairs as a matter of law* is to see its *truth as necessarily obtaining,* and to have knowledge of the *ground of the state of affairs* or of its truth: all these are equivalent expressions." The doctrine of necessity as grounded in law or generality is a viable one, devoid of the lurid vagueness attached to those who wish to ground it in some other way, on "possible worlds" or something equally obscure. Whitehead, Gurwitsch, and the present author *inter alia,* have espoused essentially this view, of necessity as grounded in law, in one form or another.

In order to handle adequately the basic laws determinative of necessity we must resort to the *"unity of a systematically complete theory."* "The systematic unity [p. 228] of the ideally closed sum of [basic] laws" rests "on one basic legality [Gesetzlichkeit] as their final ground." In a systematic theory of the kind envisaged, processes of *deductive inference* will lead from basic laws to other kinds of laws and to laws concerning specific "individual singulars." Deductive logic thus for Husserl is of paramount importance. The subject is not quite so simple as he seems to have thought, however, and in its modern form must go far beyond the "syllogisms" to which he repeatedly refers. In short, he seems not to have had a sufficient concern for some of the difficult, purely technical problems to be faced here, both internal problems, on the one hand, and those concerned with the corresponding noeses, on the other.

Toward the end of the *Prolegomena*, §65, Husserl comments on some further "sorts of acts in which theoretical knowledge is made real. We must, in particular, as thinking beings, be in general able to see propositions as truths, and to see truths as consequences of other truths, and again to see laws as such, to see laws as explanatory grounds, and to see them as ultimate principles etc." By 'see' here is presumably meant something closely akin to Frege's *Fassen* or apprehension.[9] Let

(12)   '⟨Apprh⟩e'

express that e is an act of apprehending, and more particularly,

'(⟨Apprh⟩e · e That$_{Content}$ a)'

that e is an apprehending of the content of the sentence a, i.e., of the "proposition" that a expresses. An act of "seeing" a as a truth is then an e such that

(⟨Apprh⟩e · e That$_{Content}$ $\ulcorner$Tr$_S$ $a\urcorner$).

This kind of seeing is of course quite different from seeing a *simpliciter*, being metametalinguistic, so to speak, and including as it does the notions required for the definition of 'Tr'. Seeing a simpliciter takes place in an act e such that

(⟨Apprh⟩e · e That$_{Content}$ a · Tr$_S$ a),

where the person who does this apprehending may or may not be aware of the truth of a.

An act of seeing a truth as a consequence of another truth is also a metametalinguistic notion, the notion of logical consequence itself being metalinguistic. Let 'a LogConseq b' express in the metalanguage that a is a logical consequence of b in the sense of following from b by means of the rules of inference. Then an act e such that

$(Ea)(Eb)(Ee')(Ee'')(\langle \text{Apprh} \rangle e' \cdot e' \text{ That}_{\text{Content}} \ulcorner \text{Tr}_S \, a \urcorner \cdot \langle \text{Apprh} \rangle e'$
$\cdot \, e' \text{ That}_{\text{Content}} \ulcorner \text{Tr}_S \, b \urcorner \cdot e'' \text{ That}_{\text{Content}} \ulcorner a \text{ LogConseq } b \urcorner \cdot \sim a = b \cdot$
$(e' \text{ During } e \vee e' \text{ Before}_{\text{Time}} e) \cdot (e'' \text{ During } e \vee e'' \text{ Before}_{\text{Time}} e)),$

is an act of seeing a truth as a consequence of another truth. To see a "law as such" is an e such that

$$(Ea)(\langle \text{Apprh} \rangle e \cdot e \text{ That}_{\text{Content}} \ulcorner \text{Law } a \urcorner).$$

And similarly for the other types of seeings.

Husserl takes pains (p. 233) to point out that of course "truths are what they are, and that, in particular, laws, grounds, principles are what they are, whether we have insight into them or not." Indeed they are "objective or ideal conditions of the possibility of our knowledge of them." Thus they "can be discussed and investigated apart from all relation to the thinking subject. . . . The laws in question have a meaning-content which is quite free from such a relation; they do not talk, even in ideal fashion, of knowing, judging, inferring, representing, providing, etc., but of truth, concept, proposition, syllogism, ground and consequent, etc. . . . " Change the terminology ever so little here and sharpen it somewhat, and we see that what Husserl has in mind is in essentials our modern division of labor between semantics and pragmatics. In semantics we abstract from the *user* of language, idealizing, as it were, all use of language in accord with exact semantical rules. And here of course the notions of truth and logical consequence (in both the syntactical and semantical senses) are basic. In pragmatics or epistemics the user is brought in explicitly, or at least his noetic acts, whatever it is that he *does* with items of language.

Scarcely any mention has been made in the foregoing to the actual user, but only to his noetic acts. In the laws concerning them, e.g, *Pr1–Pr15*, no parameter for a user of language has been needed. "Our treatment," Husserl writes (p. 234), "has shown that questions of the possibility of *knowledge* in general, and of theoretical knowledge in particular, ultimately lead us back to certain *laws,* whose roots are to be found purely in the content of knowledge, or of the categorical concepts it falls under, and which are so abstract that they contain no reference to knowledge as an act *of a knowing subject* [italics added]." These laws "are what are to be understood as constituting the conditions for the possibility of *theory* in general, in the objectively ideal sense." At some point, of course, laws might be forthcoming in which reference to the knowing subject would be needed. For the present, all of the foregoing laws are applicable to the acts of each knowing subject separately. All the acts considered in any one law are *co-agentive,* in the sense that they are all relativized to the same agent. This restriction, however, is merely *ad hoc* and other types of laws should be forthcoming in which the noetic acts of more than one agent are interrelated.

It is interesting to note also that Husserl seems to have grasped the need for recognizing some notions as *primitives* in the formulation of a theory. "*What* . . . [p. 235] *constitutes the ideal essence of theory as such?* What are the primitive 'possibilities' out of which the possibility of theory is constituted, or, what is the same, what are the *primitive essential concepts* out of which the concept of theory, itself an essential concept, is constituted?" We must distinguish here the primitives needed for an object language from those needed for a metalanguage. Husserl merely hints at this distinction, but strictly we should be clear concerning it. The metalinguistic primitives will be such as to lead to a characterization of the very notion itself of a theory or interpreted system. It is interesting that Husserl hints at the metalinguistic character of his project. "We are dealing with *systematic theories* [about languages] *which have their roots in the essence of theory,* [and also] with an *a priori theoretical, nomological science which deals with the ideal essence of science as such*, and accordingly has parts relating to systematic theories whose empirical, anthropological aspect it excludes." The "parts" here are presumably the object-linguistic parts of the semantical metalanguage, and hence of any pragmatical metalanguage built upon its basis. The concern in both semantics and pragmatics is of course with structural features of the theory under review and with general features concerning the noetic use of the language in which it is couched, but not with the particular subject matter with which it deals.

Husserl concludes, and in effect summarizes, the *Prolegomena* with several telling observations, the first of which concern "the [three] tasks of pure logic." To begin with (p. 236), "we must . . . lay down the more important concepts which 'make possible' the interconnected web of knowledge as seen objectively, and particularly the web of theory." Here (p. 237) "the concepts of the *elementary connective forms* naturally play a constitutive role ..., those connective forms, in particular, which are quite generally constitutive of the deductive unity of propositions, e.g., the conjunctive, disjunctive, and hypothetical linkage of propositions to form new propositions." Here the modern notions embodied in '·', 'v', and '⊃' are presumably being invoked, to say nothing of negation, symbolized by '∼', and material equivalence, symbolized by '≡'. Quantifiers no doubt should also be brought in. Moreover, some "second-order" notions have their place here, including truth, so that a semantics seems to be included under 'pure logic'. There are "other correlative concepts such as Object, State of Affairs, Unity, Plurality, Number,

Relation, Connection, etc. These are the pure, the formal *objective cate-gories.* These too must be taken into account." Such concepts are the delight of the semanticist interested in a careful specification of the *onto-logies* of the various language systems, at whatever level, that are needed. "All these concepts must be pinned down," their "*phenomeno-logical origin*" brought to light (p. 238) by "*insight into the essence*" involved. "We can achieve such an end only by *intuitive representation* of the essence in adequate Ideation, or, in the case of complicated con-cepts, through knowledge of the essentiality of the elementary [or primi-tive (?)] concepts present in them, and of the concepts of their form of combination." This adequate Ideation can take place presumably only in terms of the theory of *Begründungsakten,* more particularly, in terms of '⟨Idea⟩'.

It may seem that these are "trivial, preparatory tasks," Husserl con-tinues, and discussion of them may "seem to the layman [and even to the professional philosopher untrained in logic] to be barren, pettifogging word-exercises. But as long as concepts are not distinguished and made clear to ideational intuition, by going back to their essence, further effort is hopeless. In no field of logic is equivocation more fatal, in none have confused concepts so hindered the progress of knowledge, or so impeded the insight into its true aims, as in the field of pure logic." By 'pure logic' here we are to include of course not only formal logic in a narrow sense, but also logical syntax and semantics, the origin or *Ursprung* of which is to be brought to light within a phenomenological logic as based upon a systematic pragmatics.

The second task of "pure" logic "lies in the search for the *laws* grounded in the two classes of categorial concepts," the elementary con-nective forms (and no doubt quantifiers) and the objective (or ontologi-cal) categories. Here then we find not only strictly logical laws but pre-sumably syntactical and semantical ones as well.

The third task is to develop "the theory of the possible forms of theories or the pure theory of manifolds." Under this heading we should find no doubt a kind of *comparative* study of systems, how one relates to another in various ways. One way of doing this would be to develop something akin to a *calculus of systems.* Surprisingly little work in this direction has been done, even up to the present moment.[10] Different *kinds* of systems should be distinguished and placed in a suitably branched hierarchy. "This [p. 240] is a last, highest goal for a theoretical science of theory in general. It is also not indifferent from the point of view of the practical side of knowledge. To fit a theory into its formal class may rather be of the greatest methodological importance."

Husserl seems to have in mind, however, a somewhat different approach to the theory of systems via the theory of manifolds (*Mannigfaltigkeiten*), presumably as embedded within some all-embracing set theory. An algebraic *field* is then, roughly, any set of objects such that such and such (field-) laws obtain. Similarly for a *group,* a *lattice,* and so on. Similarly for an *n*-dimensional Euclidean or non-Euclidean space. For example, a *group,* say, is an ordered couple of a non-null set of objects *S* and an operation *o* such that

$$'(x)(y)(z) ((Sx \cdot Sy \cdot Sz) \supset (x \ o \ (y \ o \ z)) = ((x \ o \ y)o \ z))',$$
$$'(x)(y)((Sx \cdot Sy) \supset (Ez)(Sz \cdot x = (y \ o \ z)))',$$

and

$$'(x)(y)((Sx \cdot Sy) \supset (Ez)(Sz \cdot x = (z \ o \ y)))',$$

obtain as laws. And so on. A formulation is thus laid for the study of "the legal connection among pure forms of theory of determinately distinct types." The "*most general Idea of a Theory of Manifolds* [p. 241] is to be a science which definitely works out the form of the essential types of possible theories or fields of theory, and investigates their legal relations with one another. All actual theories are then specializations or singularitions of corresponding forms of theory, ... If the formal theory in question is actually worked out in the theory of manifolds, then all deductive theoretical work in constructing all actual theories of the same form has been done." The theory of manifolds is thus a kind of super-theory containing all specialized theories definitionally, so to speak (as in the example concerning groups). Such a unified theory has in fact been achieved in the Zermelo axiomatic set theory of 1908 and in its more recent progeny, although by no means in ways wholly satisfactory to all.

These three tasks are to be undertaken, in the order given, in the formulation of a given *S*, once its basic logic is determined. First the primitives must be chosen and the notions of 'term' and 'formula' of the system suitably defined. This much constitutes a *partial formalization* only. At the beginning stages the importance of a partial formalization, however, cannot be overestimated. Without a vocabulary and the formulae based upon it, we cannot go on to make any statements; we can only fumble around in the dark. With a vocabulary available, we proceed at once to the search for laws. Here two stages are to be distinguished , first, that of a tentative statement of purported laws, and, secondly, a deductive arrangement of the laws finally accepted as consequences of certain ones chosen as axioms. Both stages are fraught with difficulties. Some division of labor here is sometimes appropriate. The tentative groping after law is best done by specialists in the given field, whether it be an empiri-

cal science, a domain of philosophical analysis (or synthesis), or whatever. The task then of giving axioms comes later and requires the exact
insight of the skilled expert in deductive techniques, usually a mathematician. Husserl does not explicitly make these points, but to do so is
clearly in accord with his remarks.

Only after the degree of systematicity given by axioms is achieved is it
fruitful to reflect upon the system as a whole, upon its metatheoretic
properties, and its relations to other systems. And, of course, if this latter
is done in terms of a super-theory of manifolds, we must be sure that that
super-theory itself is in a proper working order. Also the theory of *intersystemics*, as we might call it, is of a very considerable complexity. It
must allow for *change* from one system to another, for systematic growth
and expansion, even for the simultaneous use of systems that are contradictory.[11] To a synchronic intersystemics, a diachronic one must be
added. The problems concerned with these are, of course, formidable,
and not as much careful study of them has been given as is desirable.
Much here still remains for the future.

In the discussion above no attempt has been made to follow Husserl
literally and in full detail. The aim has been, rather, merely to call attention to significant items in the *Prolegomena* that seem to be remarkably
close to items that have been clarified — or at least are under intensive
study — in recent work in semantics, systematic pragmatics, event theory, and the like. In some instances the kinship is so close as to suggest a
"wonderful affinity" of the kind Husserl sees between things and the
thoughts that make them knowable. Where the affinity is not obviously
close, suitable extensions of the techniques at hand should be able to
make it as close as one might wish. But even where the affinity is close, it
is not claimed that the problems are in any way solved or that further
work is not needed. On the contrary, the techniques here merely help to
open up the subject for exact investigation. On every topic considered,
more careful investigation can now be carried out on a more secure logical foundation than seems heretofore to have been available. Hence for
the most part we have been willing here to accept Husserl on his own
terms. Also it would be of interest to explore the contentions of the later
Formale und Tranzendentale Logik (1929), not only in comparison with
those of the *Prolegomena* and the *Logische Untersuchungen* but also
with the formal material above. It would then very likely become clear
how this material can be seen as providing a suitable foundation for what
Mohanty has recently christened 'transcendental semantics'.[12]

CHAPTER XII

On Universal Algebra and
The Whiteheadian Cosmology

"Unerring Nature, still divinely bright,
One clear, unchang'd, and universal light,
Life, force, and beauty must to all impart,
At once the source, the end, and test of art."
Pope

"Ordinary algebra in its modern developments," Whitehead observed in 1897,[1] "is studied as being a large body of propositions, inter-related by deductive reasoning, and based upon conventional definitions which are generalizations of fundamental conceptions." The use of 'based upon' here is perhaps too weak, for some "propositions" must of course be picked out as determinative of the kind of algebra in question by way of axioms. The definitions are then ancillary devices of notational abbreviation and may or may not be of terms or phrases previously introduced, and may or may not be of a "generalized" form. "Thus a science is being created [ordinary algebra in its modern developments]," Whitehead continues, "which by reason of its fundamental character has relation to almost every event, phenomenal or intellectual, which can occur. . . . Such algebras are mathematical sciences which are not essentially concerned with number or quantity; and this bold extension beyond the traditional domain of pure quantity forms their peculiar interest. The ideal of mathematics should be to erect a calculus to facilitate reasoning in connection with every province of thought, or of external experience, in which the succession of thoughts, or of events can be definitely ascertained and precisely stated. So that all serious thought which is not philosophy, or inductive reasoning, or imaginative literature, shall be mathematics developed by means of a calculus."

These remarks, among the very first that Whitehead ever penned for publication, enunciate a leading principle that underlies all his work and exhibit a tendency of thought that remained with him his entire life. They are extremely revelatory and reflection upon them will help us to discern a kind of unity in his thought and methods that is usually passed over in silence by commentators.

The interesting interplay as among 'almost', 'every', and 'all' in the

passage cited should be noted. Ordinary algebra in its modern developments "has relation to *almost* every event, phenomenal or intellectual,
which can occur." On the other hand, the ideal of mathematics is to formulate of calculus — just *one such,* notice — "to facilitate reasoning . . .
in *every* province of thought. . . . " The only exceptions are "philosophy,
inductive reasoning," and "imaginative literature." But even theories of
inductive reasoning, confirmation, and the like, are now, in the years
since Whitehead wrote, more and more being "developed by means of a
calculus," and imaginative literature, the study of metaphor, and the
like, is now being subjected to rather similar treatment along rather rigorous lines.[2]

Why now is "philosophy" taken here as an exception? Is it not a
"province of thought . . . in which the succession of thoughts . . . can be
definitely ascertained and precisely stated"? What did Whitehead have
in mind, in 1897, when he spoke of "philosophy" as though this were not
the case? One could only conjecture an answer. It is more profitable,
however, to observe instead that his attitude seems to have changed by
the time (1910–13) of the publication of *Principia Mathematica,* a sub-
sidiary aim of which was (p. 3) "to show that, with the aid of symbolism,
deductive reasoning can be extended to regions of thought not usually
supposed amenable to mathematical treatment." Foremost among such
regions surely are those areas of philosophy in which the deductive succession of thoughts can be clearly brought to light.

The interesting play, in the passages cited, between "events, phenomenal or intellectual" and between provinces of "thought, or of external
experience" should be noted. Whitehead is not here contrasting two
areas for which "a calculus to facilitate reasoning" should be set up.
Rather he is suggesting that "events, phenomenal or intellectual," and
items of "external experience" not only can be, but indeed should be,
brought under the "ideal of mathematics" expressed in terms of such a
calculus. The later cosmology is *par excellence* a theory of events, phenomenal and intellectual, and of all items of external experience, of a
philosophical kind and is thus surely no exception to the intent of these
remarks of 1897.

Whitehead's purpose, in *Universal Algebra,* is "to present a thorough
investigation of the various systems of Symbolic Reasoning allied to
ordinary Algebra. The chief examples of such systems are Hamiltonian
Quaternions, Grassmann's Calculus of Extension, and Boole's Symbolic
Logic. Such algebras have an intrinsic value for separate detailed study;
also they are worthy of a comparative study, for the sake of the light
thereby thrown on the general theory of symbolic meaning, and on alge-

braic symbolism in particular." The book is thus concerned with the comparison of a succession of special algebras, rather than with some one "grand" super-algebra in which they might all be brought together. This is not the occasion to attempt to describe Whitehead's conception of universal algebra in any detail, but merely to remark it. His discussion is complex and deeply immersed in some of the mathematics of the late nineteenth century. Also it is highly obscure at many points and not in accord with late-twentieth century standards of rigor. It is interesting that the projected second volume never appeared. During the years after 1900, Whitehead collaborated with Russell in the writing of *Principia Mathematica.* The subject then developed, no longer as universal algebra or algebras, but rather in terms of a rigorous formulation of modern logic as based on a theory of quantification of all finite levels in the hierarchy of types.

It is perhaps astonishing, from our modern point of view, that Whitehead did not include a discussion of the so-called "Logic of Relatives" in his *Universal Algebra,* a subject "which it does not enter into the plan of this treatise to describe" (p. 115). (He does call attention, however, to Peirce's work on the logic of relatives with the comment that the investigations of Peirce "form the most important contribution to the subject of Symbolic Logic since Boole's work.") But this omission is fully put to rights in *Principia Mathematica.* And although the relevant portions of the latter work are concerned only with *dyadic* relations, methods are at hand for considering also relations of any finite degree.

The ideal of a unif*ied,* and unify*ing,* universal algebra, in which relations of *all* finite degrees have their proper place, was thus beyond anything envisaged in either *Universal Algebra* or *Principia Mathematica.* Many years have had to elapse for its realization, one approach to which is given in IX above. The theory there is unified in the sense of being formulable as a special deductive system; but it is also unifying in the sense that any number of special disciplines may be accommodated in it by a suitable choice of nonlogical primitive relational constants. The logical part of the system, so to speak, consists merely of the theory of the *sums, products,* and *negatives* of relations, of *Cartesian products,* and of all manner of *domains* of relations, including *relational domains* and *converses.* The logical part is developed mainly as a result of recognizing that, given any nonlogical primitive relations determining some special "province of thought," the usual sums, products, domains, and so on, of them are immediately forthcoming. Universal algebra is thus merely the area of theory in which this recognition is made fully explicit. The theory is thus one in which the elements of the algebra, so to speak, are themselves the relations determinative of the special disciplines under consideration, and not the entities those relations are taken to relate. These latter in no wise occur, there being no variables for them in the symbolism.

It should be observed in passing that, given universal algebra in the sense of IX above, the special algebras Whitehead considers can then be handled in the nonlogical part, so to speak. For the Algebra of Logic itself, however, regarded as a theory of monadic relations, such treatment would be adscititious, the whole of that theory already appearing in the logical part. Of course some of the special algebras Whitehead discusses are mathematically of a very considerable complexity and are such as to utilize here or there portions of set theory. In 1897 mathematicians were less sensitive to their use of set-theoretic devices than they became after the turn of the century. In any case, we have seen in IX above how even an axiomatic set theory such as that of Zermelo can be provided for on the basis of universal algebra, as conceived here, as a special theory in the nonlogical part. Thus such algebras as Whitehead considers that require set-theoretic devices fundamentally raise no special problems. Of course, for each such algebra, a full axiomatization is needed. We see, then, not only that the general algebra of relations is a kind of completion of Whitehead's early work, a natural realization of what a universal algebra should be, but is also itself a kind of algebra of all algebras, a super-algebra, adequate for "the general theory of symbolic reasoning."

Let us observe next that the whole of the simple theory of types of *Principia Mathematica* itself may likewise be accommodated as a special theory within the nonlogical part of the universal algebra here. This could be shown in several ways. If set theory is assumed to be available, the whole of type theory could be embedded within it. However, we will stay closer to the spirit of *Principia Mathematica* if the theory is formulated directly rather than in terms of a set theory. Such a formulation will be closer in spirit also to the later cosmology, that of *Process and Reality,* whose doctrine of eternal objects seems envisaged, not in terms of a set theory, but rather type-theoretically. Very well, then, as a prelude to the algebraization of the later cosmology, let us consider first the algebraization of the simplified *PM* itself.[3]

Among the arguments that any primitive predicate constant may have are now expressions of various *types* and *levels*. Thus where R_3 previously stood for a triadic predicate constant with individuals as arguments, we now write $\ulcorner R_{(0,0,0)} \urcorner$ instead. The '0' indicates that the argument is an expression for an *individual* and the '0,0,0' that all three arguments are. The parentheses then indicate that the predicate itself is of the type *one higher* than 0. We may thus say that $\ulcorner R_{(0,0,0)} \urcorner$ is of the type 1 and of level 0,0,0. Similarly $\ulcorner R_{((0),0,0)} \urcorner$ is of type 2 (the first argument of which is an expression for a monadic relation of type 1, the other two arguments being expressions for individuals) and of level (0),0,0. On the other hand, $\ulcorner R_{((0,0),0,0)} \urcorner$ is also of type 2, the first argument of which is an expression for a dyadic relation of type 1 (with only expressions for individuals as arguments), the other two arguments being expressions for individuals. And so on for expressions for types and levels of any complexity.

The notions of type and level may be differentiated more clearly as follows. The *type* of a relational constant (primitive or defined) is always designated by a positive integer ≥ 1. The *level* of a relational constant, however, is designated by a sequence of expressions of the form '0', '(0)', '(0,0)', '(0,(0))', and so on and on. The number of the type of a relational constant is then always gained merely by counting the pairs of mating parentheses that occur within the expression for its level, but omitting repetitions. (Thus '((0),(0))' indicates the third type even though three pairs of mating parentheses occur. Here of course there is a repetition of '(0)'.) The level of a relational constant might also be called its *argument structure*, spelling out as it does not only its degree but also the degree and structure of each of the argument expressions. The level of a relational constant thus specifies for us precisely the full character of each of its permissible arguments.

These observations may be made more precise by the following recursive clauses taken together simultaneously.

1. The expression '(0)' as attached as a subscript to a relational constant indicates that that constant has the argument structure '0' (is of degree 1 and takes only expressions for individuals as arguments) and is of type 1.

2. If the expression $\ulcorner (a) \urcorner$ as a subscript to a relational constant indicates that it has the argument structure a (is of degree 1 and takes only expressions for relations with the argument structure a as argument expressions) and is of type m, then $\ulcorner ((a)) \urcorner$ as a subscript to a relational constant indicates that it has the argument structure $\ulcorner (a) \urcorner$ (is of degree 1 and takes only expressions for relations of degree 1 with the argument structure $\ulcorner (a) \urcorner$ as argument expressions) and is of type $(m + 1)$.

3. If a and b as subscripts to relational constants indicate that they respectively have the argument structure a and b and are of types j and k respectively ($j \geq 1$, $k \geq 1$), then $\ulcorner (a,b) \urcorner$ as a subscript to a relational

constant indicates that it has the argument structure $\ulcorner(a,b)\urcorner$ and is of type $(\max(j,k)+1)$ (where max (j,k) is j if $j \geq k$ or k if $k > j$).

In addition to notions of type and argument structure or level, we need also the notion of the *degree* of a predicate constant, the number of arguments it significantly takes. The degree of a predicate constant $\ulcorner R_{(0)}\urcorner$ is 1, of $\ulcorner R_{(0,0)}\urcorner$, 2, of $\ulcorner R_{((0),(0,0,0))}\urcorner$, 2, and so on. More precisely, we may define the notion of degree as follows. An occurrence of a comma in an argument structure a is said to be a *main* occurrence of a comma if it occurs in no proper part of a of the form $\ulcorner(b,c)\urcorner$. Thus the first comma occuring in $\ulcorner R_{((0),(0,0,0))}\urcorner$ is a main occurrence, the other two not. Now the degree of a predicate constant is $(n+1)$, where n is the number of main occurrences of commas within its argument structure.

Nothing has been said thus far concerning the nonlogical predicate constants assumed available as primitives in the nonlogical part of the theory. At least one such primitive is needed, universal algebra here being conceived as always an *applied* one, always as applied to a particular subject matter. If proper names are desired, these must be accommodated by means of suitable predicates, e.g., 'Socratizes' in place of 'Socrates'.

To make explicit the full array of expressions admitted now, of all levels and of finite types, and of all finite degrees, the following recursive specifications of 'relational term' and 'formula' are useful.

1. Any primitive predicate constant of argument structure (or level) a and of type n is a relational term of level a and type n ($n \geq 1$).

2. If $\ulcorner R_{(a)}\urcorner$ and $\ulcorner S_{(a)}\urcorner$ are relational terms of level a and type n, then $\ulcorner(R_{(a)} \cup S_{(a)})\urcorner$, $\ulcorner(R_{(a)} \cap S_{(a)})\urcorner$, and $\ulcorner -R_{(a)}\urcorner$ are also ($n \geq 1$).

3. If $\ulcorner R_{(a)}\urcorner$ and $\ulcorner S_{(b)}\urcorner$ are respectively relational terms of level a and b and of type n and m, then $\ulcorner(R_{(a)} \times S_{(b)})_{(a,b)}\urcorner$ is a relational term of level $\ulcorner a,b\urcorner$ and of type $\max(n,m)$, for $n \geq 1$ and $m \geq 1$.

4. If $\ulcorner R_{(a)}\urcorner$ is a relational term of degree n, then $\ulcorner D_i \ldots {}_k R_{(a)}\urcorner$ is a relational term of degree j, where $j \leq n$ and $i, \ldots, k$ are j distinct numbers each $\leq n$ and taken in any order of magnitude, and where $n \geq 2$.

5. If $\ulcorner R_{(a)}\urcorner$ and $\ulcorner S_{(a)}\urcorner$ are both relational terms of level a and type n, then $\ulcorner R_{(a)} = S_{(a)}\urcorner$ is a formula.

6. If A is a formula, $\ulcorner \sim A\urcorner$ is a formula.

7. If A and B are formulae, $\ulcorner(A \vee B)\urcorner$ is a formula.

The fundamental laws concerning these various notions, essentially as in IX with additions, must of course be forthcoming from suitably chosen axioms. Moreover, there must also be *nonlogical* axioms governing the nonlogical primitive predicates. The nonlogical axioms needed are suitable formulations of Axioms of Extensionality, Multiplicative Axioms, and the Axiom of Infinity. The Axioms of Class and Relational Existence, needed in most axiomatizations of the simplified theory of types, are not needed here, the existence of all permissible classes and relations being already provided for in the underlying logical part of the theory.

We should observe now that, by extending the nonlogical framework, suitable forms for the logical *syntax, semantics,* and even *pragmatics* of the *PM* object language now provided for, may be given. Thus logical syntax becomes the special algebra of the *concatenation relation* taken as applicable to the sign designs or sign events — depending upon the kind of syntax developed — of the object language. And similarly semantics, as developed, say, on the basis of the relation Den of *multiple denotation,* becomes the special algebra of that relation.[4] (Of course, suitable provision must be made here for the structural- or shape-descriptive names of or predicates for the object-language expressions.) Similarly an *intensional* semantics may be developed in various ways, one of them in terms of the Under-relation, as above, capturing the essentials of the Fregean *Art des Gegebenseins.* And similarly for areas of the *metamathematics* of the simplified *PM,* the theories of proof, of *Erfüllbarkeit* and of validity, of consistency, and of undecidability. All such theories become algebraized now in terms of the axiomatizations needed for them. No area of metamathematics is exempt from the need of an explicit axiomatization, as Frege was perhaps the first to point out in his brilliant critique of Hilbert's geometry[5] — not even the theory of undecidability itself.

Let us turn now to the later cosmology, as formulated, say, in terms of the system in *Whitehead's Categoreal Scheme.*[6] The material there can no doubt be improved upon, bringing in perhaps some suggestions due to Bowman Clarke.[7] As a rough first list, the following predicate constants are needed, some of which could be taken as primitive: $\ulcorner EO_{(a)} \urcorner$ for *eternal objects* with the argument structure a, 'AO' for *actual occasions,* 'Prhd' for the dyadic relation of *prehension,* 'PhysPrhn' for *physical prehensions,* 'CncptlPrhn' for *conceptual prehensions,* 'Ing' for the dyadic relation of *ingression,* 'EC' for the dyadic relation of being *extensively connected with,* 'Val' for *valuations,* 'SF' for *subjective forms,* 'Concr' for *concrescences,* 'Nex' for *nexūs,* 'Proptn' for *propositons,* 'Mult' for *multiplicities,* 'Purps' for *purposes,* '*cng*' for the *consequent* nature of God, and '*png*' for His *primordial* nature. (Perhaps also an adaptation of Goodman's relation W, for a relation of *withness,* is needed.) Readers will recognize in this list expressions for the fundamental notions of Whitehead's scheme.

In terms of these notions, three stages in the development of the algebra of the later cosmology may be distinguished. First we may develop a *partially formalized language* for it, as in *Whitehead's Categoreal Scheme*. The formalization is partial only in the sense of not having axioms picked out. Next certain fundamental principles are enunciated which should presumably obtain in any deeper discussion. The final stage is reached, of course, only when a suitable axiomatization is achieved. Needless to say, we are far from achieving any even remotely adequate axiomatization of the later cosmology at the present time. A full algebraization can be given, however, only on such a basis. For the purposes of discussion here we assume, as is usual in science and in the philosophy of science generally, that a suitable axiomatization is possible even though not actually at hand.

Another kind of algebraization should be mentioned, however, namely, an algebraization of the *actual text*. In view of recent work in logico-linguistics, the sentences of any text "in which the succession of [the author's] thoughts . . . can be definitely ascertained and precisely stated" can be given an exact logical form or deep structure. The actual text is then merely the succession of these forms, given perhaps conjunctively. All of the forms are to be presumed stated in terms of the list of fundamental Whiteheadian notions given, stated of course now without variables in terms of the notions of the underlying algebra of relations, together with such ancillary grammatical or quasigrammatical notions as are needed.[8] For specificity, the full theory of these latter may also be assumed algebraized and conjoined to the text.

In view of the considerations put forward above, we see that there is a central unity to Whitehead's entire oeuvre, which is foretold, as it were, in the very first paragraphs of the *Universal Algebra*. This unity, to be sure, was never explicitly recognized by Whitehead, the project of algebraization having been abandoned in favor of the quantificational material of *Principia Mathematica*. The key reason for failure to recognize this unity is that there is no discussion of relations in the former; this lack is presumably its chief defect. If we reconstrue universal algebra as an algebra of relations, of all kinds, that is, of all finite types, of all finite degrees, and of all argument structures, the programme of algebraization takes on a new vitality, in terms of which, as we have seen, the later cosmology may be accommodated.

Let us close by calling attention to the very last paragraph of Whitehead's very last book,[9] which the foregoing material helps to explicate. "Philosophy is akin to poetry. . . . In each case there is reference to form beyond the direct meanings of words. Poetry allies itself to metre, phi-losophy to mathematic pattern." One should add that science too is akin to poetry, allying itself to exact observation and experimentation as well as to mathematic pattern. The three enterprises are much more closely allied methodologically than is usually recognized.

CHAPTER XIII

The One and The Many: Logic₁ and Logics₂

"One God, one country, one logic."
Whitehead

In his "What Price Bivalence,"[1] Quine neither defends nor repudiates bivalence — belief in two-valued logic as somehow fundamental — but adheres "to it for the simplicity of the theory it affords." He thinks, however, that this can be done only at a cost, but he does not tarry to compute the cost of the alternatives. What is the cost and what are the alternatives anyhow? How are we to interpret them and therewith come to understand them? Let us reflect upon Quine's argument a little by way of a preface to an attempt to answer these questions.

"We stalwarts of two-valued logic," Quine comments, "buy its sweet simplicity at no small price in respect of the harboring of undecidables. We declare that it is either true or false that there was an odd number of blades of grass in Harvard Yard at the dawn of Commencement Day, 1903. The matter is undecidable, but we maintain that there is a fact of the matter." To be *undecidable* is meant here, presumably, either *neither known nor unknown* or *neither capable of being known nor capable of being unknown.* Both of these predicates, it should be noted, depend upon bivalence. The latter introduces the notion of *capability,* which is turn needs unpacking in terms of metaphysical possibility, logical possibility, physical possibility, physiological possibility, and so on. In the sense of *neither (now) known nor unknown* the matter is at least now undecid*ed,* but is not undecid*able* in all of the senses distinguished. It is highly probable, in some suitable sense, that the matter will never be decided. Most of the content of Quine's example can be spelled out in terms of probability, it would seem. The theory of probability used here likewise would be formulated in bivalent terms. Quine's example thus, when looked at closely, seems not to discredit bivalence in any deep sense, this latter being needed — at least metalinguistically if in no other way — at every step in his discussion.

Quine goes on to the matter of "vague" terms generally, such as 'heap', 'bald', 'table', and the like. What we need, of course, is a *theory* of vagueness properly spelled out bivalently. Quine appeals, rather, to unanalyzed notions of *fact* and *convention,* both of which cry out for

a characterization in bivalent terms.[2] In the absence of such a characterization, it is difficult to be sure of what this dichotomy consists. "Facts"
have something or other to do with factually true sentences, and conventions result from a certain type of human act.

In several previous publications, the sketch of a kind of *scalar* theory
of adverbials and adjectivals has been suggested[3] that will be of help to us
here. The leading idea is to introduce suitable *comparative* relations,
with their relata confined to certain *reference classes* or *predicates*. The
comparative relation in effect arranges these relata in a given order, so
that one can distinguish earlier from the later (or lower from the higher)
ones. Thus, let *Less-Bald-Than* be such a relation, and 'AHM' be the
class name for adult human males (restricted further perhaps to those of a
given social or other group). The sentence

'John is bald'

then can be parsed as

'John Mid Less-Bald-Than,'AHM',

that John is placed somewhere in the middle of the scale for the relation
Less-Bald-Than as restricted to 'AHM'. Similarly predicates 'High' and
'Low' can be introduced, also 'VeryHigh', 'VeryLow', 'VeryVery-
High', 'VeryVeryLow', and so on, as far as one may wish to go. A good
deal of slack is allowed at each stage, and there might be overlap as
between or among positions on the scales as used by different speakers.

The point to note now is that "vague" adjectives and adverbials can be
handled in this way with no sacrifice of bivalence, and that this kind of an
approach can easily be extended to "vague" noun or verb phrases. Let
Less-Heapy-Than be the relation of being less-of-a-heap-than, as confined, say, to virtual classes of grains of sand. Then

'This v.c. of grains of sand is a heap'

can be parsed by saying that this v.c. is placed Mid to High somewhere in
the scale for the Less-Heapy-Than relation as confined to the predicate
for being a virtual class of grains of sand.[4]

Let us reflect now upon 'table'. "Diminish a table, conceptually, molecule by molecule. When is a table not a table? No stipulation will avail
us here, however arbitrary," Quine writes. "Each removal of a molecule
leaves a physical object . . . — namely, the material content of a material
portion of space-time. A table contains a graded multitude of nested or
overlapping physical objects each of which embodies enough of the sub-

stance to have qualified as a table in its own right, but only in abstraction from the rest of the molecules. Each of these objects would qualify as a table, that is, if cleared of the overlying and surrounding molecules, but should not be counted as a table when still embedded in a further physical object that so qualifies in turn. Only the outermost, the sum of this nest of physical objects, counts as a table."

A good deal of dubious physics seems implicit in this passage that is beyond present concern. We need not just diminish the table "conceptually," it would seem; it diminishes physically in this way before our very eyes, but we do not perceive it. What we actually perceive is a physical object with a very complex inner or conceptual structure, interpenetrant in very complex physical ways with its environment. It is helpful here to distinguish the *perceived* table from the *conceived* one, and we should not conflate the logic of perception with that of conception. Each occurrence of 'table' in Quine's text here should then be prefixed by 'perceived' or by 'conceived'. Most of the purported mystery then vanishes. When is a perceived table not a perceived table? Presumably when ostension fails or when an act of perception fails to reveal it as such. If percepts are concept-laden, as we have been told again and again in recent years they are, then every perceived table is a conceived one, conceived, that is, under the very predicate 'table'. And surely all conceived tables are conceived tables. When, finally, is a conceived table not a perceived table? If it never has been perceived, presumably, or at least has not been perceived up to the time of the utterance of the question.

Quine's mention here of "a graded multitude of nested or physical objects," only some of which are perceived, makes use of course of the calculus of individuals. What Quine says about this multitude, however, seems not quite correct. He should say, it would seem, that "each of these [conceived] objects would qualify as a [conceived] table even if [not] cleared of the overlying and surrounding molecules." It can, however, be counted as a conceived table, but not a perceived one, "when still embedded in a further physical object that . . . qualifies" as either a conceived or perceived one. Nor is it the case that "only the outermost, the sum of this nest of physical objects, counts as a table," either perceived or conceived. Many of the sums can pass as a perceived table, and all of them pass as conceived ones.

The reader might question the dichotomy here of 'conceived' and 'perceived'. Both are important words of ordinary language, however, and of the theory of knowledge. It has been suggested elsewhere that forms such as

(1)   'p Prcv$_t$ x,a'

and

(2)   'p Concv$_t$ x,a',

or closely related ones, be introduced to handle the activities of perceiving and conceiving, respectively.[5] They express that person p perceives, or conceives, at time t, the object x as taken *under* the predicate description a.[6] These or closely related notions would seem indispensable ones with which to provide logical forms for ordinary sentences containing 'perceives' and 'conceives'. The dichotomy is built into our language and is needed for the theory of mental acts, and of cognition in general.

Let us note now how bivalence holds for (1) and (2). Clearly

$$\vdash (p \text{ Prcv}_t\, x,a \text{ v} \sim p \text{ Prcv}_t\, x,a)$$

and

$$\vdash (p \text{ Cncv}_t\, x,a \text{ v} \sim p \text{ Cncv}_t\, x,a).$$

But it might obtain that

$$(p \text{ Prcv}_{t_1}\, x,a \cdot p \text{ Prcv}_{t_2} x, \ulcorner -a \urcorner),$$

where t_1 is before t_2 and $\ulcorner -a \urcorner$ is the negation of the predicate a. An example is an inscription of Wittgenstein's rabbit-duck design, now perceived as rabbit representation and now as a duck one. It does obtain, however, that

$$\vdash (p \text{ Prcv}_t\, x,a \supset \sim p \text{ Prcv}_t\, x, \ulcorner -a \urcorner),$$

but not conversely, for one and the same t. And similarly for conception.

Let x be one of Quine's tables, and let a be one of the predicates describing it. A perceived table x is then one such that p Prvc$_t$ x,a. for some p and t, and a conceived one such that p Cnvc$_t$ x,a. More explicitly, we may spell out these forms by bringing in the Frege Under-relation. Thus we may let (1), for example, be short for

'$(Ee)(p \text{ Agent } e \cdot \langle \text{Prcv} \rangle\, e \cdot e \text{ Of}_{\text{Object}}\, x \cdot x \text{ Under}_e\, a \cdot e \text{ Through-}out_{\text{Pervasive}}\, t)$',

the definiens here containing expressions for suitable prepositional relations.[7] The object x here is one of Quine's logical sums.

A word now about ostension and the demonstrative phrase 'this table'. In ostension a certain kind of act takes place interrelating expression, object, and the mode of description under which the object is taken. Ostension thus is a *quadratic* relation. Let '$\langle Ost \rangle e$' express that e is an ostensive act. Then

'p Ost$_t$ x,a' may abbreviate '$(Ee)(p$ Agent $e \cdot \langle Ost \rangle e \cdot e$ Throughout$_{Pervasive}$ $t \cdot e$ Of$_{Object}$ $x \cdot x$ Under$_e$ $a)$'.

Here a may be of the form 'this table', the ostensive act e appropriately showing how a and x are interrelated. And concerning 'Ost' suitable principles based on bivalence clearly hold. We then see that the presence of vague terms in language, and the human performance of acts of perceiving, of conceiving, and of ostention, give no ground for giving up bivalence, or even of thinking that there is a high price that must be paid for espousing it.

The logic of vagueness and the logic of perceiving, and so on, are thus seen to be branches of a suitably constructed theory of language, this theory being of the classical kind. Let us go on to reflect now very briefly on other types of so-called "alternative" logics, to see how they fare with respect to bivalent classicism. Let us consider epistemic logic in general, modal logic, many-valued logic, intuitionistic logic, tense logic, deontic logics, quantum logics, Craig's Boolean-physics logic, "entailment" logics, and "gappy" semantics. The list is by no means complete and there are many subspecies within each kind and some of these kinds overlap with each other. Perforce many of the comments to follow will be somewhat sketchy, some of the points having been made in greater detail elsewhere.

The notions 'Prcv' and 'Cncv' are two very basic notions of epistemic logic. Additional notions are the Fregean *apprehension, acceptance,* and *assertion,* in addition to *utterance, belief, knowing,* and so on. As goes the theory concerning Prcv and Cncv, so goes epistemics in general. The full theory of logical forms involving expressions for epistemic notions thus can be — and no doubt should be — spelled out in bivalent terms.

Consider 'Blv' for 'believes' in the tense of tenselessness. Clearly

$$\vdash (p \text{ Blv}_t x,a \text{ v} \sim p \text{ Blv}_t x,a).$$

This principle is sharply to be distinguished, however, from

$$\vdash (p \text{ Blv}_t x,a \text{ v } p \text{ Blv}_t x, \ulcorner -a \urcorner)',$$

which need not hold. Person p's beliefs might be such that he believes neither, perhaps because he lacks sufficient evidence for one or the other. This latter form should not be mistaken for a "law of excluded middle" nor should its denial be mistaken for a denial of such. And similarly for many other epistemic terms. In general, the logic of epistemic terms, like that of vagueness, needs bivalence at its very roots.

As to modal logic, nothing need be added to what has been said in III and IV above.[8] The study of the subject, and of its many varieties, is still in its infancy. Alternative approaches to those sketched above are valuable heuristically, but seem not to date to have been founded on sound philosophical and linguistic notions that carry much explanatory value.

Let us consider now many-valued logics. At the very beginning of their monograph on the subject,[9] Rosser and Turquette comment that "it has been a truism that every statement is either true or false. It might be supposed that this principle must be disproved before we can write a serious work on many-valued logic. This is by no means the case. . . . The task of construction [of systems of many-valued logic used in this monograph] will include the logical procedures of ordinary English and those of some formalized systems of two-valued logic. . . . It does not follow that ordinary two-valued logic is necessary for the construction of many-valued logic, but it does follow that it is sufficient for such constructions." The logical procedures of ordinary English are more and more turning out to be seen as based on bivalence; there is much more evidence now that this is the case than at the time Rosser and Turquette wrote. And although the presupposition of bivalence is sufficient, it is also very likely necessary, at least at the metalinguistic level. No alternative seems to be forthcoming. An alternative not presupposing bivalence would have to have very strong constraints upon it, even unnatural ones. And in any case there is the problem of the "meaning" of both the object-language constants needed as well as those of the metalanguage.

Rosser and Turquette are concerned entirely "with the behavior of many-valued statements and not with their meaning." The problem of interpretation is left open. To spell out an interpretation is always, it would seem, to use two-valued terms metalinguistically. Not to do so is, again, to use highly artificial, perhaps obscure, notions, themselves in need of being interpreted. Meaning, in the sense in which Rosser and Turquette use the word and in the light of what we know about it to date, should surely be spelled out in clear terms and in logical forms having the requisite logical simplicity.

We might try interpreting a *three*-valued logic, for example, in terms of acceptance, say. We might stipulate that a statement *a* has the third value just when it is neither accepted nor rejected (in the sense that its negation is accepted).[10] To do this, however, is to fall right into the open arms of a two-valued pragmatical metalanguage in terms of which such an interpretation is formulated.[11] Is the use of such a metalanguage also necessary in order to give this interpretation? No alternative metalanguage, necessary in this sense, seems ever to have been formulated, or even possible without itself falling willy-nilly in turn into the arms of a bivalent metametalanguage.

The situation with regard to the interpretation of intuitionistic logics is not dissimilar, but the deeper one looks into them the more complex the situation appears. Prominent among ways of doing intuitionistic logic and mathematics is the one in which a parameter for the working mathematician himself is explicitly brought in. This approach by means of the "creative subject" is under intensive investigation and appears to be promising. In its terms, intuitionistic logic becomes a theory of a certain kind of mathematical act, of "constructing" such and such or of accepting such and such on the basis of given evidence. This approach has at least the minimal virtue of being clear and of being formulable within a metalanguage with familiar and desirable characteristics. If intuitionism is not formulated in this way, it seems that it can at least be so interpreted, so that its semantics in turn is of the bivalent type. Whether the semantics *must* be of this type is an open question. The injunction

'When in doubt, spell it out'

would seem especially applicable here. If we are in doubt as to what the interpretation is or of how we are to understand it, have a good look at it "from close to" and in terms of the simplest and least dubitable terms you can think up. To date, it seems safe to say, the theory of such terms has always turned out to be bivalent.[12]

The late Arthur Prior was one of the first to have formulated a so-called *tense* logic. The points raised in the critical appraisal of his approach, especially of the content of his basic *Time and Modality*,[13] seem never to have been answered. Here again, it seems, tense theory can be accommodated in bivalent terms without loss.

Further, tense theory, to achieve its proper goals, is to be supplemented by a theory of the *aspect* of verbs, which in turn seems to require a bivalent mereology. And still further, the theory of tense and aspect together are to be embedded within a wider, bivalent logico-linguistic system. And similarly, it would seem, for other approaches to tense theory.

Deontic logics are concerned with such notions as *obligation, permission,* and the like, usually within the confines of some moral or social code. The most appropriate linguistic forms for handling these notions would seem to be the tenseless

'p Oblgd$_t$ e,a'

and

$$'p \text{ Pmtd}_t e,a',$$

to the effect that person p is obliged or permitted to perform at time t an act e that is taken under the predicate description a. These forms are of course akin to some of the forms introduced above, especially (1) and (2).[14]

The subject of quantum logic is of course highly controversial, like that of intuitionism, and much depends upon all manner of mathematical and scientific details. Here again, however, the *primitive notions* should be properly *interpreted*, it would seem, within a suitably acceptable metalanguage. It always seems to turn out that the metalanguage is appropriately bivalent. This is the case, for example, for the Finkelstein-Putnam theory[15] and for the Lorenzen-Mittelstaedt one.[16] Of course some quantum logic might be formulated for which such an interpretation would not be easy to find. It is safe to say, however, that we would not rest content with such a logic until we had found such an interpretation.

William Craig's theory of Boolean algebra and its relation to the "everyday physical world" is an interesting example of the way in which the mathematician abbreviates to the utmost and then *seems* to arrive at an alternative kind of logic.[17] However, this is done only at the expense of shuffling off all matters of interpretation. This is a procedure Bridgman complained of years back, it will be recalled. It is the "text," according to him, that gives "what the significance of the equations is."[18] Bridgman noted that "a complete mathematical formulation requires equations plus text. . . . The necessity of a text is almost always overlooked, but I think it must be recognized to be essential, and a study of what it must contain is as necessary for an adequate conception of the nature of the mathematical theory as a study of the equations themselves." The "text" is usually the bivalent metalanguage, semantical or pragmatical or whatever, in terms of which the interpretation of the equations is given.

It is interesting to compare Craig's procedure notationally with that of DeMorgan way back at the very beginnings of the modern logic of relations. In his "On the Syllogism, No. IV, and on the Logic of Relations" of 1859,[19] DeMorgan struggled to provide a notation for some of the basic operations on dyadic relations, the negation, the logical sum, the relative product, and the converse. Two further interesting operations he introduced without naming them. Where L and M are dyadic relations, the expression 'LM'' is to "signify an L of *every* M," so we are told, and 'L$_,$M' is to signify "an L of none but M's." It is interesting that

DeMorgan used 'signify' here, putting the interpretation into the (implicit) semantics. Then, where 'X' and 'Y' are thing variables,

(3)   'X LM' Y'

can express that X bears L to everything that bears M to Y, i.e., that

(3') $(Z)(Z \, M \, Y \supset X \, L \, Z)$.

And similarly

(4)   '$X \, L_{,} M \, Y$'

expresses that X bears L to none but things that bear M to Y, i.e., that

(4') $(Z) \, (X \, L \, Z \supset Z \, M \, Y)$.

Peirce later called these notions the *ordinary* (or *forward* or *relative progressive*) *involution* and *backward* (or *relative regressive*) *involution* of L and M, respectively.[20]

DeMorgan did not have at hand the resources of modern quantification theory and bivalent logic, so as to be able to spell out (3) and (4) as (3') and (4') respectively. Yet his insight was secure, although the notations of (3) and (4) we now tend to regard as rather obscure and antiquated. The "spelling out" here can be by means of explicit definition within an object language or by means of semantical rules in a metalanguage. And so it is *mutatis mutandis* for any of the deviant or alternative logics discussed. Their authors are struggling to characterize notions not easily symbolized in the usual notations. They need new ones, some of which are taken as primitives and characterized axiomatically. Only later perhaps can it be seen — especially after logico-linguistics has made its contribution — that these notions can either be defined within the object language suitably extended or else interpreted within a suitable semantics or pragmatics.

Note that, although he had not the advantage of a happy notation, DeMorgan's insight here was very original and profound. He is actually the great founder of the modern logic of relations. Similarly, many of the deviant logicians have splendid insights into difficult material and often put forward valuable suggestions. The task usually remains, however, as we have seen, of interpreting the primitives in an acceptable way.

The Anderson-Belnap "relevance" or "entailment" type of logic incorporates important insights crying out for delineation in acceptable logico-linguistic terms.[21] The authors, however, decry any such need, and proceed as though it were adscititious. Dearly purchased progress in clarification — and paid for in hard currency, be it said — is thus tossed to the winds. This seems a pity, for everything valuable in entailment logics, it seems, can be provided for more appropriately in more acceptable terms.

Another deviant theory that has attracted attention in recent years is so-called "gappy" semantics based on "supervaluation."[22] Here truth or falsity are *withheld* from certain sentences rather than a third value assigned to them. There are thus truth-value gaps, so to speak. The theory has not been spelled out with sufficient rigor, and the question arises as to whether the metalanguage in which the gappy semantics is formulated is itself gappy. Presumably not, all purposes for having truth-value gaps being already served within the object language. At best the theory of truth-value gaps seems *ad hoc,* and the purposes for which it is designed seem best served in other, more standard, ways.

There are also some internal difficulties in gappy semantics that seem not to have been faced. If 'b' is not a referring expression and 'F' is a monadic predicate of the language, neither 'Fb' nor '$\sim Fb$' are assigned truth values. However, '$(Fb \vee \sim Fb)$' is assigned truth. This seems curious. If neither constituent is given an assignment, how can the latter, a truth-functional compound, be assigned truth? On the other hand, '$(x)Fx \supset Fb$' is given no assignment. Why not? Some clear criteria are needed as to why an assignment should be withheld for individual constituents but allowed for some compounds of them but not for others. Also, it is contended that "we cannot plausibly reject that '$t = t'$' is false when 't' has a referent and 't'' does not [quotes added]." But '$t = t'$' is equivalent to

$$\text{'}((Ft \equiv Ft') \cdot (Gt \equiv Gt') \cdot \ldots)\text{'}$$

where we fill in the blanks with equivalence clauses for all the remaining primitive predicates of the language, including suitable ones for relations. At least one conjunct here must be taken as false, then, for '$t = t'$' to be taken as false. But, if 'Ft'', 'Gt'', and so on, are not assigned a truth value, why should these compounds be? It seems more reasonable to withhold a truth assignment from them and hence from '$t = t'$' also. Thus '$(Ex)x = t$' should not properly be taken to express that t exists, as in fact it is in the paper unde discussion. Would it not be better explicitly to recognize a relation of designation Des, and then take 't exists' to mean by disquotation that (Ex) 't' Des x? There are many further important technicalia that could be queried. Of course, intuitions may well differ as to where truth-value gaps should be allowed. These differing ways should be explicitly stated and justified in the bivalent metalanguage presupposed.

The words 'deviant' and 'alternative' have been used throughout almost interchangeably.[23] Strictly they are not synonymous, however, but for present purposes there has been no need to distinguish them. The concern here has been with standard, classical logic versus other kinds of logic that might be thought to challenge its supremacy in any fundamental way.

It is clear that the standard logic is akin to Curry's "logic$_1$" and the deviant systems to his "logics$_2$," discussed previously. Also some of the points made above were made years back, in a less developed form, by Bocheński.[24]

The deviant or alternative logics discussed thus far, some of which deny bivalence, are only a few out of many. If the reader's favorite one has not been discussed, let him only view it in the light of the foregoing comments and formulate for himself the requisite abbreviatory definitions or characterize a semantical or pragmatical metalanguage within which the primitives may be interpreted. He will thus gain, no doubt, in spite of difficulties along the way, some modicum of clarity concerning the logical structure of his language.

Many of the foregoing comments are perforce sketchy, and some of the points raised have been discussed more fully elsewhere, as already noted. Even so, it is thought useful to repeat some of them here by way of summary and as background for outlining a unified position in the philosophy of logic. The position is not put forward dogmatically, but rather in the spirit of a research programme. The study of all these matters is still in its infancy, and no doubt many surprises are in store in the future. The success of bivalence to date, however, like that of the arithmetic based on it, does suggest that it is somehow at the very foundation of our conceptual and scientific modes of procedure. And we have seen how even those who question it do so on rather dubious grounds that when clarified or "interpreted" land them somewhere in the midst of a bivalent metatheory.

In spite of all this, however, an open-ended, exploratory attitude should be maintained. The spirit of adventurous boldness should be combined with that of total humility before the greatness of tradition. Rosser and Turquette speak (p. 2) of "the inevitable risk associated with novel investigations," in which "experimenting with alternative logics" is included. They recognize, however, the dangers involved and even agree that the formulation of many-valued logics is subject to them. The dangers can be mitigated somewhat — at the expense perhaps of some sheer mathematical fun — if a suitable interpretation is insisted upon right at the beginning.

A word more about the two methods suggested concerning how to formulate deviant or alternative logics. There is the method of abbreviation and that of interpretation. In the former, one seeks to extend the deviant logic with the addition of such "hidden" predicates or variables or whatever as are needed to spell out the full behavior of the primitives. The object language becomes then much more extended than before, but with a great gain in explicitness, even though longer and usually much more complicated formulae are now needed. The other method is to keep the original, deviant object language intact, but to provide a semantics for it, usually of an explicative kind,[25] with suitable rules of designation, denotation, or whatever, for the object-language primitives.

We end up, then, with an emendation to Carnap's *Principle of Tolerance:*[26] *It is not our business to set up prohibitions, but to help arrive at the intended interpretations.* Everyone — mathematician, scientist, metaphysician, theologian, social theorist, and so on — is at liberty to formulate his own logic, his own language system, as he pleases. What is required of him, however, is that he should state his methods clearly and give exact definitions and semantical or pragmatical rules. Philosophical critique of his work should be carried out only in the spirit of helpfulness, and speculative boldness should be balanced by the restraints of what in fact has proved successful in history. The great tradition of classical, two-valued logic is not some little mathematical charade thought up yesterday, but rather appears to be "the best and most irrefrageable of human theories," the raft upon which we can safely sail in all our theorizing — not, of course, without risk. Enough evidence in its favor is at hand, however, to suggest that the continued study of it and of its application in various directions is a programme worthy of pursuit.

CHAPTER XIV

A Close Look at
Goodman's Symbol Systems

"A perfect judge will read each work of wit
  With the same spirit that its author writ;
  Survey the whole, nor seek slight faults to find
  Where nature moves, and rapture warms the mind;
  Nor lose, for that malignant dull delight,
  The generous pleasure to be charm'd with wit."
                                                    Pope

In a previous paper[1] an attempt was made to provide a sympathetic
rational reconstruction of some basic features of the kind of aesthetic
theory found in Goodman's *Ways of Worldmaking*.[2] His response to this[3]
is an interesting example of criticism of criticism that results in part from
some terminological differences. But there are deeper methodological
differences also that need to be brought into the open. Goodman's theory
of "symbol systems" needs a closer look from a logical point of view
than seems heretofore to have been given it.

Let us set the stage by quoting in full Goodman's very first paragraph:

"Richard Martin, beginning with what seems a purely terminological
dispute, ends with total rejection of most of the major theses of *Languages of Art* and *Ways of Worldmaking*. He opposes using "denotation"
to cover both verbal description (predication, naming) and pictorial representation, writing

... there is a long tradition that 'denotation' be taken more narrowly to stand for
a relation only between word and object, and not between a nonlinguistic entity
and an object. ... The behavior of 'denotes' is subject to exact semantical rules
just as 'truth' is. At this stage, it would seem unwise to run counter to such well-
entrenched usage and rules.

Very well, use whatever words you like so long as you make clear how
you are using them. But that will not satisfy him. He objects not merely
to the use of "denotation" for a relation that embraces description and
representation but to the very idea of such a generic relation and to the
very idea of a still broader relation of reference or symbolization. In a
passage amazing from one so devoted to formal systematization he
writes

157

. . . it is not clear that the relations of representing, expressing, and exemplifying are *symbolic* relations in any strict sense. Rather they are *sui generis,* each having its own structure.

and later

. . . the work of art does not *stand for* [the relata of these relations] or "take the place of them". . . . To symbolize is to take the place of for some purpose or other. A painting does not take the place of whatever it represents, expresses, or exemplifies."

Goodman goes on to ask how a word can "take the place of" a denoted nonverbal object. The phrase 'take the place of' here comes from St. Augustine's famous *aliquid pro aliquo,* and is not used as a technical one. "The real issue," he contends, however, "is not over terminology but over whether description, representation, etc. are all *sui generis.* To say that several relations are *sui generis* cannot mean that they do not have exactly the same structure; difference in structure does not preclude their having significant common properties, or their logical sum from having important properties of its own. That relations are *sui generis* can only mean that their common properties and the properties of any more general relations including them are not significant but are rather, in effect, misbegotten products of *ad hoc* couplings. I maintain that, on the contrary, description and representation have evident and important affinities, and that these relations together with exemplification and expression and many another relation have important properties common and peculiar to referential relations, where something does stand for, refer to, symbolize something else, or even itself."

Goodman intends these comments seriously, so we too should try to take them so. The relations Repr, Expr, Exmpl, for representation, expression, and exemplification, are all, for him, to be "included" (presumably in the sense of relational inclusion) in some "more general relation" and to enter into a "logical sum" (presumably in the sense of the calculus of *n*-adic relations). Any such sum, however, could only be a misbegotten product of an insignificant *ad hoc* coupling. Repr is a quadratic relation, Expr a triadic one, and Exmpl and Den (for denotation) dyadic ones. Nor could there be a more general relation "including" these, in any of the usual senses of 'more general' and 'includes'. Nor is it clear what the "common properties" of these relations are. Goodman should spell these out in explicit logical detail. Of course there may be certain "affinities," but we must then be told in logically acceptable terms precisely what they are. It is surprising that a philosopher so known for his rigor in aesthetic discussion has failed either to tell us what kind of "logical sums" he is speaking of or what properties or affinities their summands are presumed to have in common.

In the next paragraph Goodman speaks of "Martin's denial that there are any nonverbal symbols and that the relations I call symbolic have anything important in common. . . . " However, there was no such denial in the senses in which Goodman construes 'symbol' and 'symbolic'. In addition to the terminological divergence, there is here a difference of emphasis and procedure. Only *after* the various relations have been suitably symbolized and the fundamental rules for them laid down, is it fruitful — or even possible, really — to determine their interconnections. Goodman has not here even taken the first step. Nonetheless, as he notes, he is "by no means suggesting that the specific differences between [among] these relations be overlooked; rather, recognition of genera that embrace several relations invites examination of the differentia among the species, with the goal an organized basis for a general theory of symbols." This splendid statement is wholly in accord with the attempt of the *SAR* paper, *to organize such a basis in what is hoped is a logically sound way.* One would have thought that Goodman himself would already have done this, but alas he has not.

But even suppose for a moment that it were denied that Goodman's symbolic relations, including denotation, "have anything important in common." "Such a stance blocks," so we are told, "the recognition that exemplification and expression are alike in running in the opposite direction from denotation, and that their difference from each other depends upon the difference between the literal and the metaphorical." But actually such a stance need do no such thing. Exmpl and Expr are "alike in running" from work of art α to predicate expression a, whereas Den "runs" from predicate expression to object x. These circumstances are built into the very notation, a circumstance that Goodman apparently fails to note. Further, "the difference between the literal and the metaphorical" should not determine the differences between Exmpl and Expr. Either can be either, depending upon how the theory requires that they be construed. The metaphorical is distinguished from the literal in very special ways, and these should be explicitly brought into the overall theory if it is to accommodate that distinction.[4]

Goodman thinks that it is "highly inappropriate" to refer to the various relations — which he calls 'referential' — as *aesthetic* relations "since they are as common in nonaesthetic as in aesthetic contexts." By parity of reasoning it would be inappropriate to refer to 'plus' as an arithmetical term on the ground that it is commonly used outside of arithmetic, or 'atom' as a term of physics on the ground that it is used elsewhere. No, the paradigmatic uses of expressions for the relations under discussion are from aesthetics — a new, technical kind of aesthetics that is in the making — and hence the relations seem properly termed 'aesthetic relations'. Referential relations, on the other hand, are those interrelating word and object — according anyhow to the usual terminology.

Goodman objects that the relation Exmpl for exemplification is not construed, as Repr and Expr are, as requiring a parameter for the painter or viewer. To construe it thus, however, is fully in accord with Goodman's own statement (*WW,* p. 65) "that the picture makes manifest, selects, focuses upon, exhibits, heightens in our consciousness. . . ." certain properties. It is the picture thus that bears Exmpl to the property. Now, however, in his comments here, Goodman wants a broader relation, which we may symbolize in context by

$$\text{`}\alpha \text{ Exmpl'}_p \; a\text{'}$$

that α exemplifies for p the "property" a. No harm can arise from adding this second exemplification relation to the list of useful aesthetic relations. However, Goodman's reason for wanting such a relation is obscure. "But if which things a given label labels involves such a parameter [for the painter or viewer], how can which labels label a given thing be independent of such?" he asks. Now of course Goodman can use 'label' in his own way. For an α to represent, however, is not for α to label. Nor is for α to exemplify for α to label. Nor need it be required that denotation be a form of labelling in Goodman's sense. Goodman's reason here seems like a grain of wheat in a bushel of straw.

The "curious passage" in the text, to which Goodman calls attention, concerns the referentiality of 'Exmpl'. However, Exmpl is not subsumed under Repr. Goodman misconstrues the remark that "to handle the referentiality of 'Exmpl' we needed to consider another representation relation, that between pictures and *properties* (or as here, predicates)." (Let this second representation relation be designated by 'Repr' ', so that

$$\text{`}\alpha \text{ Repr'}_p \; a\text{',}$$

is the appropriate atomic form in which it occurs.) He construes this "curious passage" as saying: "In other words exemplification, though not subsumed under reference, is subsumed under representation, so that depiction and expression are species of representation in general!" The "other words" here are those of Goodman, but neither those of the text nor in accord with those of the text. The use of 'representation relation' here is not "abnormal" and the passage does not "group" exemplification under representation. Nor does it obscure, as Goodman says it does, "the difference in direction of reference between a relation that runs from label to labelled and another that runs from labelled to label (or correlated feature) — the difference between a relation *R* and another that is a subrelation of the converse of *R*. "

The use of 'label' and 'labelled' here is not sufficiently exact — 'name' and 'named' would be better or the Frege-Carnap 'designator' and 'designated'. But in any case, Exmpl, Repr, Expr, and Den all "run" in the appropriate directions, as is evident from the atomic contexts in which they occur. Goodman apparently does not seem to object to these contexts. However, no one of these four relations is a "subrelation of the converse of the other." Nor is the relation Exmpl', as relativized to person *p*, a subrelation of the converse of Expr. They "run" in the same direction. But Repr', Expr, and Exmpl all have the same (first) domain, middle (or second) domain, and converse (or third) domain, and thus could significantly be taken as a subrelation of one another (as appropriate) if the theory of them so demands. This is a matter that can be left open for the moment, pending further study. But still, all of them are to be distinguished sharply from denotation, as taken either in the sense of 'Den' or in Alonzo Church's use of it (essentially that of the Frege-Carnap designation relation).

The use of 'reference' is too vague for philosophical purposes and seems best replaced by more exact words, as has been urged in VIII above. 'Referentiality' can then be retained as a loose, abstract term, for typical or paradigmatic denotation- or designation-like relationality between word and object or objects.[5]

Goodman notes two further presumed "faults" in the discussion in *SAR,* the second of which is "that expression [for Martin] is always of feelings or emotions possessed by the observer of a work." Again, this is not a correct statement of the view. It is true that *ExprR2* in the text requires that where α Expr$_p$ *a, a* must be a predicate for a feeling. Goodman fails to observe that 'Expr' is taken only in the sense of *veridical* expression, so that if

$$\langle \alpha, \mathrm{Expr}, p, a \rangle e$$

then also

$$\langle e', \mathrm{Of}_{\mathrm{Poss}}, p \rangle e$$

where *a* Den *e'*.

Goodman wishes to construe expression not in this sense but rather "metaphorically." "A feeling expressed by a work need not be experienced or literally possessed by the work itself." It behooves Goodman to give an exact definition of, or rules concerning, expression as construed in this sense. Metaphorical expression should not be confused with veridical expression in the sense of 'Expr'.

The other "fault," if such it be, is that "expression is not always of feelings or emotions; a black-and-white drawing may express motion, weight, or even color." Why not say here instead that it expresses a feeling of motion, or a feeling appropriate to motion, weight or color — using one of Zellig Harris's appropriateness relations? The difference here seems to be one primarily of wording.

"We read in vain," according to A. B. Johnson[6], "if we look into a book as we look into a mirror, and receive back nothing but a reflection of our own familiar lineaments." Goodman seems not to wish to allow aesthetics to develop beyond the confines he has given it. He seems to want no new or additional clarity of the kind that only the explicit use of logical notation, and of semantical systems embodying it, can give. Any deviation, however slight, from the letter of his law is to him unacceptable. In particular he shows no interest in the *rules needed to characterize the aesthetic relations.* Nor has he anywhere shown interest in, nor understanding of, the semantical rules governing denotation. As a consequence, he is unable to state precisely either the affinities or the differences among these various rules governing the aesthetic relations, on the one hand, and denotation, on the other. Also he seems not to realize that the very notion of a *symbol system,* to which he has given lip service, is determined wholly by its vocabulary, and the various kinds of rules governing that vocabulary. The result is that Goodman's conception of what a symbol system is is vague and inadequate. We must start over from scratch.

In his last paragraph Goodman chops off illicitly the quotation from the last paragraph of *SAR* and ends with an ironic 'Indeed'. He should have quoted the paragraph in full. "We must all be grateful," it states, "to Goodman for his valuable clarificatory comments and positive suggestions. At the same time we must lay the foundations for aesthetic analysis more firmly than he has done in preparation for the work ahead." To this one can indeed properly say "Indeed."

CHAPTER XV

On Minds and Their Brains:
Sir John Eccles

"Nature to all things fix'd the limits fit,
And wisely curb'd proud man's pretending wit.
As on the land while here the ocean gains,
In other parts it leaves wide sandy plains;
Thus in the soul while memory prevails,
The solid power of understanding fails;
Where beams of warm imagination play,
The memory's soft figures melt away.
One science only will one genius fit;
So vast is art, so narrow human wit:
Not only bounded to peculiar arts,
But oft in those confin'd to single parts."

Pope

In *The Self and Its Brain*[1], Sir John Eccles hypothesizes (p. 355–356) "that the self-conscious mind is an independent entity that is actively engaged in reading out from the multitude of active centres in the modules of the liaison areas of the dominant cerebral hemisphere. The self-conscious mind selects from these centres in accord with its attention and its interests and integrates its selection to give the unity of conscious experience from moment to moment. It also acts back on the neural centres. Thus it is proposed that the self-conscious mind exercises a superior interpretive and controlling role upon the neural events by virtue of a two-way interaction. . . . It is proposed that the unity of conscious experience comes not from an ultimate synthesis in the neural machinery but in the integrating actions of the self-conscious mind on what it reads out from the immense diversity of neural activities in the liaison brain."

Eccles bases the details needed by way of background for his hypothesis upon much experimental work on the brain and its neurology, on the one hand, and upon Popper's theory concerning the "three worlds," on the other. These latter, it will be recalled, consist of (i) "the world of physical objects or physical states," (ii) "the world of states of consciousness, or of mental states, or perhaps of behavioural dispositions to act," and (iii) the "third world of objective spirit," that of the *"objective contents of thought,* especially of scientific and poetic thoughts and of works of art."[2] The experimental work presupposed is of far-reaching significance, especially as concerns the dominant or left hemisphere of the brain, and has been provided by a number of distinguished neurologists.

It has been suggested in a previous paper that all the inhabitants of Popper's three worlds find their rightful place in the ontology of the general theory of events, discussed and presupposed in the various papers above.[3] Eccles' use of the three-worlds terminology thus seems *ad hoc* and everything he says may be said equally well, and logically more simply, in terms of a more unified ontology. Also the neurological "facts" presupposed are under continual discussion and critique, and we must always be careful not to let any metaphysical view depend too intimately upon the latest scientific statements from any one dominant laboratory or as based upon any one general point of view. At the same time, any metaphysical view that neglects such statements may do so at its peril. What should be sought is a metaphysical view that can be brought into accord with such statements in principle, so to speak, with the details of the accord left open to accommodate improvements or alternatives should this be found necessary. A metaphysical view must thus be partly in and partly beyond the science of its time — like St. Theresa, partly in and partly out of doors.[4]

Eccles comments (p. 358) that "in general terms there are two theories about the way in which the behaviour of an animal (and a man) can be organized into the effective unity, which it so obviously is." These are "monist materialism plus all varieties of parallelism" and the "dualist-interactionist explanation." Any reductionist strategy, Eccles contends, "will fail in the attempt to account for the higher levels of conscious performance of the human brain," the aim of the neural sciences being "to provide a more and more coherent and complete account of the manner in which the total performance of an animal and of a human being is explicable. . . . " The key word here is 'total'. Reductionism may succeed in accounting for some of the performance, but not its total unity. The dualist-interactionist view is based on experimental results to the effect that "there are at certain sites in the cerebral hemisphere (in liaison areas) effective interactions with the self-conscious mind, both in receiving and giving," although "its role for animals and the minor hemisphere is debatable."

There are many subdivisions to be made for both of these general types of views. Curiously, Eccles neglects to mention the third general type, for views based in one way or another upon a metaphysical or objective idealism. R.W. Sperry, however, writing of a view closely allied with that of Eccles, comments that "the present interpretation would tend to restore mind to its old prestigious position over matter, in the sense that the mental phenomena are seen to transcend the phenomena of physiology and biochemistry"[5] — and hence also of course of physics. Here too there is an enormous variety of views to be distinguished, some of which are among the great historical types of metaphysical positions.[6]

In this paper, let us attempt to get at the logical core of Eccles' hypothesis concerning the self-conscious mind, or rather concerning such minds in the plural, as "independent" entities, independent of, that is, or at least not "reducible" to, just their material substrates. In any case, minds are to be taken as *values for variables* and as *relata* of some of the primitive relational notions, along with whatever else (if anything) is so taken. Of course, all manner of dependencies will be postulated, but these will not be of a reductionist kind. And in this attempt, let us try to be sure that such capacities and activities of the mind as Eccles requires are fully provided for.

Let us return to the passage quoted in the first paragraph above and note the words that are of crucial interest for present purposes: 'self-conscious', 'reading out', 'selects', 'superior interpretive and controlling role', and 'two-way interaction', and the like. How can we provide a systematic vocabularly in which expressions for the most basic of these notions may be accommodated and the various properties needed for them provided for? Well, let 'Cnsc' be a relation expression for *being conscious of* and let 'm' with or without numerical subscripts be the new style of variables for minds. Cnsc is to be construed as an intentional relation, with a Fregean *Art des Gegebenseins* built in to provide the needed "content" or intentionality. Thus it is to be significant in contexts of the form

(1)   'm Cnsc x,a',

to the effect that the mind m is conscious of the entity x as described by the one-place predicate inscription a. This form (1) is the central one needed for the theory of consciousness to be sketched. The 'x' here is a variable of widest generality, comprising in its range physical and other objects as well as minds themselves.

What now is a *self*-conscious mind? Presumably any mind that bears Cnsc to itself as taken under the universal predicate description. Thus

'SelfCnsc m' abbreviates 'm Cnsc m,'V'',

where 'V' is the expression for the universal virtual class. The only minds admitted are presumably self-conscious ones, so that we should no doubt have a meaning postulate to the effect that

$\vdash (m)m$ Cnsc m,'V', or $\vdash (m)$SelfConsc m.

Also minds are presumably the *only* entities capable of self-consciousness in this sense, so that we may even let

'Mind *m*' abbreviate 'SelfCnsc *m*'.

Now of course minds are not only self-conscious but are also conscious of other minds as well as of other kinds of entities. Among these other entities are those modules that are "selected" or "read out" from the active centres of the liaison areas of the dominant hemisphere of the individual brain. But for a general theory minds should be taken as conscious of much else, of all manner of mental occurrences and states and even of other minds, of all manner of physicochemical occurrences and entities, and of whatever else there is taken to be — in fact, of all the inhabitants of Popper's three worlds. One postulates then a multiplicity of minds, and not just a single one.

It is important to note that the relation Cnsc is not a functional relation, except under special circumstances. In general it does *not* hold that

$$(m_1)(m_2)(x)(a)((m_1 \text{ Cnsc } x,a \cdot m_2 \text{ Cnsc } x,a) \supset m_1 = m_2).$$

However, an analogous principle does hold for *x* suitably restricted to the appropriate modules in the liaison areas of a given brain. To formulate such a principle, the specific *occasions* of the mind's being conscious of its objects must be brought in. Thus

(1')   '$\langle m, \text{Cnsc}, x, a \rangle e$'

can express that *e* is such an occasion. Clearly there are occasions in which the mind is conscious of so and so, and other when it is not. The form (1) is not sufficiently sensitive to differentiate these. Fundamental use will be made of the more pliable form (1') as we go on. Also the attendant Reichenbachian principle that

$$(m)(x)(a)(m \text{ Cnsc } x,a \equiv (Ee)\langle m, \text{Cnsc}, x, a \rangle e)$$

clearly holds.

Let 'B*y*' express that *y* is a brain and '*z* M *y*' that *z* is a module, of the appropriate kind, of *y*. The '*x*' in (1) and (1') is not to be restricted just to modules but to vast sums of such, of which *m* may be conscious during some *e*. We need then to provide for mereological sums of modules sufficiently "open" for interaction to take place. Let '*x* SO *e*' express that *x* is sufficiently open during *e* in this sense, and let '*w* P *u*' express, essentially as in Leśniewski's mereology or the calculus of individuals, that *w* is a *part* of *u*. We may then define what it means to say that *x is a mereological sum of sufficiently open modules of brain y during e* as follows.

'*x* SSOM *y,e*' abbreviates '(B*y* · (E*z*)(*z* M *y* · *z* SO *e* · *z* P *x*) · (*z*)((*z* M *y* · *z* P *x*) ⊃ *z* SO *e*) · (*z*) ((*z* P *x* · ~ *z* = N) ⊃ (E*w*)(*z* P *w* · *w* M *y* · *w* SO *e* · *w* P *x*)))'.

Here N is Leśniewski's null individual. The definiens is to the effect that *y* is a brain, *x* contains at least one sufficiently open module of *y* as a part during *e*, every part of *x* that is a module of *y* is sufficiently open during *e*, and every nonnull part of *x* is a part of some part *w* of *x* that is a sufficiently open model of *y* during *e*.[7]

A *Principle of Functional Unicity* now obtains to the effect that

$$\vdash (m_1)(m_2)(x)(y)(a)(e_1)(e_2)(e_3)((\langle m_1, \text{Cnsc}, x, a \rangle e_1 \cdot \langle m_2, \text{Cnsc}, x, a \rangle e_2 \cdot x \text{ SSOM } y, e_3 \cdot e_3 \text{ During } e_1 = e_3 \cdot e_2) \supset m_1 = m_2).$$

This principle postulates that Cnsc is in fact a functional relation of a very special kind. The theory here is thus not only a relational theory of mind, but even a functional one of a suitably restricted kind.

Along with the Principle of Functional Unicity there is a also a *Principle of Functional Existence*, that

$$\vdash (x)(y)((Ee_1)x \text{ SSOM } y, e_1 \supset (Em)(Ea)(Ee_2)(\langle m, \text{Cnsc}, x, a \rangle e_2 \cdot (e_3)(e_3 \text{ During } e_2 \supset x \text{ SSOM } y, e_3))).$$

Clearly also there are many further principles that obtain concerning the types of symmetry, assymetry, transitivity, intransitivity, reflexivity, and so on, appropriate for triadic relations. And also there are suitable principles concerning the modes of variation allowed here in the modes of description — e.g., they may be paraphrases of each other or synonymous.

We must ask now for the sense in which the self-conscious mind in an "independent" entity. Are we to postulate that

$$(Em) \sim (Ex)(Ey)(Ea)(Ee)(x \text{ SSOM } y, e \cdot \langle m, \text{Cnsc}, x, a \rangle e),$$

that there is at least one mind not conscious of any of the appropriate modules of any brain? Such a mind is not only independent but also "disembodied." Are there any such? A strong metaphysical idealism, such, for example, as that of Peirce[8], does not hesitate to make such a postulation. It is not clear that Eccles, however, has any other meaning of 'independent' to fall back upon here. Nor is it clear that he would be willing to adopt so strong an assumption. More will be said about independence in a moment.

Some further primitives are needed for the mental activities of *scanning*, of *being interested in*, of *attending to*, of *selecting*, and of *unifying* as "bringing into a unity of conscious experience." Let

(2)   '*m* Scan *x,a*',

(3)   '*m* Int *x,a*',

(4)   '*m* Att *x,a*',

(5)   'm Sel x,a',

and

(6)   'm Uni x,a',

be the new atomic contexts for these. (2), for example, expresses that m scans x, a module or sum of such, under the description a. And similarly for the others. These mental activities of course take place as special events in time, so that actually the forms

(2')   '$\langle m, \text{Scan}, x, a \rangle e$',

(3')   '$\langle m, \text{Int}, x, a \rangle e$',

and so on, are of greater utility than (2)–(6).

Note of course that all of these forms are intentional, and presuppose the various principles concerning the relation Under, as discussed in III and IV above. In fact, there is a kind of *double* intentionality involved, one provided by the modes of description, the other by the mind variables. Are both actually needed? Perhaps just the use of the latter could be made to suffice. This is a difficult matter and any decision concerning it would involve going very much more deeply into the structure of the entire language of neurology and of the theory of the brain than can be undertaken here. This is a problem that may be left open for the present. It might well be that 'm Cncs x,a', and so on, could be defined only where a is a specific shape. Thus, for example, where a is the predicate 'table', 'm Cnsc x,a' could perhaps be defined in view of the exact character of the modules of x as modules of the kind contributing to a conscious awareness of a table, table modules, so to speak, being of a very specific physicochemical character!

Covering all of these relations, Cnsc, Sel, and so on, suitable Boolean laws concerning sums, products, and negations of the modes of description (or, rather, of the virtual classes designated by the modes of description) obtain. Thus, where $\ulcorner(a \cup b)\urcorner$, $\ulcorner(a \cap b)\urcorner$, and $\ulcorner -a \urcorner$ are all defined in the usual way[9], we have that

$\vdash (m)(x)(a)(e)(\langle m, \text{Cnsc}, x, a \rangle e \supset {\sim} \langle m, \text{Cnsc}, x, \ulcorner -a \urcorner \rangle e)$,

$\vdash (m)(x)(a)(b)(e)((\text{PredConOne } a \cdot \text{PredConOne } b \cdot (\langle m, \text{Cnsc}, x, a \rangle e \vee \langle m, \text{Cnsc}, x, b \rangle e)) \supset \langle m, \text{Cnsc}, x, \ulcorner(a \cup b)\urcorner \rangle e)$,

and

$\vdash (m)(x)(a)(b)(e)((\text{PredConOne } a \cdot \text{PredConOne } b) \supset ((\langle m, \text{Cnsc}, x, a \rangle e \cdot \langle m, \text{Cnsc}, x, b \rangle e) \equiv \langle m, \text{Cnsc}, x, \ulcorner(a \cap b)\urcorner \rangle e))$.

Also there are the two rules governing the universal and null modes of description, that

$$\vdash (m)(x)(a)(m \text{ Cnsc } x,a \supset m \text{ Cnsc 'V')}$$

and

$$\vdash \sim (Em)(Ex) \, m \text{ Cnsc } x, \text{ '}\Lambda\text{'}.$$

Analogous Boolean laws hold for the other relations, Scan, Int, and so on — or, rather, for their modes of description.

The temporal sequence of the various acts of scanning, being interested in, and so on is often such that, where it holds that By, there are occasions e_1, ..., e_5 such that

$$(\langle m,\text{Scan},x,a \rangle e_1 \cdot \langle m,\text{Int},x,a \rangle e_2 \cdot \langle m,\text{Att},x,a \rangle e_3 \cdot \langle m,\text{Sel},x,a \rangle e_4$$
$$\cdot \, x \text{ SSOM } e_5 \cdot \langle m,\text{Uni},x,a \rangle e_5. \, (e_1 \text{ Before}_{\text{Time}} e_2 \vee e_1 \text{ During } e_2) \cdot$$
$$(e_2 \text{ Before}_{\text{Time}} e_3 \vee e_2 \text{ During } e_3) \cdot (e_3 \text{ Before}_{\text{Time}} e_4 \vee e_3 \text{ During } e_4) \cdot$$
$$e_1 \text{ During } e_5 \cdot e_2 \text{ During } e_5 \cdot e_3 \text{ During } e_5 \cdot e_4 \text{ During } e_5).$$

Hence each one of these relation is a kind of subrelation of Cnsc in a certain sense. Thus, for example,

$$\vdash (m)(x)(a)(e_1)(\langle m,\text{Scan},x,a \rangle e_1 \supset (Ee_2)(e_1 \text{ During } e_2 \cdot \langle m,\text{Cnsc},$$
$$x,a \rangle e_2)).$$

It might be objected that the forms (1)–(8), and also (1′)–(8′), make too much of the modules or sums of such and not enough of the activities. However, this objection can readily be overcome by noting that to scan x under a is in fact to scan x's activities. Thus

$$\vdash (m)(x)(a)(e_1)(\langle m,\text{Scan},x,a \rangle e_1 \supset (Ee_2)(Ee_3)(Eb)(x \text{ Prfm } e_2 \cdot e_2$$
$$\text{During } e_1 \cdot \langle m,\text{Scan},e_2,b \rangle e_3 \cdot e_3 \text{ During } e_1)).\text{[10]}$$

And similarly for the others.

Another remarkable role the mind is ascribed, in Eccles' theory, is that (p. 373) of "actively modifying the brain events according to its interest or desire, and the scanning operation by which it searches can be envisaged as having an active role in selection [of the modules to be modified]." Two new notions emerge here, one for *modifying,* and one for *desire.* Let

(7)   'm Mod x,a,b'

express that m modifies x as described by the predicate description a to become x as described by b. And let

(8)   'm Dsr x,b'

express that m desires that x be describable by b. Here too we need forms such as

(7')   '$\langle m, \text{Mod}, x, a, b \rangle e$'

and

(8')   '$\langle m, \text{Dsr}, x, a \rangle e$'.

Suppose now that $\ulcorner bx \urcorner$ does not obtain during e_1 but that the mind desires before e_1 that it should. To say that m modifies x *in accord with* this desire, is then to say that,

$$(\langle m, \text{Dsr}, x, b \rangle e_1 \cdot \langle m, \text{Mod}, x, a, b \rangle e_2 \cdot e_1 \text{ Before}_{\text{Time}} e_2).$$

Of course other temporal relations could hold, and the desiring might continue during the modifying. And also there are many *ways* or *kinds* of modifying that are to be brought in so that Mod here is no doubt a logical sum of considerable complexity of various relations.

Thus far we have been considering only the *agentive* character of the mind, so to speak, its active role in mind-brain interaction. There is also its *passive* or patiential role to consider. A whole new set of primitive relations is needed to provide for this. It may be presumed that such a set could readily be picked out and accommodated within the kind of framework here.

Note now that the four main characteristics (pp. 361–362) Eccles requires of the mind are here in fact provided for. "(1) There is a unitary character about the experiences of the self-conscious mind. There is concentration now on this, now on that, aspect of the cerebral performance at any one instant. This focussing is the phenomenon known as *attention*. . . . " (2) There are suitable relations providing for interaction between mind and neural events. "(3) There can be a temporal discrepancy between neural events and the experiences of the self-conscious mind." And (4) there "is the continual experience that the self-conscious mind can effectively act on the brain events. This is most overtly seen in voluntary action . . . , but throughout our waking life we are deliberately invoking brain events when we try to recall a memory or to recapture a word or phrase or to express a thought or to establish a new memory." Clearly all four of these items can be provided for in the theory here, if we presuppose that a suitably extensive primitive vocabulary is available.

Eccles claims (pp. 374–375) that his "strong dualist-interactionist hypothesis . . . has the recommendation of its great explanatory power. It gives[,] in principle at least[,] explanations of the whole range of problems relating to brain-mind interaction. . . . But most importantly it restores to the human person the senses of wonder, of mystery and of value. . . . Finally, it can be claimed that the hypothesis belongs to science because it is based on empirical data and is objectively testable. . . . " and "is not refuted by any existing knowledge."

That the hypothesis has explanatory power need not be denied, but that it "belongs to science" might well be doubted. It is unnecessary to hypothesize minds whose only role in the theory is to perform certain actions, either as agent or as patient, that in fact *can be described in a vocabulary in which all reference to minds can be deleted*. To see this, note that, although '*m*' occurs as a parameter for minds in (1)–(8), and so on, the mind is taken in these forms merely as an agent or patient for what in fact it does or performs. The *performances* are the items of importance. Thus we could take

(1″) $\qquad\qquad\qquad$ '$\langle \text{Cnsc},x,a\rangle e$',

(2″) $\qquad\qquad\qquad$ '$\langle \text{Scan},x,a\rangle e$',

and so on, as the basic forms, and reconstruct the entire foregoing theory in terms of them without the variables for minds. And similarly for the forms providing for the mind's role as the patient or recipient of neural actions. There need then be no reference to minds as such but all of the remarkable actions they are purported to perform, either as agent or patient, remain intact. The resulting view is a *performative* or *actional* theory of mind. The mind is as the mind does. Of course the event variables '*e*', and so on, are needed fundamentally, and amongst these values are mental acts and states, as in X above. Such states and acts are surely legitimate fodder for careful scientific study, but whether minds as such are, as divorced somehow or "independent" of what they do, may well be doubted. Eccles seems here to have overstated his position.

Another way of viewing this matter is to note that Eccles in effect assumes as a fundamental law a statement to the effect that

$$(x)(a)(e)(\langle \text{Cnsc},a,x\rangle e \supset (Em)m \text{ Prfm } e),$$

that every state or act of consciousness, so to speak, has a mind as its performer or doer or possessor or whatever. (And prominent among the doings here are being the agent of or being the patient of, so that

$$(m)(e)((m \text{ Agent } e \text{ v } m \text{ Patient } e) \supset m \text{ Prfm } e).)$$

The question arises as to whether this assumption is a "scientific" law. Probably it is not — at least not yet, at the present stage of research. In any case, it is surely not a law concerning the neurology of the brain. All that we wish to be able to say "scientifically" about consciousness can be said without it. Only within a wider metaphysical framework would such a law be appropriate. Similar comments obtain concerning the analogous laws for Sel, Att, and so on.

The necessity of having minds as such and as values for variables would seem to arise only when we need modes of speech, i.e., atomic sentential forms, in which minds are spoken of quite independently of their brains. (1) is such a form, but actually is dispensable. Eccles uses the phrase 'the self-conscious mind' as a whole and without analysis, the real experimental nitty-gritty of his theory being formulable in terms of (2)–(8) and the forms needed for patiency. Eccles' self-conscious minds seem thus in no way independent of their brains and are intimately linked to them in the marvelous ways he and his fellow workers have described as a result of experimental work of the highest importance surely.

Minds as such and as values for variables are needed when we turn to locutions in which two or more minds may be talked about irrespective of their brains. To say that m_1 is conscious of m_2, or that m_1 understands m_2, or the like, would be examples, provided that 'is conscious of' and 'understands' are not explained away reductively. A key problem for Eccles would seem to be that of how the various brain-dependent minds are related to each other. Also if these minds are available as values for variables, should we extend mereology to provide for such so as to con-done a "group" mind? And all minds whatsoever to form something like a Universal Mind? And from the notion of a Universal Mind that of an Absolute Mind would not be too far remote. All of these steps would, in the words of Sperry already quoted, "tend to restore the mind to its old prestigious position over matter," and would be a natural step to take if minds are taken as values for variables in the first place. All nonmental entities can then readily be provided for by an adaptation of some Hegelian-like theory of *manifestation* and/or *embodiment*. [11]

Eccles thinks that his strong, dualist, interactionism "restores to the human person the senses of wonder, of mystery, and of value." A strong metaphysical idealism does this also, and perhaps more simply. If mind — or minds — are taken as the fundamental entities, the road is well paved for a *theory* of wonder and mystery and value — a theory of them and of their interrelations and not just a comment or two. The full logical complexities of such a theory seem never to have been discussed at any depth. In such areas, to say nothing of the higher reaches of aesthetics and of theology, Eccles' hypothesis — or a suitable idealist variant of it — would no doubt come into its own.

Eccles claims, as noted above, that his hypothesis is "based on empiri-cal data and is objectively testable. ... " and "is not refuted by any existing knowledge." Here too, the empirical foundations need not be denied, but the objective testability is not of the existence of self-conscious minds but of states and actions of certain kinds. And although the hypothesis is not refuted by what we now know, neither is its denial in which of course the mental actions may be retained intact. Nor is the idealist extension of Eccles' hypothesis refuted by what we now know or perhaps ever will know. The theory of manifestation and embodiment, although not empirically based or empirically testable in any usual sense, is presumably of a metaphysico-hypothetical kind above refutation.

It might be objected that the formalization above of some of Eccles' notions is too simple and fails to capture the full neurological theory presupposed together with all that he wishes to say scientifically about the mind. To capture all of the former, of course, would be very difficult, a task of the kind undertaken by Woodger for cytology and some portions of genetics.[12] And to capture all of the latter would require that a full characterization of the scientific character of the mind be given. Such an objection thus would miss the key point concerning the need, or lack of it, of having variables taking self-conscious minds as values for variables. If we were to continue the search for all of the notions Eccles needs for the full peroration of his theory, there is no reason to think that we would at any point need forms differing in any fundamental way from $(1'')$, $(2'')$, and so on.

Finally, it is to be observed that Sir John need not disagree in the least with the points raised here. He himself comes very close to their spirit if not to their letter. "As we have developed our hypothesis," he notes (p. 552), "we have returned to the views of past philosophies that the mental phenomena now are ascendant over the material phenomena." And also "the creative imagination is being driven by the self-conscious mind into flights of imagination which of course are the greatest achievements of humanity. . . . Now this achievement again we are crediting to the self-conscious mind in the first place. . . . " Eccles then asks the very fundamental metaphysical questions: "What is the self-conscious mind? How does it come to exist? How is it attached to the brain in all its intimate relationships of give and take? How does it come to be? And in the end, not only how does it come to be, but what is its ultimate fate when, in due course, the brain disintegrates?" The mere asking of these questions veers in a metaphysical direction, and some of the abiding "past philosophies" have responded to them in ways that no advances in science or analytical philosophy have been able to improve on. It is perhaps a pity that Sir John pays no attention to these and relies wholly by way of philosophic background on a rather pallid theory of the three worlds. Something much stronger and theoretically exciting is needed to give his hypothesis its proper metaphysical setting.

CHAPTER XVI

On the Philosophical Challenge
of Intuitionistic Logic

"Se non è vero è ben trovato."

In his provocative paper "Intuitionistic Logic: A Philosophical Challenge,"[1] Dag Prawitz, following somewhat the lead of Michael Dummett, contends that there is a "real conflict between classical and intuionistic logic and that at most one of them can be "correct." Classical logic is set forth as a system of universally valid canons of reasoning" but for our "deductive practice," both in mathematics and philosophy, we "should be able to formulate explicitly what kind of reasoning is correct." Strictly, we should distinguish here between "validity" and "correctness," the former being a purely theoretical term of semantics, the latter a pragmatical or praxiological one. After distinguishing them, we can then study the way in which they are interrelated. Prawitz thinks that "neither practice nor theory has priority [over the other] but that both support each other." Yes, surely, but strictly, here again, we should distinguish not only theory from practice, but both of these from the *theory of practice*. Actually it is this latter that Prawitz is concerned with primarily.

Of what does the theory of practice consist? "In the case of our deductive practice," Prawitz tells us, "the theoretical level contains not only logical laws but principles about ontology, truth, and meaning. The dispute between classical and intuitionistic logic has to be resolved by finding an equilibrium between our inferential practice and a comprehensive theory that includes all these principles and makes our practice intelligible." Meaning, for Prawitz as with Dummett and philosophers in the Wittgensteinian tradition, is to be gotten at by the study of use. Thus the theory of practice will contain not only "logical" laws but also some semantics (concerned with ontology and truth) and some principles about use, i.e., some pragmatics. But what logical laws are contained in "the theoretical level" of the theory of use? Intuitionistic ones or classical ones? We are not told. If we view the matter from the point of view of a suitably developed pragmatics, we can gain a clear answer to this question and at the same time hope to gain a viable approach to intuitionistic logic itself.

Let us sort out the various terms of which Prawitz makes fundamental use. He speaks of "deductive practice," note, rather than of deduction *per se*. Some such practice is "correct" but not all. Deduction *per se* can be well characterized in an exact syntactical way, either within a syntax based upon sign designs or within one based on sign events or inscriptions.[2] Deductive practice, on the other hand, is something human beings, computers, and the like *do* or *carry out*. Deductive practice may or may not conform to the syntactical and/or semantical principles of deduction taken as paradigmatic. Strictly, we should speak of "correct deduction" only in connection with deductive practice. The very use of 'correct' here presupposes that some logical rules be available against which the correctness of deductive practice can be measured. It has been argued elsewhere that these rules are always best taken to be of the usual classical kind.[3]

Prawitz notes that "the conflict between classical and intuitionistic logic raises not only the question about which logic is correct but also the question how one argues about the correctness of a logical law." This question is analogous to the question as to how one might argue for the correctness of a law of real arithmetic, say. The answer is that one always considers any disputed law in the full context of the environing theory, and then reflects upon what that law adds or subtracts, so to speak, in that theory. And of course change in one law necessitates change in a good many others. The stupendous success of real arithmetic, in both mathematics and its applications, speaks well for the acceptability of its constituent laws. The success has been such as to make it paradigmatic in a certain way. So, likewise, with classical, first-order logic; there is no need to tamper with its laws and nothing to be gained by doing so, as has been urged in XIII above. Whatever is of value in the various so-called "alternative" logics can be achieved by spelling out in full the entire vocabulary needed to formulate them and then by stating explicitly the various principles or meaning postulates needed to characterize that vocabulary. Of course we should not be dogmatic on the subject so much as to observe that the achievements of classical, first-order logic are so formidable as to justify a research programme in which it is taken as fundamental and in terms of which the interpretation of alternative logics may be given. Thus there is no need to "argue" for classical laws so much as to see how, in exploratory fashion, they are able to perform the tasks required of them. The same could be said of the laws of real arithmetic and of other areas of well-developed mathematics.

Let us return now to the list of pragmatical notions Prawitz makes use of. There is the notion of *assertion*, which is to be distinguished sharply from that of a sentence or statement. There is also the notion of the *use* of a sentence or statement. Prawitz follows Wittgenstein and Dummett in construing meaning in terms of use. We are not then to think of meaning in a Frege-Church-Carnap way in purely semantical terms, but pragmatically in terms of suitable acts of use. Unfortunately we are not told much as to what these uses are. One important type would be that of *accepting,* another *uttering,* others *apprehending, questioning, exclaiming, subjunctivizing,* and so on.[4]

Prawitz also makes fundamental use of a notion of truth, but leaves it open as to how it is to be construed, whether "classically" or in some other way. As a matter of fact, however, it is not clear that there is any other way, at least none developed with the necessary rigor and explicitness of detail. Further, truth is in its very nature a classical concept. For meanings, construed technically, there are of course alternatives. The classical view of meaning, in Prawitz's terms, is that "the meaning of a sentence consists in the condition for its truth." This is attributed to Frege and Carnap, but actually is closer to the views of Schlick, Feigl, and Davidson, among others. The occurrence of 'truth' in the statement of the view is, however, the classical notion of truth, not an intuitionistic one, contrary to what Prawitz seems to suggest. Suppose 'truth' were replaced by some more or less intuitionistically acceptable phrase, such as John Dewey's 'warranted assertibility'. It would not be the case that the classical view is that the meaning of a sentence is the condition of its warranted assertibility, for this latter is already an intuitionist, or at least quasiintuitionist, view. Truth and various illicit surrogates for it should be kept quite distinct.[5] Prawitz speaks as though "the principle that a truth condition either obtains or does not obtain independently of our means of knowing which case is the actual one" is an assumption. On the contrary, it would seem, this "principle" helps us to see that a truth condition is not to be conflated with a means of knowing it, and thus that 'true' and 'known to be true' or 'accepted as true' or whatever should be handled very differently *ab initio.*

There seems to be some confusion in what Prawitz says about the Tarskian theory of truth. He seems to conflate the definition of the predicate 'Tr' for truth with the condition of *adequacy* for such a definition. He speaks as though all the full theory of truth gives us is that the extension of the predicate for truth "is a set S determined by a number of equivalences of the form '$A \in S$ if and only if P'," — "where P is the proposition expressed by A." Strictly the theory does not give us even this — there is no theory of "propositions" in Tarski's work and no theory as to how sentences "express" propositions. What Prawitz should say here is that, in the metalanguage in which 'Tr' is defined, all formulae of the form

(T)   '$A \epsilon \mathrm{Tr} \equiv p$',

where in place of 'p' the sentence (or translation of such) of which 'A' is a structural-descriptive name is inserted, obtain or are provable. The '$\equiv$' is the classical one, and the translation is that of A in the metalanguage. But of course the theory of truth gives us a good deal more than this. It contains a full syntax of the object language and in fact the full resources of the object language (or its translation) itself, hence its axioms, rules, and so on. Thus the members of Tr are genuinely the truths of the object language.

Note incidentally that Prawitz confuses the mention and use of expressions. 'A' is used in 'A or not-A' as a sentence, but in '$A \epsilon S$' as the name of a sentence. One can, of course, if one wishes blur this distinction — as Hintikka on occasion not only does but even goes so far as implicitly to recommend — but if one does one cannot grasp the full significance of Tarski's work, to say nothing of its inner details.

Prawitz comments to the effect that "if all we know about the concept of truth is ... a number of equivalences of the form '$A \epsilon S$ if and only if P', then the information A is true ... if and only if P cannot possibly give information also about the meaning of A. For all we know, S may be, e.g., the set of false sentences." If S is taken as the Tarskian Tr, however, and P is taken in the proper sense, then of course S cannot be taken as the set of false sentences, for it is provable that all axioms (including all purely logical ones) are members of it, being themselves provable. (Suppose α is an axiom. Then $\vdash \alpha$. But by (T), $\vdash (A \epsilon \mathrm{Tr} \equiv \alpha)$, where '$A$' is the structural-descriptive name of 'α'. Hence $\vdash A \epsilon$ Tr, and $\vdash\, \sim A \epsilon$ Fls, where Fls is the set of false sentences.) And even on Prawitz's grounds, S could not be the set of false sentences for then P would have to be the *negation* of the "proposition expressed by A."[6]

Prawitz's point that "the classical theory of meaning is too poor to cast any light upon the notions of meaning and truth, let alone to give any guide in resolving the conflict between classical and intuitionistic logic" seems curiously askew. The classical theory of meaning presupposes the classical theory of truth and is meaningless without it. If, however, meaning is construed as use, then of course the classical theory is poor indeed — it was never intended to supply a theory of use. The point is that for the development of a theory of meaning as use, we must go on to formulate explicitly principles in terms of specifically pragmatical notions, e.g., those mentioned above, assertion, acceptance, and so on.

Prawitz attributes to Dummett the view "that there are two main features of the use of an expression: the rules governing in what situations the expression is appropriately uttered and those governing the appropriate responses or expectations that follow upon uttering the expression; schematically, the conditions for uttering the expression and the consequences of it. If the expression is an assertive sentence, the first feature is the conditions for asserting it, i.e., the grounds on which it is correct to assert it, and the second feature is determined by the conclusions that can be inferred from the sentence." In the main Prawitz accepts this view and thinks that a theory of use can be gained in terms essentially of "Gentzen's introduction rules or Heyting's explanation of the notion of proof. . . . " However, as we shall now try to show, any adequate theory of meaning as use must contain a good deal more than can be provided in any such way as this.

In the first place, the linguistic "expressions" must be subdivided in some suitable way, the most important being sentences as wholes. In fact, it is only these latter that Prawitz speaks of here, and, to simplify, let us follow him in this. However, as a final theory such a simplification will never do. The notion of a "situation" is ambiguous, there being also the *nonlinguistic* circumstances that enter into and in part determine use as well as usage. When we speak of use we should also be taking actual usage into account, the theory of the two being so closely intertwined. Also there is much more than just utterance to take into account; as already suggested, there are questioning, exclaiming, and so on. The notion of being "appropriately uttered" must be supplemented by a theory of the appropriateness of the other types of linguistic acts. Also there are the appropriate "responses or expectations" aroused in the hearer or recipient of the utterance, assertion, question, or whatever. A pragmatical vocabulary for all of these notions should be at hand, together with many more, if we are to get on with the task of delineating a theory of meaning as use, and therewith of the Dummett-Prawitz interpretation of intuitionistic logic.

Let us tarry a moment longer with the notion of utterance. The minimal adequate form for present purposes, in a systematized pragmatics, would seem to be

(1) $\qquad\qquad$ '$p \, \text{Utt}_e \, a,b,e',q$',

expressing that person p utters on occasion e the sentence a (of the object language) on the accepted appropriate evidence b, in the appropriate circumstances e', to person q as hearer or recipient.[7] Utt is thus a hexadic relation, with a person as agent, an occasion, a sentence, an evidential sentence, a nonlinguistic circumstance, and a patient or recipient as its relata. All of these factors are at least implicit in Prawitz's account, and it is good to bring them out into the open in a suitable notation. (1) can no doubt be defined in terms of some of the fundamental relations needed for the theory of logical form, as

'(p Agent e · ⟨Utt⟩e · a Object e · b ApropEvid$_e$ a · e' Approp e · e' Cir e · q Patient e)'.

Here Agent is the relation of being an *agent* of, and Patient, of being a *patient* of. The clause

'b AppropEvid$_e$ a'

may be defined as

'(b Approp e · b Evid a)',

that b bears of one of Zellig Harris's *appropriateness* relations to e and that b gives (suitable) evidential support to a.[8] The clause 'e' Cir e' expresses that e' is the (mereological sum of the) nonlinguistic circumstances surrounding e.

What a task we have on our hands to give a full, or even partial, account of all these, and allied notions! Nothing less, however, would even begin to do justice to the complexities of a theory of meaning as use. And even so, we have left out any account of the appropriate responses and expectations aroused in the hearer and of the circumstances surrounding such. And then we should go on to questions, exclamations, and so on, as already noted, and, then, to reflect upon the use of expressions other than full sentences. The sentence as a whole, however, does seem to be the main vehicle of use, although by no means the only one.

Prawitz proposes that "the notion of truth ... [be] replaced by the condition for a correct assertion" and then used "as a constitutive element in a meaning theory." The motive for such a replacement, however, is not clear. It seems best to keep the predicate 'Tr' in essentially its classical sense — although we shall have to part from Tarski's account in all manner of details — and to characterize 'correct assertion' as clearly as we can within a pragmatics already containing a predicate for truth and its ambient theory. What now is a correct assertion? One way of construing an assertion is as a simultaneous acceptance and utterance.[9] Person p then asserts correctly a sentence a provided he both accepts and utters it on some occasion under the appropriate provisos. Thus we may let

(2)   'p CrctAssrt$_e$ a,b,e',q' abbreviate '(p Utt$_e$ a,b,e', q · p Acpt$_e$ a,b,e' · Tr a)',

where the clause containing ' Acpt ' has its obvious reading.

The theory concerning the various logico-linguistic relations Utt, Agent, and so on, is developed in terms of the standard truth functions and quantifiers and is such that a classical predicate for the truth of the sentences of the object language is automatically forthcoming, as already suggested. The distinction between object and metalanguage used in all this is quite essential for any notion of truth of the classical kind. Prawitz seems not to distinguish with sufficient clarity the different levels of language, but tends to want all packed into a language at some one level. Such packing is legitimate provided the level be a metalinguistic one sufficiently high in the hierarchy and that a metalanguage of next higher level be in the offing if needed.[10]

Prawitz complains that "the classical theory of meaning and truth is certainly unable to explicate the conditions for correct assertions." But of course it was never intended to, as already noted. The theory governing the forms (1) and those of the definiens of (2) (and hence that of its definiendum) involves much more, as we have seen. It is thus quite incorrect to contend that "the notion of truth gets its fundamental characteristics from its relation to the conditions for correct assertions and is explicated in terms of these conditions." Truth here is being mistaken for "in-principle-possible-to-assert-correctly". This latter may well be a notion of sufficient interest to justify an extensive analysis of it. In particular the use of 'possible' here needs explication — possible in what sense? A pragmatic theory of meaning should not, it would seem, be based upon an unexplicated notion of possibility. Also the admission of deictic expressions in the sentences must be considered. A classical notion of truth for occasion sentences is directly forthcoming.[11] But an occasion sentence may be in principle possible to be asserted correctly in some circumstances, as well as its negative in others, contrary to what Prawitz suggests.

Let us reflect for a moment on the law of excluded middle as construed within intuitionistic mathematics. Fundamental to this latter is the notion of a proof, or rather the notion of *constructing* a proof, a kind of activity performed by the working mathematician. Let

(3)   '⟨Constr⟩e'

express that e is an activity of constructing an intuitionistically acceptable proof. In context, e will be something performed *by* someone and *of* a certain mathematical statement. Thus

(4)   'p Constr$_e$ a' may presumably abbreviate '$(p$ Agent $e \cdot$ ⟨Constr⟩$e \cdot e$ Of$_{Object}$ $a)$'.

What now would any purported intuitionistic law of excluded middle state? Not that

$$(p)(e)(p \; \mathrm{Constr}_e \, a \lor \sim p \; \mathrm{Constr}_e \, a),$$

nor that

$$((Ep)(Ee)p \; \mathrm{Constr}_e \, a \lor \sim (Ep)(Ee)p \; \mathrm{Constr}_e \, a),$$

nor that

$$(p)(e)(p \; \mathrm{Constr}_e \, a \lor p \; \mathrm{Constr}_e \, \ulcorner \sim a \urcorner),$$

nor that

$$((Ep)(Ee)p \; \mathrm{Constr}_e \, a \lor (Ep)(Ee) \, p \; \mathrm{Constr}_e \, \ulcorner \sim a \urcorner).$$

The first and second of these are classically acceptable, but the third and fourth come closer to capturing what intuitionists would seem to understand by an unacceptable "law of excluded middle." Neither of these, however, is classically acceptable either.

If (3) and the definiendum of (4) — or suitable alternative forms — can be fleshed out in such a way as really to capture the inner content of intuitionistic mathematics, we see that this latter presupposes at the metalevel the standard classical logic. There need then be no quarrel between the two kinds of logic, the one being presupposed fundamentally by the other.

The question naturally arises as to whether, conversely, in some fashion, we could presuppose intuitionistic logic in a suitable form and then generate classical logic in full generality out of it. This would seem unlikely. In other words, given the notion of, say, in-principle-possible-to-be-asserted, it would seem unlikely that a full Tarskian truth predicate 'Tr' could be defined with its adequacy condition (T) forthcoming for all sentences of the language. In any case, this has not been shown. The burden of proof here would seem to be upon those intuitionists who somehow think their logic is more fundametnal than the classical one.

The key difference between the attitude taken here and that of Prawitz is that for him the "meaning" of the notion of truth is held in abeyance, whereas in the above it has been taken explicitly in classical terms. There would appear to be no reasons for construing truth in any other way, and it thus seems best to use some other term for some other idea.

Incidentally, throughout the discussion here there is a considerable ambiguity as to just how a classical truth predicate is to be defined. The standard Tarskian method is within a semantics as based on shapes or sign designs and within a metalanguage containing variables of higher logical type than those of the object language. Many useful alternatives to this type of semantics are available, in particular those based on inscriptions or sign events and within a language of the same logical level as the object language, but with an additional semantical primitive. For definiteness, at any point in the discussion the exact character of the metalanguage being employed should be further specified.

It is interesting to note that classical logic gives rise in a very simple way to classical syntax, a classical semantics, and a classical pragmatics. The utility and importance of these fields for the exact study of natural and scientific languages and for both analytic and constructive philosophy have been well established. Has there been any comparable development along intuitionistic lines? No, there seems to be no intuitionistic syntax, semantics, or pragmatics — of sufficient strength anyhow — and no deep analysis of the logical forms of scientific or of natural sentences in intuitionistic terms. At best intuitionism seems interesting in mathematics, and not elsewhere. These are remarkable facts to be noted as a matter of historical record. Most discussions of intuitionism, other than within mathematics, are concerned with its *interpretation,* with the meaning of its basic logical constants and quantifiers, with attempts to justify its rejection of some key logical laws, and so on. None of these items can be handled in the simple, clear-cut way that they have been handled — and successfully so — for classical logic. It can be legitimately concluded then, it would seem, that intuitionism has a long development ahead before it should be taken as a challenge to classical logic in any genuine sense, and the various points above are such as to lend strong support that no such development is needed or is even possible. The situation with intuitionistic mathematics is somewhat different, if it can in fact be fully fleshed out in terms of forms such as (3) and (4). But in such an event intuitionistic mathematics is no longer based on intuitionistic logic but rather upon a classical one containing a suitable pragmatics and theory of mental acts.

Prawitz worries at one point how we go about establishing what the logical constants are and what they mean. Recall that meaning is taken as use and therefore the question of what they mean reduces to the question of how they are used. Any attempt to answer such a question can be given only in terms of some background theory. Let us consider first the constants of intuitionistic logic, and then go on to make some suggestions concerning the use of the constants of classical logic.

The basic uses of the constants of intuitionism can be explicated in terms of the notion of an intuitionistic construction as symbolized in (3). Let now

$$\text{`}e \text{ Constr } a\text{'} \quad \text{abbreviate} \quad \text{`}(\langle \text{Constr} \rangle e \cdot e \text{ Of}_{\text{Object}} a)\text{'},$$

the definiendum here expressing that e is a construction of a. It will be helpful to have also available a disquotational form of this, so that

⌜*e* Constr *A*⌝ is defined as ⌜*e* Constr *a*⌝,

where in place of '*A*' a sentence of the language is inserted and in place of '*a*' its shape- or structural-descriptive name. Intuitionistic *logic* may now be taken as the theory of the relation Constr as taken in this disquotational sense.

Let us consider the constants for intuitionistic disjunction and negation, which are used only in contexts concerning acts of construction. We may in fact immediately define

$$⌜(A \; v_{Int} \; B)⌝ \quad \text{as} \quad ⌜(Ee)(e \; \text{Constr} \; A \; v \; e \; \text{Constr} \; B)⌝$$

and

$$⌜\rightharpoonup_{Int} A⌝ \quad \text{as} \quad ⌜(Ee)e \; \text{Constr} \sim A⌝.$$

An intuitionistic disjunction ⌜(*A* v_{Int} *B*)⌝ is thus used to express merely that there is a construction of either *A* or *B*, and an intuitionistic negation ⌜→_{Int} *A*⌝ to express that there is a construction of ⌜∼ *A*⌝. In similar fashion we may let

$$⌜⊦_{Int} A⌝ \quad \text{abbreviate} \quad ⌜(Ee)e \; \text{Constr} \; A⌝,$$

achieving thus a kind of intuitionistic assertion of theoremhood.

Concerning the relation Constr a good deal of theory of course must be forthcoming, to give these constants the requisite properties. A full axiomatization of this theory would no doubt be tantamount to an axiomatization of intuitionistic mathematics itself. Of course along the line further primitives would no doubt be needed. To attempt such an axiomatization would be a formidable task, and yet such an axiomatization is needed if intuitionistic mathematics is to be given a sufficiently clear exposition. One principle that would seem to hold concerning Constr is a *Principle of Consistency,* that

$$((Ee)e \; \text{Constr} \; A \; \supset \; \sim (Ee)e \; \text{Constr} \; ⌜\sim A⌝,$$

so that if there is a construction for a statement there is no construction for its negation. From this the stronger principle that

$$(e)(e \; \text{Constr} \; A \; \supset \; \sim e \; \text{Constr} \; ⌜\sim A⌝)$$

follows immediately. The converses of these clearly do not hold.

We see then that all formulae of the form

$$⌜(⊦_{Int} A \; \supset \; \sim \; \rightharpoonup_{Int} A)⌝$$

obtain, but not of course their converses. These forms may be strengthened to allow iterated intuitionistic negations, with suitable definitional extensions admitting constructions of constructions.

A kind of intuitionistic existential quantification may also be introduced in terms of 'Constr'. Let '*F*' stand for any virtual class of the language. Then

⌜(E*x*)$_{Int}$ *Fx*⌝ may abbreviate '(E*e*)(E*x*)(E*a*)(*a* Des *x* · *e* Constr ⌜*Fa*⌝)'.

Here Des is the semantical relation of designation.

These various definitions are highly tentative and are put forward merely as suggestions for further reflection and development. And of course they need not be acceptable to a thorough-going intuitionist, i.e., by one who rejects classical logic *in toto* or thinks that its notions "make no sense" and have no place anywhere in the whole fabric of our thought and speech. Such intuitionists tend to be rather narrow, however. The situation here is similar to that of an analysis of a poem, say, which may or may not succeed in being acceptable to its author, or to a logical analysis of a piece of scientific research which may or may not be acceptable to those who have carried it out. Also intuitionists tend to confuse the use and mention of expressions, as already noted, and to confuse 'known to be true' and similar notions with truth itself. These are both grave errors that should be corrected *au fond*. Until they are corrected, there is no possibility of any liaison with the intuitionist on his own grounds.

A final comment, in answer to the question: How can we go about the study of the meaning or use of the logical constants construed classically? Well, by reflecting upon how they are used by speakers and hearers of the language. [12] Certain *patterns* of acceptance are regarded as *normal* under appropriate conditions. Thus a person uses '·' normally, say, with regard to his or her acceptances, provided he or she accepts sentences of the form ⌜(*A* · *B*)⌝ just where he or she accepts *A* and accepts *B*. And similarly for the other constants, and for suitable pragmatical relations other than acceptance. In this way various patterns are distinguished, some of them paradigmatic, some of them characteristic only of a particular user, some of them characteristic of an entire social group. Very little detailed, experimental work in studying such patterns seems to have been carried out. Such work would seem urgently needed, however, if only to show how the pragmatics of language is intimately related to exact studies in psycho- and socio-linguistics.

CHAPTER XVII

On Purpose, Obligation, and Transcendental Semantics

"Semper aliquid certi proponendum est."
Kempis

At the very end of his useful new book on the Frege-Husserl connection, J. N. Mohanty calls attention to the field of "transcendental semantics,"[1] ending up with a position somewhat critical of Frege. "A transcendental philosophy," he writes, "will find . . . [Frege's] theory [of intensionality and sense or *Sinn*] interesting, possibly ingenious, requiring some technical virtuosity. But it is not *radical* enough. Indeed, it even presupposes that the entities in the world are objects of reference as much as the timeless senses [*Sinne*] and are just "there" available for use and "grasping." Transcendental semantics, if I may coin such a phrase, goes back to the origins of the phenomena of reference and meaningful discourse . . . in the intentional acts of consciousness and their structures. It brings to light *from within* intentionality how senseful [or meaningful] discourse is possible. This is the deeper significance of the contrast between Frege and Husserl."

It is not necessary for present purposes to reflect at all extensively upon the contrast between Frege and Husserl nor upon Mohanty's critique. But the very phrase 'transcendental semantics' is a happy one, it would seem, and helps call attention to a kind of study that has been rather neglected in most of the recent literature in both philosophic logic and in phenomenology. It is not the contrast between the views of Frege and Husserl that needs emphasis, so much as the development of a view in which the desirable features of *both* may be incorporated. It is, to put it much too simply, a Frege-*cum*-Husserl kind of theory that is very much needed and devoutly to be sought.

Mohanty agrees in recognizing this need and points out that in the Navya-Nyāya tradition of logic, which has flourished in India more or less since the fourteenth century, the necessary kind of syncretism of the logical and the cognitive, of Frege and Husserl, is achieved "by construing the mental process of reasoning as *a rule-governed succession of cognitive events* (jñānāni), the rules governing this succession being, not empirical generalizations, but Brentano-like intuitive inductions. *A cognitive occurrent* or jñāna *has a logical structure of its own, a structure that is evident to reflective analysis* . . . [italics added]. If this theory psychologizes logic [in some appropriate sense], it also logicizes the psychology of cognition."

Neither of these traditions, that of transcendental semantics nor that of Navya-Nyāya, has yet been developed at much depth, with the necessary attention to detail, and in "modern terms." This last phrase 'in modern terms' is due to Father Bocheński and is used extensively by him, in his monumental *History of Formal Logic*.[2] The use of this phrase helps to call attention to the need to reconsider whatever is under review in the light of the newer developments in logic, syntax, semantics, and pragmatics and in their applications to philosophical problems. Neither Mohanty nor workers in the Navya-Nyāya tradition have concerned themselves as yet with such matters to any great extent. Mohanty speaks of Frege's work, with a touch perhaps of condescension, as having been developed with "some technical virtuosity." Here we must distinguish Frege's contributions to the foundations of mathematics from his work in the theory of *Sinne* and the philosophy of language. And similarly for Husserl, who also contributed notably to both. Actually much of Frege's greatness is due to his stupendous technical contributions to the foundations of mathematics. And although Husserl's *Philosophie der Arithmetik* is a remarkable book, of a very different kind from those of Frege, it suffers from a lack of technical skill, unfortunately, in just the places in which it is most required. And even to this day no one with the necessary technical knowledge seems to have looked at this book in modern terms. In their philosophies of language and theories of senses or of meanings, however, neither Frege nor Husserl exhibited much technical skill, and this is perhaps one of the reasons their work in this area seems to us nowadays so unsatisfactory and in need of a careful overhaul. In the case of Frege's kind of theory, Carnap and Alonzo Church have both carried the matter further technically. The first attempt to do likewise for the Husserlian approach is apparently that of XI above. A beginning at least is made there that is in need of further development.

Quite independently of the traditions of transcendental semantics and of the Navya-Nyāya, a related type of research has recently issued in a logico-metaphysical theory of events, states, acts, and processes — call it 'event logic' or 'event metaphysics', whichever you will. It is this theory that is used in XI and will be needed in what follows. It is of a very broad generality, a kind of all-embracing theory, and is able to do what the various so-called "alternative logics" are claimed by their proponents to be able to do. (Recall XIII above.) In any case, event theory is thought to be of special utility in the study of mental acts, acts of accepting, believing, asserting, evaluating, purposing, being obliged to do, being permitted to do, and so on. A good deal will be said about these in a moment.

In particular, it should be emphasized that in event theory "the mental process of reasoning" is construed "as a rule-governed succession of cognitive events" — Mohanty's very words — "the rules governing this succession being, not empirical generalizations, but . . . intuitive inductions" resulting in *meaning postulates* in essentially Carnap's sense. In any case, "a cognitive occurrent has a logical structure of its own, a structure that is evident to reflective analysis. . . ." It is the aim of this present paper explicitly to exhibit the logical structure of certain types of mental occurrences connected with sentences concerning purpose, obligation, and allied notions.

In a recent but not yet published paper devoted to the analysis of evaluating, another type of mental process, Paul Weiss has called attention to the highly *practical* character of theoretical work of the kind under discussion — thereby helping to verify Whitehead's famous dictum to the effect that the paradox is now fully resolved that our most abstract concepts are our best and most useful instruments with which to come to understand concrete matters of fact, especially perhaps in the study of actual inference, cognitive acts, and the like. Weiss comments (MSS., p. 13) that "most of our inferences do not begin with premises known or accepted as being certainly true. Often we fail to move straightforwardly to necessitated conclusions. We begin with what is dubious, merely believed or supposed. We backtrack and qualify to end with what is only tentatively accepted. Rules governing the legitimate moves [— Mohanty's "rule-governed succession of cognitive events" —] are today being formulated by modal, intensional, and multi-valued logicians, with the result that logic is more pertinent today to the [analysis of the] reasoning of actual men than it ever had been before. So far as what logicians have achieved is ignored, . . . " — if one refuses to take the medicine the doctor prescribes — no benefits will result.

It is interesting that Weiss mentions modal, intensional, and multi-valued logics, but not the event-theoretical or transcendental-semantic ones, which may be extended to embrace *inter alia* the logics of probability and induction. What one needs is an all-inclusive logic in which the positive achievements of these various alternative logics can be accommodated without having to pay the high, inflationary prices they usually demand — excessive ontic commitment and involvement, "fuzzy" semantics, excessive and perhaps unsound or at least dubious axioms and rules, and failure to achieve the kind of "maximum logical candor" that should be aimed at. It is thought that the approach via event theory provides the kind of unified outlook required and at a reasonable price. Weiss is surely correct in thinking that logic, as construed in a sufficiently broad sense, is nowadays of greater practical as well as philosophical utility than ever before. Moreover, the more it is used the greater its helpfulness is seen to be in assuring correctness of statement and of inference and adequacy of assumptions needed for a given purpose, in bringing to light unforeseen relationships and interconnections, in leading to new insights and new problems to be investigated, and so on.[3]

In speaking of the burgeoning literature on evaluating, Weiss comments (MSS., p. 12) that the subject "suffers from two unexamined limitations: it explicitly recognizes only a few of the methods that it actually uses, and it misconstrues the import of what it does acknowledge. It is not alone [in this]. Every practical [and indeed philosophical] enterprise, I think, suffers from the same defects, though usually in different places [and ways] and with different results." On one item, however, almost all practical enterprises — insofar as they are talked or written about — seem to share the *same* defect at the *same* place, namely, an inattention to the character of the basic vocabulary needed or being used, its syntax, its semantics, its pragmatics. Let us reflect a little on this circumstance in connection with the topics of obligation and purpose, considering the latter first because of its simpler structure.

How can 'purpose' be incorporated within a suitable system? This question is altogether different from asking what our purposes *should be* in a given context. To attempt to answer this latter question in a suitably articulate way would be to have at hand the resources of that very system. And since we seem to be rather in the dark about how to characterize these and allied notions, some little attention to the system in which they may be discussed would not seem out of place.

Purposes come and go. One and the same person can *purpose* on one occasion to do such and such, but not on another when he may purpose something quite different. Some purposes or purposings are thus abiding, some not. But, clearly, to purpose is to be purposed *by* someone and *toward* such and such a desired end. Further, purposing is clearly intentional, a mental activity, the handling of which requires an intentional logic of some sort. Let

$$(1) \qquad\qquad\qquad \text{'}p \text{ Purps}_e \ e', a\text{'}$$

express that e is an act or occasion of person p's purposing to bring an occasion e' about as described by the one-place predicate a. The use of form (1) as a basic locution for talking about purposes brings in a parameter 'p' for the person, the occasion e of his purposing, and the desired state or act e' as suitably described. Alternatively, we could write (1) as '*p* Purps$_e$ (*e'* quā *a*)',

that *e* is a purposing *by p* to do *e'* quā *a*, *e'* regarded as having *a* apply to it.

An example will help us to see the usefulness of this form (1) or its alternatives. To say that I now purpose or intend to go home this evening is for me, person *p*, now to be in a certain mental state or to perform now a certain mental act *e'*. The *e'* is described by me — if I am the utterer or asserter of some appropriate instance of (1) — under the predicate 'a going-home by me this evening'. It might happen, of course, that something will come along to prevent or thwart my going home this evening, so that the *e'* will not take place. If so, the *e'* is the *null* event or state. The use of a null entity is a helpful adjunct to the theory, the null entity being, according to Leśniewski, the one entity that does not exist or occur.[4] The *e'* here, however, may be taken under all manner of predicate descriptions, whether in fact it ever occurs or not. We see thus that in the form (1) parameters are present for all the items needed in sentences stating purposes, the person *p* purposing, the act or state *e'* purposed, the *content* or mode of description *a* of the purposing, and the very act or state *e* of the purposing itself.

Readers of the foregoing papers will have observed that (1) may also be written as

'⟨*p*,Purps,*e'*,*a*⟩*e*'.

A few tentative principles concerning the relation Purps suggest themselves as follows, if we bear in mind the corresponding principles concerning the relation Under (as in III and IV above). (The notation throughout is essentially as above. 'Per' is the general predicate for human persons, 'Int' for intentional acts or states, 'Act' for acts, 'St' for states, 'PredConOne' for one-place predicate constants, 'Agent' and 'Object' for the quasigrammatical relations of being the agent of and of being the object of, and 'Before$_{Time}$' and 'During' for suitable temporal relations. '−', '∪', and '∩' are the familiar Boolean signs, significant here as applied to or as between PredConOne's. '{*e* ∋ --*e*--}' stands for the virtual class of all *e*'s such that --*e*--.)

Pr1. ⊢ (*p*)(*e*)(*e'*)(*a*)(*p* Purps$_e$ *e'*,*a* ⊃ (Per *p* · Int *e* · (Act *e'* ∨ St *e'*) · PredConOne *a* · (*e* Before$_{Time}$ *e'* ∨ *e* During *e'*) · *p* Agent *e* · *e'* Object *e* · *e'* Under$_e$ *a*)),

Pr2. ⊢ (*p*)(*e*)(*e'*)(*a*)(*p* Purps$_e$ *e'*,*a* ⊃ ∼ *p* Purps$_e$ *e'*,⌈−*a*⌉),

Pr3. ⊢ (*p*)(*e*)(*e'*)(*a*)(*b*)((PredConOne *a* · PredConOne *b*) ⊃ ((*p* Purps$_e$*e'*,*a* · *p* Purps$_e$ *e'*,*b*) ≡ *p* Purps$_e$ *e'*,⌈(*a* ∩ *b*)⌉)),

Pr4. $\vdash (p)(e)(e')(a)(b)((\text{PredConOne } a \cdot \text{PredConOne } b \cdot (p \text{ Purps}_e e',a \lor p \text{ Purps}_e e',b)) \supset p \text{ Purps}_e e', \ulcorner(a \cup b)\urcorner)$,

Pr5. $\vdash \sim (Ep)(Ee)(Ee')p \text{ Purps}_e e', `\{e'' \ni \sim e'' = e''\}'$.

Pr6. $\vdash (p)(e)(e')(a)(p \text{ Purps}_e e',a \supset p \text{ Purps}_e e', `\{e'' \ni e'' = e''\}'$.

It is to be noted that *Pr2–Pr4* have to do with the fundamental Boolean notions of the negation, logical product, and logical sum of the virtual classes under whose predicate descriptions purposed events or actions are taken. And similarly, *Pr5* and *Pr6* for the null and universal virtual classes. *Pr1*, on the other hand, is a Limitation Law, serving to stipulate the kinds of relata or arguments the relation Purps takes on.

Any theory of purpose or purposing would seem to need a relation of being a *means* of achieving what is purposed. Here too we have to do with an intensional relation in which both the means and ends are taken under given predicate descriptions. Also means and ends are *person*-relative as well as *occasion*-relative. Thus it would seem best to take as the form for handling the means-end relation a form such as

(2) $\qquad\qquad\qquad$ '$p \text{ Mns}_e e_1,a,e_2,b$',

to express that e is an occasion or act or state of person p's taking e_1 under a as being a suitable (or desirable or viable) means to achieving e_2 under b, where a and b are the relevant predicate descriptions. (2) could perhaps also be more perspicuously written in terms of '*quā*', as

'$p \text{ Mns}_e (e_1 \text{ quā } a), (e_2 \text{ quā } b)$',

or as

'$\langle p,\text{Mns},e_1,a,e_2,b\rangle e$'.

What now would the fundamental laws governing the relation Mns and analogous to *Pr1–Pr6* look like? As a first attempt to formulate such laws, within the kind of vocabulary admitted here, let us consider the following.

Pr7. $\vdash (p)(e)(e_1)(e_2)(a)(b)(p \text{ Mns}_e e_1,a,e_2,b \supset (\text{Per } p \cdot \text{Int } e \cdot (\text{Act } e_1 \lor \text{St } e_1) \cdot \text{PredConOne } a \cdot (\text{Act } e_2 \lor \text{St } e_2) \cdot \text{PredConOne } b \cdot p \text{ Agent } e \cdot e_1 \text{ Under}_e a \cdot e_2 \text{ Under}_e b \cdot (e \text{ Before}_{\text{Time}} e_1 \lor e \text{ During } e_1) \cdot (e \text{ Before}_{\text{Time}} e_2 \lor e \text{ During } e_2) \cdot (e_1 \text{ Before}_{\text{Time}} e_2 \lor e_1 \text{ During } e_2)))$,

Pr8. $\vdash (p)(e)(e_1)(a)(e_2)(b)(p \text{ Mns}_e e_1,a,e_2,b \supset (\sim p \text{ Mns}_e e_1,a,e_2, \ulcorner -b \urcorner \cdot \sim p \text{ Mns}_e e_1, \ulcorner -a \urcorner,e_2,b))$.

Pr9a. $\vdash (p)(e)(e_1)(e_2)(a)(b)(c)((\text{PredConOne } a \cdot \text{PredConOne } b \cdot \text{PredConOne } c) \supset ((p \text{ Mns}_e e_1,a,e_2,b \cdot p \text{ Mns}_e e_1,a,e_2,c) \equiv p \text{ Mns}_e$

$e_1,a,e_2,\ulcorner(b \cap c)\urcorner))$,

Pr9b. $\vdash (p)(e)(e_1)(e_2)(a)(b)(c)((\text{PredConOne } a \cdot \text{PredConOne } b \cdot \text{PredConOne } c) \supset ((p \text{ Mns}_e e_1,a,e_2,b \cdot p \text{ Mns}_e e_1,c,e_2,b) \equiv p \text{ Mns}_e e_1,\ulcorner(a \cap c)\urcorner,e_2,b))$,

Pr9c. $\vdash (p)(e)(e_1)(e_2)(a)(b)(c)(d)((\text{PredConOne } a \cdot \text{PredConOne } b \cdot \text{PredConOne } c \cdot \text{PredConOne } d) \supset ((p \text{ Mns}_e e_1,a,e_2,b \cdot p \text{ Mns}_e e_1,c,e_2,d) \equiv p \text{ Mns}_e e_1,\ulcorner(a \cap c)\urcorner,e_2,\ulcorner(b \cap d)\urcorner))$,

Pr10a. $\vdash (p)(e)(e_1)(e_2)(a)(b)(c)((\text{PredConOne } a \cdot \text{PredConOne } b \cdot \text{PredConOne } c \cdot (p \text{ Mns}_e e_1,a,e_2,b \text{ v } p \text{ Mns}_e e_1,a,e_2,c)) \supset p \text{ Mns}_e e_1,a,e_2,\ulcorner(b \cup c)\urcorner)$,

Pr10b. $\vdash (p)(e)(e_1)(e_2)(a)(b)(c)((\text{PredConOne } a \cdot \text{PredConOne } b \cdot \text{PredConOne } c \cdot (p \text{ Mns}_e e_1,a,e_2,b \text{ v } p \text{ Mns}_e e_1,c,e_2,b)) \supset p \text{ Mns}_e e_1,\ulcorner(a \cup c)\urcorner,e_2,b)$,

Pr11. $\vdash \sim (Ep)(Ee)(Ee_1)(Ee_2)(Ea)(Eb)(`\{e' \ni \sim e' = e'\}' = b \cdot (p \text{ Mns}_e e_1,a,e_2,b \text{ v } p \text{ Mns}_e e_2,b,e_1,a))$,

Pr12. $\vdash (p)(e)(e_1)(a)(e_2)(b)(c)(`\{e' \ni e' = e'\}' = a \supset ((p \text{ Mns}_e e_1,c,e_2,b \supset p \text{ Mns}_e e_1,a,e_2,b) \cdot (p \text{ Mns}_e e_2,b,e_1,c \supset p \text{ Mns}_e e_2,b,e_1,a)))$.

In addition we should presumably wish the relevant kinds of asymmetry and transitivity to hold of the Mns relation.

Pr13. $\vdash (p)(e)(e_1)(a)(e_2)(b)(p \text{ Mns}_e e_1,a,e_2,b \supset \sim p \text{ Mns}_e e_2,b,e_1,a)$,

Pr14. $\vdash (p)(e)(e_1)(a)(e_2)(b)(e_3)(c)((p \text{ Mns}_e e_1,a,e_2,b \cdot p \text{ Mns}_e e_2,b,e_3,c) \supset p \text{ Mns}_e e_1,a,e_3,c)$.

Presumably also we should have that

Pr15. $\vdash (p)(e)(e_1)(e_2)(a)(b)((p \text{ Purps}_e e_1,a \cdot p \text{ Mns}_e e_1,a,e_2,b \cdot p \text{ Do } e_1) \supset p \text{ Purps}_e e_2,b)$.

These various "principles" are put forward tentatively and as a basis for further discussion rather than as final statements of apodictic certainties. (In particular, some restrictions on the PredConOne's may be needed.) They are, as it were, mere first attempts at trying to eke out a few samples of general laws that, at first blush anyhow, would seem to hold.

The notions of purpose and its allied one concerning means are not ordinarily taken as belonging to *deontics* or deontic logic, whereas notions of *obligation* and *permission* are. There is a very considerable literature on the logic of these latter, but little on the former. The two types of notions are very closely allied, however, being fundamental ones in any theory of morality and therewith in any of the human sciences for which such a theory is relevant. Some purposing are no doubt obligatory in some sense and much that is obliged may be purposed. Some purposings are permitted in some suitable sense, some not. Obligation and permission, however, seem always relative to some *code* or set of norms taken as paradigmatic. Alter that set of norms and the whole character of one's obligations and permissions alters also.

What form is needed for the theory of obligations analogous to (1) and (2) in the theory of purposes and means? The new item needed here would seem to be the *code* providing for the basis or norm or *ground* of an obligation. Or course purposings too have grounds, but they may be whimsical or arbitrary. Obligations, however — that is, "true" or "real" obligations — have the normative factor built into their very structure. Hence let us use

(3) $\qquad\qquad$ 'p Oblgd$_e$ C,e',a'

as the fundamental form for obliging. (3) expresses that e is a state or act of person p's being obliged, in accord with the code C, to do the act e' or be in the state e' with its content described by the one-place predicate a. In place of (3) we could write

$\qquad$ '$\langle p,$Oblgd$,$C$,e'$,$a\rangle e$'

equally well.

The code C could be taken as a virtual class of very general, declarative sentences that are taken as definatory or determinative or normative in the given context. The context may be a legal one, a moral one, a social one, a set of conventions regulative of a certain kind of behavior, a theological one concerned with a certain way of life or of achieving unity with the Godhead, an epistemic one concerned with what should be believed, accepted, or whatever, on the basis of given principles, and so on. We must thus distinguish a *general* theory of obligation from specific theories as based on specific types of codes. The English word 'ought' is highly ambiguous and takes on definiteness only when the code is specified.

The code can also be taken somewhat more simply, not as a class of sentences, but as a set of normative one-place *predicates, a* in (3) being such a predicate. Let us take codes, then, as virtual classes of suitable one-place predicates, some of which are picked out as normative in a given kind of context.

Let

'*p* Pmtd$_e$ C,*e'*,*a*' abbreviate '(PredConOne *a* · ~ *p* Oblgd$_e$ C, *e'*, $\ulcorner - {}_{\shortmid}a \urcorner$)'.

For *e'* as described by *a* to be *permitted* for person *p* on the basis of code C on some occasion *e* is for *e'* not to be obligated as described by $\ulcorner -a \urcorner$ for *p* on that occasion.

Concerning Oblgd we have Boolean laws analogous to *Pr1–Pr6* above for Purps, but where of course the form '*p* Purps$_e$ *e'*,*a*' is supplanted by '*p* Oblgd$_e$ C,*e'*,*a*'. These laws are *Pr16–Pr21*. Concerning Pmtd we have rather the following purported principles.

Pr22.   ⊢ (*p*)(*e'*)(*e*)(*a*)(*b*) ((*p* Pmtd$_e$ C,*e'*,*a* · *p* Pmtd$_e$ C,*e'*,*b*) ⊃ *p* Pmtd$_e$ C,*e'*,$\ulcorner (a \cap b) \urcorner$),

Pr23.   ⊢ (*p*)(*e'*)(*e*)(*a*)(*b*)((PredConOne *a* · PredConOne *b*) ⊃ ((*p* Pmtd$_e$ C,*e'*,*a* v *p* Pmtd$_e$ C,*e'*,*b*) ≡ *p* Pmtd$_e$ C,*e'*,$\ulcorner (a \cup b) \urcorner$)),

Pr24.   ⊢ (*p*)(*e'*)(*e*)(*a*) (*p* Oblgd$_e$ C,*e'*,*a* ⊃ *p* Pmtd$_e$ C,*e'*,*a*),

Pr25.   ⊢ (*a*)(*p*)(*e*)(*e'*)(PredConOne *a* ⊃ ((*p* Oblgd$_e$ C,*e'*,$\ulcorner -a \urcorner$ ≡ ~ *p* Pmtd$_e$ C,*e'*,*a*) · (~ *p* Oblgd$_e$ C,*e'*,*a* ≡ *p* Pmtd$_e$ C,*e'*,$\ulcorner -a \urcorner$))),

Pr26.   ⊢ ~ (E*p*)(E*e'*)(E*e*) (*p* Pmtd$_e$ C,*e'*, '{*e''* ∋ ~ *e''* = *e''* }'),

Pr27.   ⊢ (*a*)(*p*)(*e'*)(*e*)(*p* Pmtd$_e$ C,*e'*,*a* ⊃ *p* Pmtd$_e$ C,*e'*, '{*e''*∋*e''* = *e''*}').

The reader may verify for himself or herself the aptness of these various principles. As already noted, some of them may need modification or restriction upon further reflection. (The same, incidentally, is true of most mathematical theorems, which are usually first put forward without all the hypotheses or restrictions needed.) Also there are many more principles to be distinguished, concerning mereological sums, products, and negatives of persons and of events including acts and states. Also suitable laws should be forthcoming for virtual-class sums and products of codes. Laws of most of these types seem never to have been formulated.

Let us consider now in some detail an example from Morton White's new book *What Is and What Ought to Be Done*, just off the press.[5] To do so will help to clarify the purport of (3) and also to show the adequacy of the event-theoretic framework in handling some very basic types of moral reasoning. Here of course the code C is presumed to be a moral one.

Consider the following:

(i)   Whoever takes the life of (T) a human being (HB or Per) does something that ought not to be done.

(ii) The mother (ιM) took the life of (T) a living fetus (LF) in her womb ($\iota x \cdot x$ W (ιM)).

(iii)Every living fetus in the womb of a human being is a human being.

(iv) The mother took the life of a human being.

(v) The mother did something that ought not to be done.

(v) may be validly inferred from (i)–(iv), and such inferences are typical of acts of moral reasoning.

Let us symbolize these, respectively, as

(i') '$(p)(q)(e)((\text{Per } p \cdot \text{HB } q \cdot \langle p,\text{T},q \rangle e) \supset (Ee')(Ea) (p \text{ Do } e' \cdot$ '$\{e_1 \ni (Ep')(Eq')(\text{Per } p' \cdot \text{HB } q' \cdot \langle p',\text{T},q' \rangle e_1)\}$' $= a \cdot \sim (Er)(Ee_2)$ $(\text{Per } r \cdot \langle r,\text{Pmtd},\text{C},e',a \rangle e_2)))$',

(ii') '$(Ep)(Ee)(\text{LF } p \cdot p \text{ In}_{\text{Place}} (\iota x \cdot x \text{ W } (\iota \text{M})) \cdot \langle (\iota \text{ M}),\text{T},p \rangle e \cdot e \text{ Before}_{\text{Time}} now)$',

(iii') '$(p)((\text{LF } p \cdot (Eq)(\text{HB } q \cdot p \text{ In}_{\text{Place}} (\iota x \cdot x \text{ W } p))) \supset \text{HB } p)$',

(iv') '$(Ep)(\text{HB } p \cdot \langle(\iota\text{M}),\text{T},p \rangle e \cdot e \text{ Before}_{\text{Time}} now)$',

(v') '$(Ee)(Ee')(\langle(\iota\text{M}),\text{Do},e \rangle e' \cdot e' \text{ Before}_{\text{Time}} now \cdot \sim (Ep)(Ea)$ $(Ee'')(\text{Per } p \cdot \text{PredConOne } a \cdot \langle p,\text{Pmtd},\text{C},e,a \rangle e''))$'.

In these transcriptions 'ought not' has been equated with 'not permitted' according to *Pr25*, which helps to bring out how the truth-functional '$\sim$' is related to the virtual-class '$-$'. These symbolizations may appear strange, complex, and unnatural to anyone not familiar with the notation of event logic. Readers familiar with that notation, however, will recognize its appropriateness. 'Per', the general predicate for human persons, is of course coextensive with 'HB', but not cointensively so.

An additional premiss is needed, that Per (ιM), and the code C here is presumed to contain a normative predicate of the form

$$'\{e \ni \sim (Ep)(Eq)(\text{Per } p \cdot \text{HB } q \cdot \langle p,\text{T},q \rangle e)\}'.$$

It is then easily seen how (v) is a logical consequence of (i)-(iv) on the basis of the usual first-order quantification theory, within the event-theoretic framework.

The theory of obligation and permission here does of course make a good deal of the code C. Change this code and the whole theory changes content. How do the codes arise? Where do they come from? What is their "origin"? The answer to these questions is to be found in the theory of *valuation* and *preference*. Some predicates, so to speak, are valued over others, just as a matter of fact, in given contexts. The theory of obligation thus seems to presuppose a theory of preference. Here the fundamental form needed is

$$(4) \qquad \qquad \text{`}p \, \text{Prfr}_e \, e_1, a, e_2, b\text{'},$$

expressing that e is an act or state of person p's preferring e_1 as described by a over e_2 as described by b. There are very considerable difficulties to be found in giving suitable axioms governing this notion, axioms analogous to the principles above for Purps, Mns, Oblgd, and Pmtd. Of course we must distinguish various types of preference, legal preference, moral preference, and so on, each leading to the corresponding kind of code C. Precisely how the membership in a code is determined from suitable patterns of preference or valuation is, of course, a very difficult matter, requiring careful study.

Attention has been confined thus far wholly to the purposings, obligations, permissions, and valuations of the individual person. But there are of course *group* purposings, obligations, and so on, that must be considered. The theory of group purposings, for example, is not reducible to that concerning the individuals comprising that group. The group can purpose even where some of the individuals in it do not. Again, the problem of how the theory of group purposings, obligations, and so on, is constructed is a difficult one that cannot be discussed here. One item is clear, however. The group can be handled as the logical sum of the persons comprising it, taking 'logical sum' here in the sense of Leśniewski's mereology. This latter was already needed above anyhow, it will be recalled, in order to accommodate the null entity.

It might be objected that too much has been made in this paper of the *language* which we use to talk about concepts and mental events and actions and not enough of the "logical structure" of those events themselves. Such an objection would seem ill-founded, however, in view of the very intimate relationship between logic and language and hence between "logical structure," in Mohanty's sense, and the logical forms needed to express or describe those structures, in event logic. This point has been well expressed by Bocheński in his *The Logic of Religion*.[6]

In his talk about concepts the philosopher is after all using language, a highly special one usually, with a very special vocabulary. This vocabulary, together with its attendant variables, determines an *ontology*. In formulating a language this ontology is usually presupposed as spread out before us in timeless splendor. Mohanty, it will be recalled, seems to object to this circumstance in Frege, that Frege "even presupposes that the entities of the world are objects of reference as much as its timeless *Sinne* are and are just [out] "there" available for use and "grasping"." To get around this Mohanty seems to think we must get back to the "origins" of the phenomena of reference and meaning. But to do so we will of course wish to *talk* about such phenomena. We would not wish to claim that our talking about them "constitutes" their origin, or creates them, or anything of the kind. No, to talk about them we would assume that our language has the means already available to discuss them. Thus, in a certain sense, Frege's presupposition of an ontology both of objects to refer to and of *Sinne* there to be grasped is legitimate for his purposes. If we wish to talk now about "origins," the very principles governing such talk must be investigated. The very logic of the concept of an "origin," in the sense Mohanty and Navya-Nyāya wish — that is, the logic containing the structural principles governing it — seems not to have been studied at any depth. And in any case, it is doubtful that this could be done in any other way than the Fregean one, with its ontology spread out before us. To talk about states and acts of consciousness, and successions of these in time, is to have all such entities either within the basic ontology or constructible in terms of fundamental entities that are. There is nothing objectionable, however, in requiring this, which anyhow is a mere logical device, as it were, a useful logical fiction that utilizes the tense of timelessness.

It is clear that nothing more has been done in this paper than to have scratched the surface of the topics under consideration, and surely very difficult problems lie ahead. Because we know so little about the logical structure of the deontic concepts and of the cognitive acts and states involving them, any little progress in clarification here should be welcome.

CHAPTER XVIII

A Review of
Five Reviews

" 'Tis hard to say if greater want of skill
Appear in writing or in judging ill;
But of the two less dangerous is th' offence
To tire our patience than mislead our sense;
Some few in that, but numbers err in this,
Ten censure wrong for one who writes amiss."
Pope

A kind of one-up-manship is often the characteristic stance of the reviewer. If only he or she had written the work under consideration the result would have been considerably better in this or that respect. The constraints upon the reviewer are of course that he or she must reflect upon the work in question rather than upon some other, and that he or she must stay with it long enough to understand it and represent it fairly. It is of course always pertinent to suggest tasks and problems beyond those the author considers, but this must be done with discretion, especially in philosophical or linguistic work where the material tends almost always and naturally to overflow in multifarious directions. These points are of interest in connection with three recent reviews of the author's *Semiotics and Linguistic Structure*, one of *Events, Reference, and Logical Form*, and one of *Primordiality, Science, and Value*. The material of this paper will constitute a kind of review of these five reviews.

The comments concerning *SLS* made by Frederic B. Fitch[1] would seem more appropriate for some book other than the one under discussion. His first paragraph is perfunctory and merely scans a part of the table of contents. He then turns immediately to the handling of relations in terms of event descriptions, essentially as in the papers above, and comments that "in order to handle relations [in the manner of the text], . . . we consider some event which evidently relates an agent to a patient. Then to assert that the relation does relate the agent to the patient, we simply assert the event and assert that the agent is the agent of the event and that the patient is the patient of the event." This highly inaccurate comment is intended to describe the method by which dyadic relations are introduced in terms of acts or events.

In the first place, the talk of agents and patients is relevant only for sentences about human actions and other closely related ones, not for all relations. Further, we never "assert" an event. What should have been said here is that to say that person *p* bears an action relation *R* to *y* is parsed as saying that there is an act *e* such that it is an *R*-ing, to speak in terms of the appropriate gerundive, of which *p* is the (or an) agent and *q* is the (or a) patient.[2] Fitch then states that "the logically more natural approach" to the analysis of relations is to regard any sentence "that mentions two entities . . . as implicitly asserting that a relation holds *from* one *to* the other [italics added], or conversely, thus avoiding any choice as to which is agent and which is patient, a difficult or impossible choice for many common relations." Quite, and nothing contrary to this latter is stated in the text. Fitch fails to note the passage (*SLS*, pp. 208ff.) in which there is no talk of agents and patients, thus giving way to use of the Russellian From- and To-relations. These latter, it is thought, enable us to handle the very prepositions 'from' and 'to' that Fitch himself uses in the sentence cited.

"Of course," Fitch goes on, "a relation seen in this logically more natural way [Fitch's way] is an abstraction from a proposition, and is avoided by Martin since he wishes to have nothing to do with anything so Platonic as either a (real) abstraction or a (real) proposition." Fitch regards relations as abstractions from propositions, and his view is intriguing,[3] but it is by no means the "more natural" one. Relations are not so regarded by such great masters of the subject as DeMorgan, Peirce, Frege, Whitehead, Leśniewski, Russell, Zermelo, Carnap, Tarksi, and others. Also it is not correct to say that "Martin . . . wishes to have nothing to do with" things Platonic. The view is rather that such "things" are extra-logical, to be located in one's metaphysics, and that logic and semantics should be kept metaphysically neutral. Fitch, on the other hand, wishes his logic to be metaphysically loaded.

The very next comment is that "the whole purpose [of the text] is to develop an intellectual scheme which basically countenances (to use that weasel word of Quine) only concrete entities such as events and physical objects." This contention would apply perhaps to some of Quine's work, to some of Goodman's, to Rolf Eberle's, and so on, but not to the text under discussion. Fitch fails to note the *conceptualist* approach to semiotics developed especially in Chapters V and VI of the book, where sign events are taken as the products of conceptual acts of a certain kind. And why is 'countenance' a weasel word? It serves well as a word for the relation between an abstract system and the ontology intended for it in some suitable interpretation, and in fact is now widely used in this sense.

Fitch discusses as a "prejudice . . . for the concrete" a view, then, that is not put forward in the book. Further, he states that such a prejudice "is on a par with the finitist dislike of the infinite and perhaps includes this dislike as a special case." Actually, however, the two are very different and by no means on a par. One can espouse the "concrete," whatever it is, and be either a finitist or an infinitist, and one can be either of the latter and not espouse the former. Strictly, 'finitist' and 'infinitist' are ambiguous words, as between a view based on some fixed finite number and denumerablism, or as between denumerablism and nondenumerablism. Fitch's own espousal of denumerablism, as over and against either finitism as based upon a fixed finite number and nondenumerablism, could then with equal justice be dubbed a "prejudice."

Fitch states that it is "not really so virtuous, however, to eschew the abstract and cleave to the empirical." No such virtue was claimed, however, and nothing whatsoever about the empirical was said in the book. And in any case the empirical should not be equated with the concrete. Moreover, the concrete is scarcely even mentioned in the book and no substantive claims concerning it are made.

"The important thing," Fitch continues, "is to avoid paradox and contradiction in our theorizing, and this can best be done by constructing demonstrably consistent systems that are adequate for whatever purposes are at hand. Of course concretists and finitists hope that their highly limited techniques will guarantee consistency . . . , but this is only a hope, in contrast to an actual proof of freedom from contradiction." Surely one would not deny that proofs of freedom from contradiction are devoutly to be wished for wherever possible, together with a clear delineation of their exact logicomathematical structure. Such proofs are few and far between, however, even for suitable areas of mathematics. Fitch himself has contributed to this subject. The full character of his proofs of consistency, however, has not been spelled out in sufficient mathematical detail to assess accurately either their validity or the soundness of the assumptions needed. Thus, as a matter of fact, acceptable guarantees of consistency in mathematics, and *a fortiori,* in any domains of philosophy or science that presuppose mathematics, seem to be mere hopes at the present stage of research rather than actual achievements.

Fitch notes that "science would be intolerably impoverished by elimination of all abstraction, as in relativity theory and quantum mechanics." Quite. The question is a moot one as to whether Fitch's own preference for the denumerable impoverishes science or not, the full nondenumerable array of real and complex numbers being probably needed fundamentally. Even so, the comment, construed as a criticism of the book under discussion, fails to take into account the conceptualist handling of the full nondenumerable totality of real numbers suggested in Chapter VII.

One cannot justly contend, surely, that the methods there impoverish science. On the contrary, they provide more, in certain respects, than Fitch's denumerablist methods do.

Fitch's final substantive point is that "even the limitation of logic to first-order functional calculus, as apparently advocated by Martin, does away with self-referential arguments that are so important in philosophy, and destroys much of the usual Platonic foundation for mathematics, without offering any clear or viable alternative." The inapplicability of this last contention has already been pointed out. The knotty matter of self-reference remains to be commented on. Perhaps it is not so important in philosophy as is commonly supposed. Even Gödel's incompleteness theorem is regarded by some as a kind of *succès de scandale,* resulting from failure to probe deeply enough into the philosophical problems concerned with the so-called *insolubilia.* At least fifteen "solutions" to these and allied *insolubilia* were summarized in the *Logica Magna* (1499) of Paulus Venetus. These were apparently studied at great depth by the Polish logician Jan Salamucha, whose manuscript on the material was bombed in Warsaw in World War II. No competent scholar has apparently studied them since. There can be no doubt but that there is a very intimate connection between some of these "solutions" — to say nothing of more recent ones — and the methods employed by Gödel. At best Gödel chose one method which may not be the "best" and may not even be an acceptable one. There is an urgent need for a careful study and appraisal of this interconnection.

The eminent linguist, Zellig Harris, the great founder of modern mathematical linguistics, at the end of an important recent paper, "A Theory of Language Structure,"[4] makes some very strong claims concerning self-reference, including by innuendo the kind of self-reference that leads to Gödel's theorem. All talk of reference for Harris is to be handled in terms of suitable relations of cross-reference. "Sentences," he writes, "can carry [contain] operators which refer to locations within the sentence. This is so because every sentence has a linear order of words and, more important, a partial order of entry and [italics added] *every sentence is complete before the next higher operator acts on it.* . . . Language thus has a metatextual machinery for cross-reference, for stating that a word in one argument (of an operator) is the same, or has the same reference, as a word in another argument of that operator." A basic principle concerning CrRef, the relation of cross-reference, is that

$$(a)(b)(a \text{ CrRef } b \supset (\sim a \text{ Occ } b \cdot \sim b \text{ Occ } a)),$$

where Occ is the syntactical relation of *occurring in.* For *a* to be *cross-referential* to *b* it is necessary (not only that *a* and *b* be distinct but also) that *a* have no "address" or location in *b* nor *b* in *a*. (The clause ' $\sim a =$ *b*' is not needed here, being entailed by ' $\sim a$ Occ *b*'.) No genuine cross-reference could take place otherwise, for there would be nothing for a given term or expression to cross over to, so to speak, so far as concerns reference. To allow it to cross-refer to a part of itself, or to a whole of which it is a part, would be for it to fail to *cross*-refer in any but a Pickwickian sense. This fact may be enunciated as the *Principle of Limitation for Cross-Reference,* and would appear to be fundamental for natural language. It imposes, as Harris in effect notes, "certain limitations on what can be pronouned. Since nothing can be pronouned which has not been cited, as a complete linguistic entity, under the given metatextual operator, it follows that the self-referring pronoun [or pronomial phrase] of impredicative sentences does not exist in natural language. For example, in *This sentence is false,* the *this* cannot refer in English to the sentence of which it is a part."

In the form '*a* CrRef *b*' the *a* and *b* may be either actual inscriptions of sentences, or one of them may be a pronoun or a demonstrative phrase for a sentence. By the Principle of Limitation for Cross-Reference, '*this sentence*' cannot cross-refer to a sentence of which it is a part. Strictly, then, any such purported "impredicative" sentence cannot correctly state of itself that which it purports to do. In other words, any such statement is false. This is in effect what Harris should mean when stating that the self-referring pronoun of impredicative sentences "does not exist in natural language." Of course *This sentence is in English* also becomes false, in spite of a rather vague but widespread feeling (without much theory to back it up) that it should be regarded as true.[5]

If Harris' theory, one of the strongest (be it said) yet put forward by any structural linguist, is itself acceptable or at least on the right track, then of course Gödel's proof becomes at best somewhat suspect.

Of the three fundamental notions of mathematical syntax and semantics, that of being a *sentence* (Sent), of being a *theorem* (Thm), and of being *true* (Tr), Gödel's incompleteness theorem concerns primarily that of Thm, that in suitable languages there exist Sent's which say of themselves that they are not Thm's. Harris' indictment of the truth of any sentence of the form 'This sentence is not true' may be turned against 'This sentence is not a theorem' by noting that all Thm's are Tr's. A notion of Thm (containing no free variables) lacking this property would not be suitable. Hence if 'This sentence is not Tr' is false, 'This theorem is not a Thm' must be false also. The very core of Gödel's method must thus give way to a more reasoned and mathematically sound theory of reference within a properly worked out theory of language. Again, there is an urgent need for a deep and careful study of these latter preparatory to a critique of Gödel's work and of the various contentions stemming from it.

Another point should be mentioned, one quite independent of the foregoing. The full axiomatics of all the assumptions needed for carrying out Gödel's proof should be looked into. It is almost a scandal that this has never been done in full detail. At best only sketches of proofs have been given. There would seem, however, to be many semantical and other hidden assumptions that are needed, which should be spelled out in explicit logistic detail. Also there are powerful set-theoretic assumptions that are probably needed. It is extraordinary that very powerful axioms are viewed with some suspicion when used elsewhere in mathematics but admitted without qualms in Gödel's proof. In any case, we have no way of judging the validity of the latter short of an exhaustive characterization of *all* assumptions, syntactical, semantical, and otherwise, that are required for it. It is really astonishing that this matter seems never to have been looked into with the necessary care. There remains even now — 50 years *ex post facto* — an urgent need to do so, if only to keep tabs on the tools needed.

These comments on self-reference should be expanded in several ways. There are *pragmatical* considerations that are relevant,[6] as well as all manner of epistemic ones. We are so in the dark, it would seem, on almost everything here that any little step forward towards the light should be welcomed in experimental fashion.

Let us turn now to the second review under review, that by Rita Nolan.[7] Her first misstatement is that "the linguistic orientation underlying Part B [of the book] is guided by ideas of Zellig Harris and George Lakoff." It is true that Chapters VIII and IX of *SLS* are concerned respectively with some of the work of these two distinguished authors. The material there is rather critical of both, however, in their very fundamental failure to delineate in any adequate way the kind of underlying logic needed for the very "source" forms or "grammatical structures" they cite. The two chapters try to show how such forms may be given on the basis of the material of Part A. The only use made of the work of the two authors is thus to consider some of their examples, together with some occasional, rather superficial, agreement as to points of doctrine. To state that Part B is "guided" by the ideas of these two authors is highly inaccurate, as is the further suggestion that their ideas are there "combined."

Nolan considers only three points: the "crucial" devices of "(1) introducing event logic as an extension of mereology, (2) relativizing syntax and semantics to individual users of language and occasions of use, and (3) construing the theoretical domain as token sign events."

Concerning (1) it is stated that "Martin's event logic is intended to capture our intuitions about the nature of events; since its basis is the calculus of individuals, it analyzes events in the manner of compositional analysis of physical aggregates. The aggregational analysis of events is counterintuitive." There are three fundamental errors in this statement. It is not correct to say that the aim of event logic is "to capture our intuitions" about events, that its "basis" is the calculus of individuals, or that events are analyzed in the manner of physical aggregates. It is very difficult to say what "our" intuitions about events actually are, and they surely vary greatly from one person to another. The aim rather was to put forward a theory (in Chapter IV) concerning the internal structure of events, states, acts, and processes. If the theory does in fact capture some of "our" intuitions, this is all to the good. If it does not, some of our intuitions may have to be given up or readjusted to fit the theory — not necessarily this theory but perhaps a better one. It is a great philosophic error, as Peirce was perhaps the first to have observed, to regard appeals to intuition and to the ordinary uses of speech as determinative of logical doctrines. In fact, so Peirce maintained, "they are utterly useless for the investigation of logical questions."[8] Peirce's contention here is a bit strong, perhaps, but no doubt in the right direction.

The second error in the passage cited is that the "basis" of event logic is the calculus of individuals. Even a most casual reading of Chapter IV shows that the very first item in the discussion of event theory is the introduction of the event-descriptive predicates. Only after these have been discussed is it noted that "the calculus of individuals is now extended to events." A most significant part of event theory can thus be formulated quite independently of mereology. Note also that event identity is taken as a primitive and not defined in terms of the expression for a part-whole relation. An appropriate mereology is taken as a part of the theory of events, but is by no means a "basis" for it. Thus also, it is not the case that the analysis of events "is in the manner of compositional analysis of physical aggregates." The analysis is, rather, primarily in terms of the event-descriptive predicates applicable to them. Even so, mereology need not be taken as applicable *only* to physical aggregates, as Nolan's comment suggests.[9]

Nolan gives an example as to why the aggregational analysis — let us forget its physical aspect now — is counterintuitive. Her example fails to make its point, however, for the mereological part-whole relation between events is construed as being "deemed by speakers to be" or to have been parts of such and such. To be deemed by a speaker to be a part of is of course a very different relation from being a part of, just as being deemed a truth is a very different property from being true. Nolan's objections to some of the principles suggested in Chapter IV are thus based upon a misconstrual of the part-whole relation used there.

The second "crucial device" with which Nolan takes issue is that of pragmatizing or conceptualizing semiotics, as in *SLS,* Chapters V and VI. Her reasons for this are somewhat obscure. She seems to object somehow to the notion — an almost Peircean one, be it said — that anything whatsoever can be taken as a sign "provided it behave in the proper way," and that what determines the proper way are "the rules of the language at hand." She then states that "there are . . . only two ways that rules of a language can be derived [?] from the spare apparatus admitted. One is by selecting a person as an ideal user; the other is by head-count." The connection she sees between "pragmatizing semiotics" and the derivation of the rules of language is, however, obscure. The rules of a language are not pragmatized, only its inscriptions. Nolan writes as though it were contended otherwise. How can the rules of language be "derived" from a less sparse apparatus? How are the rules of language derived — in any strict sense — at all? As a matter of fact, many of them are not derived, but must play the role rather of primitive sentences of the theory. The contention, then, is that "although pragmatization of the theory extends the range of what can be described, the theory lacks explanatory power." What explanatory power? How and why is a non-pragmatized treatment of inscriptions more explanatory than the one put forward? Further, what here is the "range of what can be described"? It seems that Nolan here has read much more into the notion of a pragmatized semiotics than is contained in it.

"The device in linguistics of abstracting from extralinguistic conditions of utterance in providing semantic and syntactic representations of sentences," she goes on, "makes use of the idealized notion of standard conditions of utterance. Martin's analyses in Part B, however, are of token sentences taken in some way by a person or on occasion; as a result of this pragmatizing, an unlimited number of interpretations of each sentence (type) is theoretically required. The principles upon which Martin selects the interpretation that he represents are not explained, either systematically or presystematically." Unfortunately all of these contentions go astray. No greater number of interpretations of a sentence type are required in the pragmatized version than in any other. Just as a matter of fact there is no one "idealized notion of standard conditions of utterance" for a sentence type; there are many. Consider the example 'The ball rolled underneath the table'. Two readings are considered in *SLS* (p. 249), on both of which it is assumed that the ball was not under the table when it started rolling. "But on other assumptions," Nolan notes correctly, "such as that the ball is in a turning roulette wheel under the table, numerous other readings arise; some idiosyncratic readings will violate any logical rule proposed." For the circumstances involving the roulette wheel, probably 'The ball was rolling around and around underneath the table' would be more appropriate. However, the contention that some *outrès* readings will violate any form — not rule (!) — proposed, is not the case. The problem, in considering this example, is to determine which of the many underneath-relations is the appropriate one. Clearly for the roulette-wheel case, it is the underneath-relation of *location*. In even unusual circumstances, *some* underneath-relation is being used. If it is not clear which, we can always use the general underneath-relation, namely, the logical sum of all the special ones. This is what we usually do anyhow, unless it is very clear which special one is being used. As noted in the text, there are usually many readings of a sentence. The ones chosen for analysis were the most common ones or those obviously intended by the author from whom they were borrowed.

Nolan concludes her remarks on pragmatizing semiotics by commenting that "the issue is . . . whether . . . [Martin's] strong normative thesis identifying logical form with linguistic structure is actually supported by the pragmatized system offered." The aim of pragmatization is neither to give nor to withhold support to such a thesis. The two may be held quite independently of each other. Nor is this identification a "strong normative thesis." What else is a linguistic structure if not a logical form? No cogent answer to this question has been given by linguists upon a secure theoretical basis, and without presupposing all manner of vague and ill-begotten matters concerning *inter alia* the traditional parts of speech. In any case, Nolan gives no reasons as to why this thesis should not be maintained or even why it is in some sense suspect.

The third point Nolan raises, concerning "construing the theoretical domain [of expressions] as token sign events," need not be discussed in detail here. She answers her own objections as she reads on. She does ask, however, "in what way linguistic expressions are *identified with actual entities in the world,* i.e., with object-language events and objects? Are inscriptions and the like sign events, or are sign events a special kind of "taking"? This ambiguity is of fundamental importance, for the gain in logical simplicity and ontological economy could be lost in the obscurity of the basic individuals. It is not clear that Martin's conceptualistic nominalism (pp. 95–97) surmounts this problem."

The answer to the key question here is clearly given on the very pages referred to. Inscriptions and sign events are one and the same. Neither, however, is a special form of "taking" for this would make them an *activity.* Rather they are the *objects* or *patients* of such activity. An LP or left parenthesis is a sign event taken to behave the way left parentheses behave. The standard notation for such is of course the usual one. Nothing in the inscriptional approach need violate standard notation. In fact the very meaning of 'standard' here can be explicated in its terms. Also nothing in the inscriptional approach prevents making fundamental use of sign designs also in the guise of virtual classes of suitably similar sign events. And note that sign designs can even be quantified over in this treatment, using a familiar type of definition. (See below.) Thus nothing is lost in the inscriptional approach — and much is gained, e.g., in the handling of deixis, a point Nolan fails to observe.

Finally, Nolan complains that "the author's nominalistic tendencies lead him to other consequences that some will find empirically unacceptable." The three examples she cites, however, have no more to do with nominalism than with any other view. She complains that "the same form given (on p. 155) for 'I am in process of writing a poem' . . . does not generalize to other locutions that are analogously problematic, such as 'baking a cake' or 'hunting a deer'." Quite, and perhaps the best procedure is to take '$\langle \text{Proc} \rangle e$' to express that e is a process as a primitive locution, one acceptable surely to both nominalists and nonnominalists alike. Also she objects to another form on the grounds that "from the fact that something can be boring it does not follow that it can bore everyone who does it." Surely not, and no such principle was maintained in the text. However, it *might* obtain that 'Every member of the royal family is now doing something that can bore him' means precisely what 'What the members of the royal family are now doing can be boring' means. The 'boring' in this last sentence can be taken as 'boring to them' with 'them' construed either collectively or distributively.

The third example of something purported to be nominalistically inspired but "empirically unacceptable" is that "Martin notes (p. 315) that according to one analysis of a person's not believing a certain thing ((14.3), p. 311), if someone does not believe a certain thing then it follows that there are believings that no one has or someone does believe that thing." This contention is incorrect. From the analysis given by (14.3) — which was intended to be a logical form for a sentence stressed in a certain way — it does not follow that there are believings no one has but rather that there are believings not everyone has. It does, however, follow that someone *does* believe that thing, due to the stress. From 'Ralph [stressed] does not believe that Ortcutt is a spy' it should indeed follow that someone else does. (14.3) seems thus to be as it should be quite irrespective of any nominalistic "prejudices."

Nolan notes what she thinks to be an underlying "methodological problem." "Martin fuses a theory of logical forms that reflects metaphysical preferences with a theory of linguistic structure for which independent empirical correctness is apparently claimed. But it is unclear what relation is intended between the metaphysical constraints chosen and the structure of natural language. Is it suggested that other metaphysical preferences are incompatible with the structure of natural languages?" No, it is not. "Issues such as this are not discussed in the text." No, they were not. The aim was merely to put forward *one* view in what was hoped to be a reasonably satisfactory way. Of course, there may be other, better ones. However, any such view need not reflect metaphysical preferences in any precise sense. But no "independent empirical correctness" — whatever that is — was claimed for the theory. The aim rather was to try to characterize in logical forms structural and other aspects of sentences needed to capture their meanings and logical consequences. In Chapter XV, twenty-one desiderata for such a theory were put forward. No commentator has yet questioned the appropriateness of these or suggested that some should be excluded or others added. Nor, apparently anyhow, has any other author suggested a theory alternative to the one put forward that meets these conditions with even a modicum of success.

We see then that all of the problems Nolan considers evaporate under analysis, so that they may not, contrary to what she states, "prompt others who are interested in grounding theory in a spare, clean, and clear metaphysics to pursue the changes that Martin's work invites [and that she urges]. This is a demanding task that should be undertaken only by the sophisticated and serious student." As a matter of fact, however, there is no grounding of the theory under a metaphysical rubric at all, nor even a suggestion of such, anywhere in the book. As we have noted in II above, suitable *bridge rules* are needed to connect the logico-linguistic material with some metaphysical view. The exact statement of these would help to pave the way for an exact metaphysics. *This* is the demanding task to be approached seriously, and which will surely loom important in the future of metaphysics.

A few remarks are now in order concerning the more competent review of *SLS* by Susan Haack.[10] She notes that "Martin's theory — especially in view of its insistence on respect for word order — seems in some danger of parochialism, of offering no more than logical analyses of English sentences, without any means of generalization to other languages, instead of the intended, general theory of language as such." This is an interesting observation and preservation of word order is by no means essential. It is useful as a heuristic for the discovery of the (or a) form for a sentence and for diagramming the transition from the sentence to a form (as, for example, on p. 309). Ultimately, however, word order is specified, not in the system of forms, but in the transformation rules leading from sentence to form and back again.[11] Such rules of course vary from language to language. Thus, where only one language is under consideration, no harm arises from requiring sameness of word order and representation of word order, in sentence and form respectively, thereby eliminating or simplifying some transformation rules. Where more than one language is under consideration, no such requirement is desirable.

Haack comments that "a sceptical reader may suspect that Martin's criteria of adequacy for a theory of logical form [(P1)–(P21) of Chapter XV, the twenty-one desiderata mentioned a moment back] are such as to allow only his own semiotic as adequate; and go on to reflect that the same might be said of the constraints Davidson imposes." Davidson's constraints are clearly inadequate, consisting apparently of only (P1)–(P5). The question to ask of any sceptical reader who queries (P1)–(P21) is: which of them do you wish to excise? And why? Any excision here — bearing in mind the slight weakening of (P15) as concerns word order if more than one language is under consideration, in accord with the pre-ceding paragraph — would seriously affect both one's theory of form and the whole theory governing word order. Any argument for the one not only is but should be an argument for the other. But of course there are alternative approaches to both, as already observed above, which should be developed in experimental fashion, so that serious comparative study can be carried out.

(An additional, parenthetical, note, also concerning word order, is occasioned by a comment by "P.J." in *The Review of Metaphysics* (1982):883–884. P.J. extols the desideratum laid down (p. 302 of *SLS*) that "a theory of logical forms must be developed in accord with an atti-tude of respect for natural language *precisely as it is.*" He or she then complains that "this principle seems invariably the first to be sacrificed for the sake of theory construction, and it is a pity Martin himself neglects it." Most of the logical forms given in *SLS* were intended as only first approximations, as noted again and again, and can be brought into conformity with the word-order requirement merely by means of the commutative and associative laws concerning the truth-functional '·' for the basic 'and'. Where word order was not preserved, it can thus trivially be provided. Often "a" logical form rather than "the" logical form was spoken of. "The" logical form could be identified with the form most closely preserving the word order of the original. After this misunder-standing, P.J. comments that "whatever its intrinsic interest, the further development of Martin's approach risks irrelevance to its subject matter in the absence of greater sensitivity to common speech," having already agreed that "event logic is more adequate to the task of structural analy-sis than is either Harris's system of report or George Lakoff's general semantics." One would like therefore to know of what the purported "irrelevance" would consist. No insensitivity to common speech is pointed out other than the purported one concerning word order. Haack thinks too much is made of word order in *SLS*, and P.J., too little. Take your pick. The truth is somewhere in the middle. Finally, P.J. regards as "sweeping" the claims that "every formula of logic is a lesson for the student of language," failing to note the play on Stuart Mill's famous observation that "the structure of every sentence [of a natural language] is a lesson in logic." Greater sensitivity on the part of P.J. to the associative and commutative laws concerning '·' and their relevance for language would have been welcome.)

Let us turn now to the fourth review. In her comments concerning *Events, Reference, and Logical Form,* LaVerne M. Shelton[12] makes several erroneous observations that are apt to mislead the reader as to the true content of the book. Let us comment briefly upon these one by one.

(1) "One of Prof. Martin's major assumptions," she writes, "is that analysis and the setting out of logical forms are two different enterprises, the second being prior to the first." Actually, however, no such assumption is made, nor is either taken as "prior" to the other. Both are significant enterprises going hand in hand, as Skelton herself observes later on.

(2) "The account [in terms of events] presumes virtual classes." Yes, but any first-order account of anything at all does likewise. The reviewer seems not to realize that the use of so-called virtual classes and relations is merely an ancillary notational device. [13]

(3) It is stated that "persons are quite different from the things normally called events. Prof. Martin suggests we use the criterion that persons, unlike any other type of thing, utter sign events (p. 7), or (later on) perhaps that they concatenate signs or that they refer. But could there not be "events" of the shape of sign events made by the wind?" The answer to this last is "Yes, of course," but, even so, several errors are concealed in these sentences. 'Event' is taken throughout in an extended philosophical sense, so as to include (as suitable mereological sums) physical objects, persons, inscriptions, and so on. And, indeed, in the context of the theory 'Utt' for utterance is taken only for human utterances, and similarly for 'C' for concatenation and 'Ref' for reference. But no "criterion" or "defining feature" for personhood, outside of the context of the theory, is given or even remotely suggested. Of course the wind can do remarkable things, but it cannot concatenate with self-conscious intent in the way in which a knowing syntactician or semanticist can.

(4) Shelton thinks that "the assumption that there is *any* "one-criterion" specification of a category such as personhood is suspect." In any case, it would be difficult to give such a specification — agreed. She

then goes on to state that "if many of our concepts are at best cluster concepts, we cannot expect simple renditions of their "logical form"." Agreed also. But who is it that expects simple renditions anyhow? Usually those who never even try to give any at all. And of course we must distinguish "renditions" of category words that are primitives from those that are defined. The predicate 'Per', for being a person, perhaps could be taken primitively, but also it may be definable, in the broad sense that Shelton wishes, within a sufficiently extended metaphysical scheme. Even so, in the last sentence quoted, there is confusion between a logical form and the "representative" of a natural-language word. Thus 'Per' is a representative but not a logical form. Concepts do not have logical forms, only sentences do.

(5) "Suppose . . . we want to determine what sorts of "events" must occur when knowledge claims are true. Suppose that all attempts to analyze our concept seem to require a reference to the physical context in which the putative knowledge and prerequisite beliefs are obtained. And yet the determined logical forms allow no place for parameters varying our contextual features. Then the "logical forms" must be incorrect or would have been prematurely suggested." Very well, let us suppose all this. We would go on to seek more adequate forms containing the requisite parameters. Shelton's suppositions here are inappropriate for the theory of forms in the book under review, in which as much context as is relevant may always be accommodated. However, her comments are highly relevant for narrower theories of form that wish to have no truck with context.

(6) "Why just events? The project seems doomed from the outset if only actual events are considered. There are describable properties never instantiated, and these may be important to the completeness of some physical theory." It would be helpful to have been told just *what* project is being doomed here, that of a metaphysics based on events — *pace,* then, Whitehead and all process metaphysicians — or that of a physics based wholly on events — *pace,* then, relativity theorists — or that of a semantics or pragmatics based wholly on sign events, to mention merely a few. In all of these theories there are "properties" — better, predicates — that in fact are never instantiated; they are then merely null. No language adequate for science could lack this feature; otherwise it would lack the resources needed for forming a null predicate. Shelton's point here is thus vacuous and, further, has no relevance as to whether the events are all "actual" or not.

(7) If nonactual events — whatever these are — are admitted, Shelton thinks, following Hilary Putnam, they are nonactual possibles, and "nonactual possibles are no more concrete that the sets which the

nominalists eschew." But of course they are; they are potentially more concrete, we might say, just as a piece of candy that I might eat (a possible candy, if you like) is potentially sweeter than a draught of hemlock. (We will return to the notion of being "concrete" in a moment.)

(8) The phrase 'nonactual event' is presumably supposed to denote events that have not yet been *actualized* or that have not yet come into being. The discussion of them must thus presumably make use of temporal locutions. A theory of coming into being and passing out of being, all done up in suitable logical detail, seems never to have been worked out. (Recall, however, IV above.) It would be interesting to have such a theory at hand in which the very distinction between 'actual' and 'nonactual' could be made. Any such theory, however — and this is the point Shelton misses completely — *will have all events whatsoever spread out as values for the variables in full Fregean splendor in the tense of timelessness.* (Recall the penultimate paragraph of XVII above.) The purported nonactual events are always temporally relative and hence are regarded as actual in the tense of timelessness.

(9) Let us turn now to nonactual or possible inscriptions or sign events. "Prof. Martin responds," we are told, to the abortive criticism that "nonactual possibles are no more concrete than the sets which nominalists eschew," "that as far as inscriptions are concerned, even those that are not "explicitly exhibited" are values for variables. But this seems to be no answer. If Prof. Martin is allowing also inscriptions not perceived, we still do not have enough. If, on the other hand, he does mean nonactual inscriptions, then indeed there are very strangely abstract objects passing as events."

Two quite different ways of construing inscriptions were considered in the book under review, the conceptualist way of its earlier chapters, and the strictly nominalist way, in the final chapter on Putnam. (The former was merely sketched but developed more fully in the later *SLS*.) The strictly nominalistic way, which Putnam was criticizing, is the view of Goodman and Quine in their "Steps toward a Constructive Nominalism."[14] In that paper all inscriptions are presumed actual in the tense of timelessness, but even so, an infinity of them is not assumed. Without an infinity of inscriptions syntax may well be hampered at certain key points. A legitimate kind of nominalistic syntax, however, results from explicitly postulating an infinity of inscriptions. The theory then differs radically, however, from that of Goodman and Quine. In *SLS,* in which syntax is treated in a more conceptualistic than nominalistic manner, an infinity of inscriptions is assumed in terms of mental acts of concatenating. (See especially *SynR9* on p. 81.) Thus the purported Putnam-Shelton criticism may be relevant to the nominalistic syntax of Goodman and Quine, but fails of its target for the two alternatives just mentioned.

(10) Let us reflect now upon the question 'Why just events?' in the sense of 'Why just sign events?' Well, the answer is that in infinitistic inscriptional syntax, a full theory of shapes or sign designs is automatically forthcoming by regarding these latter as virtual classes of similar inscriptions. And, further, even quantification over shapes is forthcoming. Let '$\{b \ni b \text{ Like } a\}$' be the expression for the virtual class of all inscriptions typographically like a. (This Like-relation, or a closely related one, it will be recalled, is a fundamental one in the theory.) Then

'(S)---S---' may be taken as short for '(a)---$\{b \ni b \text{ Like } a\}$---', where '---$S$---' differs from the formula '---$\{b \ni b \text{ Like } a\}$---' only in containing some new sign 'S' wherever '$\{b \ni b \text{ Like } a\}$' occurs in '---$\{b \ni b$ Like $a\}$---', there being no free occurrences of 'a' in '---$\{b \ni b$ Like $a\}$---' other than in the context '$\{b \ni b \text{ Like } a\}$'.

The definiendum here contains in effect a quantifier over all shapes. The answer to 'Why only sign events?' is then that sign events are all that are needed for syntax.

Note that if classical syntax, of the familiar Tarskian kind as based on shapes, is assumed, the theory of inscriptions cannot be introduced by definition, for altogether new variables must be present to handle them. The question 'Why only shapes?' is thus not to be asked. The proper question is 'Why inscriptions in addition to shapes?' And the answer is, of course, to handle deixis, and in general, occasion and other sentences of similar type.

(11) Shelton inadvertently identifies the syntax of *Events, Reference, and Logical Form* with that of Goodman and Quine, from which, however, it differs radically, as already noted. There is no one nominalism, but a whole family of different kinds. All talk of "concrete" and "abstract" entities is at best rather vague, and has been useful only as a heuristic. No clear-cut or satisfactory demarcation between them seems ever to have been given, all tied up in the necessary logical detail. The overriding reasons for nominalism, in a suitably extended, highly theoretical sense, rest on suspicion of set and class theory. If these latter have been utter failures in mathematics — as more and more seems to be becoming the prevailing opinion among mathematicians — it seems a bit *retardataire* for philosophers to hang on to their coat strings. They are unlikely to prove helpful in philosophy if they have failed for the very purposes for which they were designed. A suitable nominalism can, however, be as realist as one wants it to be as regards the real existence of physical and/or mental entities, and as Platonic as one wishes in its seeking of laws or patterns of universal generality covering them.

(12) A number of further errors and misstatements stud Shelton's last paragraph. "The values of the variables of the [nominalistic] language systems would be found only among nominalistic events. These are specified within the system by using virtual classes, which are not values of variables. In the metalanguage we can explain that these are like sets, but do not exist." All three of these statements seem inadequate. There would seem to be no specifically nominalistic events — if there are, it would be good to be told what they are, as opposed to nonnominalistic ones. Further, how does a virtual class "specify" an event? It may have it as a member, or not, but to be a member is not to be specified. Nor do we, in the metalanguage, explain that virtual classes are "like" sets, nor do we say in the metalanguage that virtual classes "do not exist." The key terms 'like', 'sets', and 'exist' in the desired senses and contexts are simply not present in the metalanguage. Strictly, all talk of virtual classes must be carried out in the notations allowed for them and is meaningless otherwise.

From these and further misstatements Shelton is emboldened to say that "clearly the nominalist loses the well-foundedness of concepts that the realist has." (The shift to talk of "concepts" here obviously bypasses the discussion of them in *ERLF* (pp. 15ff.).) If this "well-foundedness" is that of set theory, it is probably illusory, and even vague as Shelton seems to suggest in her next sentence. But, she goes on, "whatever vagueness the realist specification may suffer, the nominalist "manner of speaking" has the further trouble of being in principle inexplicable, since it must always be said that classes are really nothing." It is true that all talk about a manner of speaking is somewhat tenuous. The point is, of course, as already noted, that all talk of virtual classes should be carried out in terms of their notation. There is a virtual-class notation — this and this only — but there are no virtual classes.

(13) Shelton's last sentence is admirable and can be agreed with wholeheartedly. "It would seem that elegance, perspicacity, and understandability are prerequisites for the acceptability of a theory . . . [and] are at least as important as parsimony." But now surely, the first three prerequisites can scarcely be claimed of philosophical theories just because they are based on set theory, nor can they be denied to theories not so based — *ceteris paribus,* of course. Each theory must be examined as to its own merits. The minimal courtesy a reviewer of a book can do the reader is to apprise him or her of its accomplishments and content. The present review focuses exclusively on material that adds up to at most one page; it would have been helpful to the reader to have been told something of the inner content of the others, which, it is hoped, are not altogether lacking in "elegance, perspicacity, and understandability."

The fifth review, by Jeff Foss,[15] is of *Primordiality, Science, and Value*. Unfortunately this review also is studded with heinous blunders.

Fundamental use is made in *PSV* of the theory of virtual classes and relations. Foss complains that "the principal generator of ... [Martin's] logic is the 'virtual set'. . . ." But of course the virtual set is not the "principal generator" — first-order quantification theory is. "So," Foss contends, "despite Martin's claiming parsimonious brotherhood with Quine and Goodman . . . he works with a very large expense account nevertheless. There are problems with this pretense of riches. For one thing, it seems essential that the concept of a set and of set inclusion be *presumed* in Martin's metalanguage, as indeed it *is* presumed, or else we have no reason whatever to understand [that] a statement of set-inclusion is being made by '$y \ni \{x:Fx\}$' given that it is introduced as merely the abbreviandum of 'Fy'." But of course the notation '$y \ni \{x:Fx\}$' is nowhere used in *PSV*, nor in *SLS* either to which Foss makes reference. Foss uses '$\ni$' as the symbol for class inclusion rather than the more customary '$\subset$'. No definition given anywhere — so it seems — introduces '$y \subset \{x:Fx\}$' as an alternative notation for 'Fy'. Foss seems here to be confusing set membership with set inclusion. Very well, let us then construe his '$\ni$' as standing for set membership in place of the more customary 'ϵ'. Even so, no definition given anywhere introduces '$y \epsilon \{x:Fx\}$' as an alternative notation for 'Fy'. '$\{x:Fx\}$' is the usual expression for the *real* set of x's such that Fx, not for the virtual set of such. Very well, let us suppose now that Foss is purporting to say that '$y \epsilon \{x \ni Fx\}$' is taken as an alternative notation for 'Fy', where '$\{x \ni Fx\}$' is a virtual-class expression (even a primitive one perhaps). Such a definition would be permissible, and indeed harmless, merely allowing us to write the definiens and definiendum interchangeably wherever we wish. Inclusion would still have to be handled separately. But still there would be no quantification primitively over either 'F' or '$\{x \ni Fx\}$', so that both F and $\{x \ni Fx\}$ remain virtual not real. As a result of all this misunderstanding Foss claims that "it comes to pass that . . . [Martin's] metalanguage is free to make ontological commitment that the object language would not touch with a dungfork." This of course is incorrect, virtual classes and relations being introduced in essentially the same way in object language and metalanguage alike.

Foss's misunderstandings get deeper and deeper. "If we do not assume that Martin is talking about sets in the normal sense, but about imaginary [virtual] ones, then definitions such as, e.g., that of 'God' as 'the fusion of the set of all primordial valuations [p.34, *PSV*], are as vacuous as the 'set' involved." Well of course the virtual class involved is not vacuous, in virtue of the ambient theory of primordial valuations. Foss's point is rather that "the fusion of a virtual class ... is a class" and because quantifiers are available over fusions they are also available over classes. But this contention is incorrect. Foss is apparently unfamiliar with the technicalia concerning the notions of fusion and nucleus that play an important role in mereology or the calculus of individuals. The fusion is an individual along with the members of the virtual class of which it is a fusion.

Foss goes on to state that "even if we are insensitive to the metaphysical disputes of the logicians, Martin's work still does not accomplish all we would like to see accomplished by a formal treatment of a subject." The reason is that axioms are not provided but merely a "parade of principles." "Now, we may forgive a logician [but not a metaphysician?] for not fully formalizing such work, for choice of axioms is somewhat arbitrary, and completeness perhaps irrelevant to special applications. However, it would be nice to know whether the parade of formulae behind turnstiles is even consistent." Yes it would, but very difficult to find out, even in the simplest, most studied areas of mathematics. Foss's point here is similar to one raised by Fitch, lamented above. Somewhat similar laments are in order concerning metamathematical notions of the completeness of logical systems, the full theories of which are not spelled out with the axiomatic exactitude Foss wishes of metaphysical theories containing these systems. Foss is thus making a demand here impossible of fulfillment until we know a great deal more than we do about the foundations of completeness theory itself.

Foss's last paragraph, part of which concerns the papers in *PSV* on Kant's second antinomy, again runs afoul of his confusions concerning virtual classes. Until these are corrected, it is next to impossible to fathom what he is trying to say here.

In his first paragraph, Foss speaks of the "evangelical motif" to the book which is supposed to show that the treatment of the various topics in it is "by no means an impartial one." What is this "evangelical motif?" Part of it seems to be the maxim for philosophers to "use quantification theory and generalize as far as possible" and not to "ride in a horse and buggy." Without quantifiers there would be little reason to think that modern logic is of much use to the philosopher in helping him to get his ideas clear. Without them — or their surrogates, say, perhaps in the manner of the relational algebra of IX above — one can coast along in the easy comfort of yesteryear's modes of transport. The injunction to "generalize as far as possible" is of course essentially that of Peirce and Whitehead, the aptness of which surely needs no defense here.

Foss also errs in misconstruing the "parsimonious brotherhood with Goodman and Quine," just as the other reviewers have. No attempt is made in any of the books discussed to reduce all entities to physical objects, to qualia, to "ways of worldmaking," or to any combination thereof — to say nothing of the different ways in which inscriptions are taken. The parsimonious brotherhood turns out to be not even a family resemblance.

The author is indebted to the five reviewers for their comments, even for those with which agreement has not been possible. It is gratifying that Nolan found the "project" of *SLS* "rich in controversial theoretical implications and . . . an exciting addition to current literature in the metatheory of logic and language, taking off in a different direction from other efforts in exact methodology." The controversial items she noted mostly evaporate under analysis, so that the material is perhaps less controversial than she imagines. Only let her try to construct a commensurate theory satisfying the ten desiderata laid down in the Preface (pp. xviii–xix) and leading to a theory of logical form in accord with (P1)–(P21). The desiderata and principles, it is thought, are so fundamental that any adequate theory of language should seek to accommodate them. They are "controversial" only in the sense, it would seem, that no theory heretofore has been able to do so, or has even tried to do so. The result perhaps is too much novelty, even some "offensive novelty" perhaps, to use Hobbes' perspicuous phrase.

It is also gratifying to note that Haack thinks that "the austerity of Martin's logical apparatus [in *SLS*] is exhilarating, especially in view of the present popularity of doubtfully explanatory 'possible worlds' semantics." She might have noted here also the "doubtfully explanatory" character of set theory itself within mathematics and metamathematics, and *a fortiori* beyond such in linguistics. She states, moreover, that "this is an intriguing and idiosyncratic book, which ontologically scrupulous readers will find particularly refreshing." It is not clear wherein the idiosyncrasy is supposed to lie — the book is by the author and no one else. Also too much should not be made of ontological scrupulosity, important as it is. Equally important is the simplicity of the various basic grammatical and other relations and notions made use of, some of this simplicity of course stemming from the nature of the relata or arguments. Ontological scrupulosity and simplicity of overall theory seem to go hand in hand and cannot be divorced.

It is interesting also that Foss suggests that *PSV* would better be entitled 'Logician, Will Travel', dealing as it does with "issues from all corners of the philosophic sphere." Well, as a matter of fact, logicians *should* travel, and a great deal more and a great deal farther than they are usually willing to do. Travelling broadens the mind and increases one's sympathies and tolerance. "Everything is an exercise in formal logic, even chemistry," Peirce noted years back with extraordinary acumen. It is unwillingness to travel that has helped block the road to inquiry. It has helped to hold back the development of philosophic logic and has contributed to the widespread opinion that this latter is for the most part irrelevant to all but very constricted parts of "analytic" philosophy. The more appropriate — and even traditional — view is that logic, in the sense of a *logica utens,* can be of great help in all areas of philosophical inquiry, especially if used with the requisite delicacy and sensitiveness to their individual demands.

Notes

Chapter I

1. Morton White, *Toward Reunion in Philosophy* (Harvard University Press, Cambridge: 1956).
2. See Gottlob Frege, "Über Sinn und Bedeutung," second paragraph, and *Begriffsschrift*, §8.
3. Cf. III and IV below and *Logico-Linguistic Papers* (Foris Publications, Dordrecht: 1981), Chapter VII.
4. See *Events, Reference, and Logical Form* (The Catholic University of America Press, Washington: 1976) and *Semiotics and Linguistic Structure* (State University of New York Press, Albany: 1978), *passim*.
5. (Princeton University Press, Princeton: 1979).
6. This point is not to be confused with the related but rather vague one, much discussed in the literature, due to Quine.
7. See *Semiotics and Linguistic Structure*, *Events, Reference, and Logical Form*, and *Pragmatics, Truth, and Language* (D. Reidel Publishing Co., Dordrecht: 1979). See also II below.

Chapter II

1. The Presidential Address to Section A, British Association, Newcastle, 1916. Reprinted in *The Aims of Education and Other Essays* (The Macmillan Co., New York: 1929), pp. 152–179.
2. Cf. *Belief, Existence, and Meaning* (New York University Press, New York: 1969), pp. 28 ff.
3. "On Philosophical Ecumenism: a Dialogue," in *Primordiality, Science, and Value* (State University of New York Press, Albany: 1980).
4. See especially *Semiotics and Linguistic Structure*.
5. See again Gottlob Frege, "Über Sinn und Bedeutung," second paragraph, and *Begriffsschrift*, §8.
6. See *Semiotics and Linguistic Structure* and *Events, Reference, and Logical Form*.
7. See *Whitehead's Categoreal Scheme and Other Papers* (Martinus Nijhoff, the Hague: 1974).
8. C. S. Peirce, *Collected Papers* (Harvard University Press, Cambridge: 1931–1958), Vol. I, §492.
9. On explicative semantics, see "Towards an Objectual Dynamics of Logical Systems," in *Logico-Linguistic Papers*.
10. See "Fact, Feeling, Faith, and Form" and "Towards a Constructive Idealism," in *Primordiality, Science, and Value*.
11. See especially Laszlo Tisza, "The Conceptual Structure of Physics," *Reviews of Modern Physics* 35(1963): 151–185.
12. See H. Scholz, *Metaphysik als Strenge Wissenschaft* (Wissenschaftliche Buchgesellschaft, Darmstadt: 1965, but first published in 1941) and *Mathesis Universalis* (*Ibid:* 1969), pp. 341–387.

Chapter III

1. P. Butchvarov, *Being qua Being, a Theory of Identity, Existence, and Predication* (Indiana University Press, Bloomington and London: 1979).
2. This phrase 'in modern terms' is Father Bocheński's. See his *A History of Formal Logic* (Notre Dame University Press, Notre Dame: 1961), *passim*.

3. See Again G. Frege, "Über Sinn Und Bedeutung," second paragraph, and *Begriffsschrift*, §8.
4. Cf. especially *Semiotics and Linguistic Structure*, Part B.
5. See "On Disquotation and Intensionality," in *Pragmatics, Truth, and Language*.
6. See esp. his *Mathesis Universalis*.
7. See *Truth and Denotation* (University of Chicago Press, Chicago: 1958 and 1975), Chapters IV and XI, and *Semiotics and Linguistic Structure*, Chapter VI.
8. Cf. "Some Comments on Abstract Nouns," in *Logico-Linguistic Papers*.
9. See especially *Events, Reference, and Logical Form, Semiotics and Linguistic Structure*, and *Pragmatics, Truth, and Language, passim*.
10. *Ibid.* and *Logico-Linguistic Papers*.
11. See "Of 'Of' " in *Pragmatics, Truth, and Language*.
12. Cf. "Of Time and the Null Individual," in *Pragmatics, Truth, and Language*.
13. Recall *Whitehead's Categoreal Scheme*, Chapter II.

Chapter IV

1. The Presidential Address given at the meeting of the Metaphysical Society of America at the Union Theological Seminary, New York, 21 March 1953.
2. Cf. *Truth and Denotation*, Chapter X, and III above.
3. In her Presidential Address, "Dispensing with *Possibilia*," *Proceedings and Address of the American Philosophical Association* XLIX (1975–76): 39–48. Cf. also *Pragmatics, Truth, and Language*, Chapter XIV.

Chapter V

1. At King's College, London.
2. For a still useful summary, see *Truth and Denotation*.
3. Recall, for example, *Belief, Existence, and Meaning*, Chapter III, and III and IV above.
4. On pragmatics, see especially *Toward a Systematic Pragmatics* (North-Holland Publishing Co., Amsterdam: 1959) and *Pragmatics, Truth, and Language*.
5. Cf. *Belief, Existence, and Meaning*, Chapter VIII.
6. As in *Truth and Denotation*, Chapters III or XI, depending upon whether the syntax is one of shapes or of inscriptions — or of both.
7. Cf. *Events, Reference, and Logical Form*, pp. 29ff.
8. See R. Carnap, *Introduction to Semantics* (Harvard University Press, Cambridge: 1946), pp. 41ff.
9. See G. Frege, *Grundgesetze der Arithmetik*, Vol. I, p. xii.
10. Recall III and IV above.
11. A. Gurwitsch, "Philosophical Presuppositions of Logic," in his *Studies in Phenomenology and Psychology* (Northwestern University Press, Evanston, Ill.:" 1966), Chapter 14.
12. As in *Semiotics and Linguistic Structure*, pp. 113ff.
13. *Ibid.*, p. 84.

Chapter VI

1. Subsequently published as *The Logic of Natural language* (Oxford University Press, Oxford: 1982).
2. (The Belknap Press of Harvard University Press, Cambridge: 1963 and 1969). See also *Truth and Denotation*, Chapter IV.
3. Cf. *Primordiality, Science, and Value*, Chapter XIII.
4. Readers familiar with the Hilbert-Bernays 'η' and 'ϵ' will already have noted kinship with the

theory here and will no doubt have surmised that the whole of first order quantification theory is implicit in it. See especially Hilbert-Bernays, *Grundlagen der Mathematik* (J. Springer, Berlin: 1939), Vol. 2, §1.

5. Any occurrence of a variable x_i in a formula C said to be *bound* in C provided it occurs in a part of C of the form $\ulcorner \{x_i \ldots x_m \ni D\} \urcorner$ where D is a formula and $1 \leq i \leq n$; otherwise free. And an occurrence of a *term* in C is then free in C provided every occurrence of a variable in that term is a free occurrence of that variable in C.

6. Here '$=_{VC}$' is the sign for virtual-class identity.

7. Here x is assumed to be any variable not free in F or G.

8. Here x is any variable not free in F or G.

9. Cf. *Truth and Denotation*, Chapter IV, or *Belief, Existence, and Meaning*, Chapter VI.

10. As in *Truth and Denotation*.

11. Cf. *Truth and Denotation*, Chapter X. The inclusion in the treatment here of some proper names as primitives is of course not essential, definitions for such being always possible in terms of the requisite predicates. The elimination of such would bring the treatment closer to that of Sommers. And similarly for '$=$'.

12. The subscript 'A' is to suggst 'all' just as the subscript 'S' in 'Des$_S$' was to suggest 'some'. And similarly for 'T' for 'the' in the next paragraph.

13. Cf. *Semiotics and Linguistic Structure*, Part II.

14. Cf. Frege's *Begriffsschrift*, §8, and "Über Sinn und Bedeutung," second paragraph.

15. Here likewise x and y are to be any distinct variables not free in F or G.

16. Essentially as in *Semiotics and Linguistic Structure*, Chapter III.

Chapter VII

1. P. Strawson, *Subject and Predicate in Logic and Grammar* (Methuen and Co., London: 1974), p. vii.

2. See especially *Semiotics and Linguistic Structure*.

3. As in the work of Tarski and Carnap.

4. As in *Toward a Systematic Pragmatics*.

5. See "And" in *Pragmatics, Truth, and Language*.

6. See "Of 'Of' " in *Pragmatics, Truth, and Language*.

7. Note that the context allowed here for 'That$_{Content}$' contrasts with that allowed previously with respect to the first argument. "Socrates swims' b' here expresses that b is an inscription of the shape 'Socrates swims'.

8. Cf. "On Virtual-Class Designation and Intensionality," in *Primordiality, Science, and Value*.

9. See *Logico-Linguistic Papers*, Chapter I, and "Some Protolinguistic Transformations," in *Pragmatics, Truth, and Language*.

10. See *Semiotics and Linguistic Structure*, Chapters XI and XII.

11. See his *The Logic of Religion* (New York University Press, New York: 1965), p. 3.

12. Cf. *Events, Reference, and Logical Form*, Chapter I.

Chapter VIII

1. Presented at the Boston University Colloquium for the Philosophy and History of Science on 9 December 1980, and appearing in his *Theories and Things* (Harvard University Press, Cambridge: 1981).

2. Cf. *Truth and Denotation*, p. 106.

3. (The Belknap Press of Harvard University Press, Cambridge: 1963 and 1969).

4. See *Belief, Existence, and Meaning*, Chapter VI.

5. See "On Virtual-Class Designation and Intensionality," in *Primordiality, Science, and Value*.

6. In view of the well-known work of Schönfinkel and Curry. See also Quine's *Selected Logic Papers* (Random House, New York: 1966), pp. 227–235.

7. See *Constructivity in Mathematics*, ed. by A. Heyting (*Studies in Logic and the Foundations of Mathematics*, North-Holland Publishing Co., Amsterdam: 1959), pp. 1–14.

8. Cf. "Toward an Objectual Dynamics of Logical Systems," in *Logico-Linguistic Papers.*

9. In view of the enormous richness needed in the semantical metalanguage, then, we may as well eliminate 'Den' and 'Des' as primitives and define them in terms of the full Tarskian regalia of quantifiers.

10. In *Selected Logic Papers, loc. cit.*

11. Cf. his *The Ways of Paradox* (Harvard University Press, Cambridge and London: 1976), p. 304.

12. Again, see "Toward an Objectual Dynamics of Logical Systems," and also III and IV, in *Logico-Linguistic Papers.*

13. Here '=' as between abstracts of higher order is presumed to be a new object-language primitive axiomatized in familiar ways.

14. Cf. *Primordiality, Science, and Value*, pp. 195 f.

15. "Predicate Functors Revisited," *The Journal of Symbolic Logic* 46 (1981): 649–652.

16. See H. B. Curry, *Foundations of Mathematical Logic* (McGraw-Hill Book Co., New York: 1963). Cf. also III and IV in *Logico-Linguistic Papers.*

17. *The Ways of Paradox*, pp. 308–321.

18. *Truth and Denotation*, Chapters VIII, IX, and XII.

Chapter IX

1. See especially Chapters I and II.

2. No harm arises from regarding '=' for the identity of individuals as one of the primitive non-logical predicates of the language.

3. Cf. *Semiotics and Linguistic Structure*, pp. 36–37.

4. See, e.g., A. Church, *Introduction to Mathematical Logic*, Vol. I (Princeton University Press, Princeton: 1956), §39.

5. Some remarks somewhat to this effect were made by Ivor Leclerc at the meeting of the International Society for Metaphysics at King's College, London, July, 1980.

6. See especially P. Bernays, "Über eine Natürliche Erweiterung des Relationenkalküls" in *Constructivity in Mathematics* and the works there referred to.

7. On shape (or structural) descriptions, see Tarski, *Der Wahrheitsbegriff*, §2, or *Truth and Denotation*, Chapter III.

Chapter X

1. (Yale University Press, New Haven: 1976).

2. Cf. Chapter VIII in *Logico-Linguistic Papers.*

3. See especially *Events, Reference, and Logical Form, Semiotics and Linguistic Structure*, and *Pragmatics, Truth, and Language.*

4. Cf. *Semiotics and Linguistic Structure*, pp. 27 ff.

5. See *Belief, Existence, and Meaning*, Chapter VI.

6. See *Truth and Denotation*, Chapters XI and XII.

7. See *Truth and Denotation, passim.*

8. Cf. Chapter V in *Logico-Linguistic Papers.*

9. See *Semiotics and Linguistic Structure*, pp. 152 ff. and 273 ff.

10. Here 'e That $_{Content}$ a' expresses that a is the content of e, or that the striving e bears the That-relation of content to a. Similarly 'she Agent e' expresses that she is the agent or doer of e and 'e During now' expresses that e takes place during the now of the present moment. "she perceives --'a' expresses that a is of the shape 'she perceives --'.

11. A point well made in Sommers' book discussed in VII above.

12. See "Über Sinn und Bedeutung," second paragraph and *Begriffsschrift*, §8.

13. Cf. *Semiotics and Linguistic Structure*, p. 63.
14. Recall III above.
15. See *Primordiality, Science, and Value*, p. 196.
16. See *Semiotics and Linguistic Structure*, Chapter XV.
17. See *Truth and Denotation*, pp. 17 f.

Chapter XI

1. All quotations are from the translation of J. N. Findlay (Routledge and Kegan Paul, London: 1970).
2. On event-descriptive predicates see *Events, Reference, and Logical Form, Semiotics and Linguistic Structure*, and *Pragmatics, Truth, and Language*.
3. Cf. R. Carnap, *Introduction to Semantics*, pp. 22ff.
4. See Frege's "Der Gedanke," and "On Frege's Pragmatic Concerns" in *Peirce's Logic of Relations and Other Studies* (Foris Publications, Dordrecht: 1980).
5. Cf. "Of 'Of' " in *Pragmatics, Truth, and Language*.
6. All of the predicates used here are essentially as in previous publications and are more or less self-explanatory.
7. See his *Meaning and Necessity* (University of Chicago Press, Chicago: 1947 and 1956), pp. 222ff.
8. Cf. *Pragmatics, Truth, and Language*, Chapter III.
9. As in "Der Gedanke."
10. See *Logico-Linguistic Papers*, Chapters III and IV.
11. *Logico-Linguistic Papers*, Chapter XII.
12. See J. Mohanty, *Frege and Husserl* (Indiana University Press, Bloomington: 1982).

Chapter XII

1. A. N. Whitehead, *A Treatise on Universal Algebra and Its Applications* (Cambridge University Press, Cambridge: 1898), p. viii.
2. Cf. "On Metaphor and Logical Form" and "On the Logic of Fictive Locutions," in *Logico-Linguistic Papers*.
3. The first formulations of a simple or simplified theory of types, it will be recalled, are due to Chwistek and Ramsey.
4. See especially *Truth and Denotation*, Chapter IV.
5. G. Frege, *On the Foundations of Geometry and Formal Theories of Arithmetic* (Yale University Press, New Haven: 1971). Cf. also *Logico-Linguistic Papers*, Chapter XII.
6. Chapters I and III.
7. See his "R. M. Martin on the Whiteheadian God," *The Southern Journal of Philosophy* XVI (1978): 293–305 and *Primordiality, Science, and Value*, Chapter X.
8. Some of these are reflected upon in *Semiotics and Linguistic Structure* and *Logico-Linguistic Papers*.
9. *Modes of Thought* (The Macmillan Co., New York: 1938), pp. 237–238.

Chapter XIII

1. *The Journal of Philosophy*, LXXVIII (1981): 90–95.
2. Cf. *Belief, Existence, and Meaning*, Chapter VIII.
3. See *Semiotics and Linguistic Structure*, pp. 268ff.
4. These comments are closely akin to some of those of J. van Heijenoort, "Ostension and Vagueness," a mimeographed communiqué dated 13 June 1979.

5. See "On Dialogism and Perception," in *Logico-Linguistic Papers.*

6. On 'under' see *Logico-Linguistic Papers,* Chapter VII, and recall III and IV above.

7. Cf. *Semiotics and Linguistic Structure,* Chapters XI and XII.

8. Recall also the material of *Belief, Existence, and Meaning,* Chapter III.

9. J. B. Rosser and A. R. Turquette, *Many-Valued Logics (Studies in Logic and the Foundation of Mathematics,* North-Holland Pub. Co., Amsterdam: 1952), p. 1.

10. See H. Putnam, *Mathematics, Matter, and Method* (Cambridge University Press, Cambridge: 1975), Chapter 9. Cf. also *Logico-Linguistic Papers,* Chapter XI.

11. Recall the material of *Toward a Systematic Pragmatics.*

12. See *Events, Reference, and Logical Form,* Chapter XII, and XVI below.

13. (The Clarendon Press, Oxford: 1957). See the present author's review in *Mind* LXVIII (1959): 271–275.

14. Recall *Belief, Existence, and Meaning,* Chapter XI, and see XVII below.

15. Putnam, *op. cit.* Chapter 10.

16. See especially Peter Mittelstaedt, *Quantum Logic* (D. Reidel Publishing Co., Dordrecht: 1978).

17. William Craig, "Boolean Logic and the Everyday Physical World," *Proceedings and Addresses of the American Philosophical Association,* 52 (1979): 751–778. See also *Logico-Linguistic Papers,* Chapter IV.

18. P. W. Bridgman, *The Nature of Physical Theory* (Princeton University Press, Princeton: 1936), pp. 59–60.

19. *Transactions of the Cambridge Philosophical Society,* 1860: 361–*358.

20. *Collected Papers,* 3.77, 3.113, and 3.640.

21. See Alan R. Anderson and Nuel D. Balnap, Jr., *Entailment,* Volume I (Princeton University Press, Princeton: 1975).

22. See B. C. van Fraassen, "Singular Terms, Truth-Value Gaps, and Free Logic," *The Journal of Philosophy* LXIII (1966): 481–495.

23. Cf., however, Susan Haack, *Deviant Logic* (Cambridge University Press, Cambridge: 1974), Chapter I.

24. See *Logico-Linguistic Papers,* Chapter III and IV, and Bocheński's *The Methods of Contemporary Thought* (D. Reidel Pub. Co., Dordrecht: 1965), p. 79.

25. See *Logico-Linguistic Papers,* Chapter XII.

26. See *The Logical Syntax of Language* (Harcourt, Brace and Co., New York: 1937), pp. 51–52.

Chapter XIV

1. "On Some Aesthetic Relations," *The Journal of Aesthetics and Art Criticism* (1981): 258–264. A longer version of this paper is in *Primordiality, Science, and Value,* Chapter XV.

2. (Hackett Publ. Co., Indianapolis: 1978).

3. *The Journal of Aesthetics and Art Criticism, ibid.:* 275-277.

4. Cf. "On Metaphor and Logical Form," in *Logico-Linguistic Papers.*

5. Cf. "Some Comments on Abstract Nouns," in *Logico-Linguistic Papers.*

6. In *The Meaning of Words* (John Windsor Chamberlin, Milwaukee: 1948), p. 11.

Chapter XV

1. By Karl L. Popper and John C. Eccles (Springer International, Berlin, Heidelberg, London, New York: 1977), especially Part II, Chapter E7.

2. See *Events, Reference, and Logical Form,* Chapter XI.

3. See also *Events, Reference, and Logical Form, Semiotics and Linguistic Structure,* and *Primordiality, Science, and Value.*

4. As in Gertrude Stein's *Four Saints in Three Acts.*

5. In "A Modified Concept of Consciousness," *Psychological Review* 76 (1969): 532–536.

6. For a valuable but neglected classification of these, see W. H. Sheldon, *God and Polarity* (Yale University Press, New Haven: 1954).

7. Cf. *Semiotics and Linguistic Structure*, p. 202, for a related definition.

8. See *Primordiality, Science, and Value*, Chapter XIX, and *Peirce's Logic of Relations, etc.*, Chapter X.

9. As in *Semiotics and Linguistic Structure*, Chapter I.

10. 'Prfm' here is a general predicate for all manner of performances, actions, and the like. When fully spelled out it may be handled in terms of a very complex logical sum of relations.

11. As in *Primordiality, Science, and Value*, Chapter V.

12. J. H. Woodger, *The Axiomatic Method in Biology* (Cambridge University Press, Cambridge: 1937) and *Biology and Language* (*ibid.*: 1952).

Chapter XVI

1. Presented at the meeting of the Institut Internationale de Philosophie in Düsseldorf in August, 1978, and appearing in *Logic and Philosophy*, ed. by G. H. von Wright (Martinus Nijhoff, The Hague: 1980), pp. 1–10.

2. See *Truth and Denotation*, Chapters III–V and XI–XII. But cf. also *Semiotics and Linguistic Structure*, Chapters V and VI.

3. Recall XIII above.

4. As in *Semiotics and Linguistic Structure*.

5. See "Truth and Its Illicit Surrogates," in *Pragmatics, Truth, and Language*.

6. For details see Tarski's original paper, "The Concept of Truth in Formalized Languages," in *Logic, Semantics, Metamathematics* (The Clarendon Press, Oxford: 1956), Chapter VIII, or *Truth and Denotation*, Chapters IV and V.

7. Cf. the forms in *Semiotics and Linguistic Structure*, Chapter VI.

8. See Z. Harris, *Papers in Structural and Transformational Linguistics* (D. Reidel Pub. Co., Dordrecht: 1970), esp. Chapter XXX.

9. As in *Toward a Systematic Pragmatics* or *Semiotics and Linguistic Structure*.

10. As in *Semiotics and Linguistic Structure*.

11. Again, as in *Semiotics and Linguistic Structure*.

12. See especially *Toward a Systematic Pragmatics*, pp. 39ff.

Chapter XVII

1. In his *Frege and Husserl* (Indiana University Press, Bloomington: 1982), Chapter 5.

2. J. M. Bocheński, *A History of Formal Logic* (Notre Dame University Press, Notre Dame: 1961).

3. Cf. *Truth and Denotation*, Chapters I and XIII.

4. Recall "Of Time and the Null Individual," in *Primordiality, Science, and Value*.

5. (Oxford University Press, New York and Oxford: 1981).

6. *The Logic of Religion*, p. 3.

Chapter XVIII

1. *Philosophy and Phenomenological Research* XLII (1982): 453–454.

2. It is interesting to compare this suggestion with the one in Peirce. See his *Collected Papers*, 1.492–1.493 and 3.492, and also *Primordiality, Science, and Value*, Chapter XVIII, and *Logico-Linguistic Papers*, Chapter X.

3. See his "Propositions as the Only Realities," *American Philosophical Quarterly* 8 (1971): 99–103 and *Events, Reference, and Logical Form*, Chapter IX.

4. *American Philosophical Quarterly* 13 (1976): 247–255. Cf. also *Logico-Linguistic Papers*,

5. These two and a half paragraphs are borrowed from the paper on Harris just cited.

6. Cf. "On the Pragmatics of Self-Reference," in *Pragmatics, Truth, and Language.*

7. In *The Journal of Symbolic Logic* 46 (1981): 167–171.

8. *Collected Papers,* 2.67–70.

9. For an illuminating discussion of a kind of causal mereology as applied to events, see Judith Jarvis Thomson, *Acts and Other Events* (Cornell University Press, Ithaca and London: 1977).

10. In *Philosophical Books* 20 (1979): 127–129.

11. See *Logico-Linguistic Papers,* Chapter I, and *Pragmatics, Truth, and Language,* Chapter XVIII.

12. In *The Philosophical Review* 89 (1980): 485–487.

13. Cf. *Belief, Existence, and Meaning,* Chapter VI.

14. *The Journal of Symbolic Logic* 12 (1947): 105–122.

15. *Canadian Philosophical Reviews,* Vol. 1, No. 6, 1982, pp. 268–271.

Index

INDEX OF SPECIAL SYMBOLS